tic
ng
ctive
onal

ack

Wiley Publishing, Inc.

To Laurel, Emma, and Charlotte

Pragmatic Software Testing: Becoming an Effective and Efficient Test Professional

Published by
Wiley Publishing, Inc.
10475 Crosspoint Boulevard
Indianapolis, IN 46256
www.wiley.com

Copyright © 2007 by Rex Black
Published by Wiley Publishing, Inc., Indianapolis, Indiana
Published simultaneously in Canada

ISBN: 978-0-470-12790-2

Manufactured in the United States of America

10 9 8 7 6 5 4 3 2 1

For general information on our other products and services or to obtain technical support, please contact our Customer Care Department within the U.S. at (800) 762-2974, outside the U.S. at (317) 572-3993 or fax (317) 572-4002.

Library of Congress Cataloging-in-Publication Data is available from the publisher.

About the Author

With a quarter century of software and systems engineering experience, **Rex Black** is president and principal consultant of RBCS, Inc., a leader in software, hardware, and systems testing. For over a dozen years, RBCS has served its worldwide clientele with consulting, outsourcing, assessment, and training services related to testing and quality assurance. RBCS has over 100 clients spanning 20 countries on 6 continents, including Adobe (India), ASB Bank, Bank One, Cisco, Comverse, Dell, the U.S. Department of Defense, Hitachi, NDS, and Schlumberger.

With four books to his credit, Rex is the most prolific author currently practicing in the field of testing and quality assurance today. His popular first book, *Managing the Testing Process*, now in its second edition, has sold 25,000 copies around the world, including Japanese, Chinese, and Indian releases. His other book on test management, *Critical Testing Processes*, along with previous editions of this book, marketed as *Effective and Efficient Software Testing*, have also sold thousands of copies, including Hebrew, Indian, Japanese, and Russian editions.

Rex is the president of both the International Software Testing Qualifications Board (www.istqb.org) and the American Software Testing Qualifications Board (www.istqb). Being a primary coauthor of both the current Foundation syllabus (version 2005) and the upcoming Advanced syllabus (version 2007), he was well qualified to coauthor the definitive text for ISTQB certification candidates, Foundations of Software Testing, with Isabel Evans, Dorothy Graham, and Erik van Veenendaal.

In addition to books, Rex has written over 25 articles; presented hundreds of papers, workshops, and seminars; and given over a dozen keynote speeches at conferences and events around the world.

When Rex is not traveling the world for work or vacation, he lives in Bulverde, Texas, with his wife, Laurel Becker; his daughters, Emma Grace and Charlotte Catherine; and his dogs, Cosmo and Hank.

Credits

Senior Acquisitions Editor
Jim Minatel

Development Editor
Maureen Spears

Production Editor
Martine Dardignac

Copy Editor
Judy Flynn

Editorial Manager
Mary Beth Wakefield

Production Manager
Tim Tate

**Vice President and Executive
Group Publisher**
Richard Swadley

**Vice President and Executive
Publisher**
Joseph B. Wikert

Compositor
Craig Woods, Happenstance
Type-O-Rama

Proofreader
Kathryn Duggan

Indexer
Jack Lewis

Anniversary Logo Design
Richard Pacifico

Contents

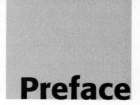

Preface

Testing even a simple system is a potentially infinite task. With tight budgets and schedules, testers need practical techniques, hands-on experience and the right strategies to effectively and efficiently test software.

This book puts those things right in the palm of your hands, literally. Through a sequence of thorough, practical, and, I hope, well-explained chapters, you'll learn the following skills that are critical to software testing:

- How to analyze the risks to system quality and allocate your testing effort appropriately based on the level of risk.

- Different testing strategies and how to choose the right strategies every time, including effective strategies for handling regression testing.

- How to design tests based on a system's expected behavior (black box), including boundary values, equivalence partitioning, decision tables, use cases, state diagrams and tables, all-pairs tables, orthogonal arrays, and domain analysis

- How to design tests based on a system's internal structure (white box), including levels of code coverage, data-flow coverage, and basis-path coverage

- How to plan and perform integration testing

- How to use your intuition, experience, and knowledge to explore and attack the system

- How to make all your hard work serve the needs of the project

Because testing is a hands-on activity, this book includes 11 complete chapters of realistic, life-sized exercises illustrating all the major test techniques, with detailed solutions.

If you've never read a book on test design, if you've read other books on test design and found them too hard to follow, or if you've read a book on test design and found it stopped just when things got really interesting, this book is for you. By the end of this book, you will know more about the nuts and bolts of testing than most testers learn in an entire career, and you will be ready to put those ideas into action on your next test project.

Acknowledgments

If you're reading this because you just bought this book, it's only right for me to start by saying thanks to you. Ultimately, readers are the reason people such as me write books like this one. I hope I repay the favor you are doing me as a reader of my work by teaching you some new and useful testing techniques as you read this book.

This book grew from training materials that date back to the mid-1990s. Therefore, I would like to thank all the students all around the world who took my courses, who number in the thousands, for their help in improving the base material of this book.

The book itself grew by a circuitous route, from an e-learning project that never quite made it to delivery. I wrote the scripts and was ready to record the audio tracks, but then things fizzled. Having done about four or five successful e-learning projects, I wasn't going to write off the work on this one, so those scripts became the first draft of this book. As the saying goes, "Success has a thousand fathers, while failure is an orphan." So I won't name names, but if you're reading this, thanks for the push that made this book happen.

After this became a book, a number of people reviewed the material. In no particular order, my thanks go out to Judy McKay, Mitsuaki Narita, Barton Layne, Julie Gardiner, Michael Bolton, Mikhail Pavlov, Joe Mata, and Jamie Mitchell for their thoughts.

In another interesting twist, this book happens to be the first book on testing published in Hebrew. I would like to thank David Bassa for pushing the deal forward, Alon Bar-Shamai for the legwork, Tal Pe'er for his insightful comments and questions during the review of the Hebrew translation, and the rest at SELA who helped to make this happen. *Toda raba* to my friends and colleagues in Israel!

I would also like to thank Charles Arnao, Michael Caruso, and the rest of the team at Bisk Education and Villanova University for selecting this book as a text for our (successful) e-learning project "Essentials of Software Testing." In addition, thanks go out to Professor Charles Pfohl of the University of Canberra for his use of this text for his course on testing there. Finally, thanks to Noel LeJeune of the Metropolitan State College of Denver for selecting this book as a text for his course too.

This book started its wider life in the United States as a self-published, spiral-bound, soft-copy beast sold on Amazon. I didn't knock any dents in Dan Brown's royalty stream with *Effective and Efficient Software Testing* (this book's name at that time), but a number of folks were kind enough to buy it. I thank each of you, especially those of you who were even more kind and sent comments and suggestions.

Jim Minatel, my editor at Wiley, has worked with me for years on one of my previous books, *Managing the Testing Process*. In the years that I polished this book in its various forms, I would go back to Jim from time to time and ask him if Wiley was ready to publish it. A number of "not yets" has finally become "yes," and I thank Jim for his efforts to bring this book to a wider audience.

Of course, while all these readers, students, and reviewers contributed ideas, thoughts, and opinions, I made the final call about what I would write, positions I would adopt, and jokes I would make. So, please hold me responsible for the content.

Thanks to my wife and business partner, Laurel Becker, for all her help. Self-publishing a book is an interesting experience, and I'm sure it was especially interesting for Laurel. From getting ISBNs to setting up the printing to arranging a listing on Amazon.com, among untold other contributions, thanks for your help, love, and support, on this project as on so many others, and in my life.

Last but not least, thanks to my charming, hilarious, and loving daughters, Emma and Charlotte, and my equally hilarious (though somewhat less charming) dogs, Cosmo and Hank, for providing amusement, friendship, and a wet nose (the dogs, not the girls) when requested — and when not requested. Which makes me realize that every child needs chores. My father made me mow the lawn when I was a kid: I wonder if I can have Emma and Charlotte write the next book?

Introduction

What Kind of Book Is This?

This is a book about software and system testing. This is an ambitious book. In it I cover the strategies, techniques, and concepts that effective and efficient test professionals need to do their job. That covers a lot of ground, and so does this book.

This book is about practical concepts. This book is hands-on. If you work your way through the whole book, you'll do many realistic exercises to apply these concepts immediately. You'll be able to compare your solutions with mine.

Appropriately enough, this book is tested. I have used these concepts in my career as a test professional, which began in 1987, four years after I started my software career in a Fortran and C programming job. Since 1997, literally thousands of software and systems professionals around the world have taken the training courses that provide the base material for this book. We have discussed the concepts and worked through the exercises.

What Topics Will I Cover?

In Part I, I discuss the goals, strategies, and tactics of effective and efficient testing. Even experienced testers will find something new here, and I encourage people who are new to testing to work through these chapters completely.

In Part II, I lay the foundation of my technique for risk-based testing. You'll learn how to analyze, prioritize, and document risks to the quality of the system, using both informal and formal techniques. Unless you are already an experienced risk-analysis professional, I recommend that you work carefully through this section, including the exercise.

In the heart of the book, with the goals of testing defined through quality risk analysis, you'll start to fill your testing toolkit. In Parts III, IV, and V, you'll learn to design, develop, and, ultimately, document various kinds of tests. You'll learn static, black-box, and white-box test techniques, including the following:

- Requirements, design, and code reviews
- Equivalence classes and boundary value analysis
- Decision tables
- Live data and customer workflow testing
- State-transition diagrams
- Domain testing
- Orthogonal arrays
- Statement, branch, condition, and loop code coverage
- McCabe complexity and unit basis tests
- Data-flow coverage
- Integration test techniques
- McCabe integration basis tests

These are fundamental test techniques, the knowledge of which distinguishes the test professional from the part-timer or amateur tester. I suggest that you work through all of these chapters, even if you are an experienced tester, including the exercises. If you've already mastered these topics, this material and the exercises should be easy for you, but you might find new nuances in these chapters. I know I did as I was preparing them.

Part VI has Omninet Marketing and Systems Requirements Documents as well as a bibliography and suggestions for further reading.

Can I Skip Topics?

If you feel that one or two major test techniques are inapplicable to you, feel free to skip them. For example, you might work in a group focused entirely on black-box techniques. You can skip the sections on static and white-box testing. The section on black-box testing stands on its own, and each technique can be studied independently, too. Similarly, you could go through static testing and black-box testing and skip white-box testing. It's up to you.

While all are fundamental test techniques, they are not all of the same degree of applicability. I would group them into three categories:

- Generally applicable — equivalence classes, boundary values, reviews, code coverage, and integration test techniques

- Often applicable — decision tables, state-transition diagrams, live data and customer workflows, McCabe Cyclomatic Complexity, and orthogonal arrays

- Sometimes applicable — domain analysis, data-flow coverage, and McCabe integration basis tests

You certainly could decide to study only the generally and often applicable techniques if that's what you feel you need to learn right now. The material is designed to be modular and selectively usable.

However, if your goal is to be a well-rounded test professional, you need to be familiar with all these major test techniques, not just for your current job, but for your future ones as well. Should you want to pursue one of the major test certifications, such as the Foundation or Advanced certificates granted by National Boards of the International Software Testing Qualifications Board, you'll be tested on most of these concepts.

At one point or other in my 20-plus-year career as a test professional and software engineer, each topic covered in this book has been important and practical. As we go, I'll point out why I find these topics important, oftentimes with anecdotes from projects I've worked on or heard about from credible sources. As the saying goes, "Any fool can learn from his own mistakes [and I hope *I* have], but the wisest amongst us can learn from the mistakes of others." So, I'll share not just success stories, but also some cautionary tales.

Can I Practice with Realistic Exercises?

This book uses a lifelike project, Omninet, to structure many of the exercises. Omninet is a project to deploy a network of public access Internet kiosks in places like malls, theaters, and other public places. Users will be able to buy Web surfing time using cash, debit cards, or credit cards. The realism and complexity of this hypothetical project will give you a chance to try out many of the test concepts we talk about, especially the test design techniques.

The Marketing Requirements Document and the System Requirements Document are included in appendices of this book. I recommend that you review them before you start the first chapter.

Since Omninet wasn't the perfect way to illustrate every concept, I've included a few other examples. I'll explain those in the exercises when we get there.

In live courses, the time allocated for the exercises in the training materials is tightly constrained, usually between 30 and 120 minutes. This might at first seem artificial, but in reality, most of our work as test professionals is constrained by time (and often money) too. For this reason, I suggest time constraints for each exercise. These time constraints mean that you'll have fit-and-finish issues in your solutions.

I've followed these constraints when preparing my solutions too. The fit-and-finish issues in my solutions indicate the level of fit-and-finish issues that I expect in a typical time-constrained test project. In real life, we don't always need to — or have a chance to — polish our work, especially when it's for our own internal use.

In many cases, more than one correct solution exists. So just because your solution differs from mine, that doesn't make your solution — or mine — wrong. The differences might indicate differences in our assumptions about what's important. If you get a solution different from mine, ask yourself what differences in perspectives and priorities might lead to those differences.

Does It Matter That I Have (or Haven't) Read Another Book on Testing?

This book stands on its own, so you needn't have read any other test books. If you have read my other books, *Managing the Testing Process* and *Critical Testing Processes*, there is very little overlap, except in the material on quality risk analysis. Even if you are familiar with my earlier writings on this topic, you'll probably find some new ideas here.

If you have read other test design books, you will find new ideas on those topics too. I start with the basic ideas for each test design technique, but I go well beyond the basics, especially in my discussion of the exercise solutions.

Goals, Strategies, and Tactics

In this Part

What Does It Mean to Be Pragmatic?

Let's start at the beginning by exploring some obvious questions with some not-so-obvious and not-so-universally-accepted answers about pragmatic testing. From a pragmatic, or practical, standpoint, it involves being effective and efficient when testing software. What is effective software testing? What is efficient software testing? What is software testing, anyway? What is quality?

While these might seem like impractical, philosophical questions, in my experience, they are not. Your answers to these questions determine what *you expect to do* as a tester. Other people's answers to these questions determine what *they expect you to do* as a tester. Having common expectations up, down, and across the organizational chart and throughout the project team is essential to success. Without such commonality, no matter what you do, someone's sure to be disappointed. With common expectations, you can all strive for the same goals, and support others in their endeavors.

What Do Effective and Efficient Mean?

Webster's dictionary defines the word *effective* as "producing a decided, decisive, or desired result; impressive." So, to be an effective software tester, you must decide what results you desire from your testing efforts.

Likewise, Webster's defines *efficient* as "productive of the desired effect; especially to be productive without waste." So, to be an efficient tester, you must allocate resources (time and money) appropriately.

In the next few pages, you'll get a closer look at each of these concepts.

First, though, note that testing usually occurs within the context of some larger project or effort. That larger project could be developing a new system, maintaining an existing system, deploying a system in a new or existing environment, or deciding whether to accept or reject a proposed system. So, when the testing subproject exists within the context of the larger project, you should look at test effectiveness and efficiency from the project perspective, not the test subproject perspective.

What Effects Do You Want?

On most projects I've worked on, I've typically wanted to do the following:

- Produce and deliver information to the project team about the most important aspects of the quality of the system under test.

- Produce and deliver information to the development team so they can fix the most important bugs.

- Produce and deliver information to the project management team so they can understand issues such as the current levels of system quality, the trends of those levels, and the level of quality risk reduction being achieved.

- Produce and deliver information that can help the technical support team, help desk, and other folks on the receiving end of the project deal effectively with the system they received, warts and all.

In short, I often find myself a producer and provider of useful information for the project team. This has some interesting implications, which you'll examine in a minute.

Reading this list, you might have thought of some effects that you — or other people with whom you've worked — typically want from testing that are missing. Good! There is no one right set of answers for this question.

What Is the Right Level of Efficiency?

The definition of efficiency that was presented earlier included the ideas of productivity and a lack of waste. What does that mean?

Avoiding Redundancy

Of course, you don't want to waste time, so you should try to avoid redundancy. You should try to run the right tests and run them as rapidly as possible. You should try to discover bugs as early as possible and find the more-important bugs before the less-important bugs.

That said, you've probably seen more than one project where the old cliché "more haste, less speed" applied. You rushed into things without planning and preparation. You didn't attend to details. You abandoned carefully thought-out strategies at the first sign of trouble or delay. In short, in an attempt to save time, you made mistakes that cost you more time than you saved.

Reducing Cost

You also don't want to waste money, so you should buy only the supplies — software and hardware tools, test environments, and so on — that you really need and that you have the time and talents to gainfully employ. You should carefully evaluate tools before you buy them and be ready to justify them with cost-benefit analyses.

When you do such analyses, you'll often find that good tools and test configurations can pay for themselves — sometimes dramatically. On one project, a manager decided to "save money" by having us use a test server that was in a different country. This server cost about $20,000, and he said there was no money in the budget for another one. However, they paid more than $20,000 in lost time and productivity when people had to wait for the system administrator in the remote location to respond to their calls for help — sometimes for more than a day.

This matter of cost-benefit analyses brings us to another question: What is the cost-benefit analysis for testing? Is testing an investment that pays for itself?

While these questions are more a test management topic, let me briefly mention the concept of *cost of quality*. Cost of quality recognizes two types of quality-related costs that organizations pay:

- Costs of conformance: These are the costs you pay to achieve quality. They include *costs of detection*, which are the costs of testing, or looking for bugs. Conformance costs also include the *costs of prevention*, which are the costs of quality assurance, of improving the people, technologies, and process.

- Costs of nonconformance: These are the costs you pay when you fail to achieve quality. These costs include the costs associated with finding and fixing bugs, plus retesting those bugs and doing regression testing, before you release, deploy, or go live with the system. These are also called the costs of *internal failure*. The costs associated with finding bugs after that point are called costs of *external failure*. External failures can cost you in terms of finding, fixing, retesting, and regression testing, as well as the additional associated costs of support or help desk time, maintenance or patch releases, angry customers, lost business, and damage to reputations.

Usually, costs of conformance are less than the costs of nonconformance and costs of internal failure are less than costs of external failure. So, testing can have a positive return on investment by reducing the total cost of quality.[1]

What Software Testing Isn't...But Is Often Thought to Be

So far, I've talked about effectiveness and efficiency and what those concepts mean in terms of software testing, but what exactly is software testing?

Let's start with what it's not: Software testing is not about proving conclusively that the software is free from any defects, or even about discovering all the defects. Such a mission for a test team is truly impossible to achieve.

Why? Consider any system that solves complex business, scientific, and military problems. There are typically an infinite or practically infinite number of sequences in which the programming language statements that make up such a system could be executed. Furthermore, large amounts of tremendously diverse kinds of data often flow not only within each subsystem but also across subsystems, with features influencing other features, data stored earlier being retrieved again later, and so forth. Finally, users will use systems in unintended, often impossible-to-anticipate fashions, eventually even on system configurations that did not exist when the software was being written.

As if this were not enough, the complex flows of control and data through your systems create intricate dependencies and interactions. Careful system designers can reduce coupling, but some of these flows arise due to essential complexity. So, minor changes can have significant effects, just as a pebble can produce rings of ripples across a whole pond or, perhaps more aptly, just as the lightest touch of a fly's wing vibrates the whole spider web.

Perhaps you're thinking, "Okay, Rex, I get it, let's move on." The problem isn't that we testers seldom understand the impossibility of complete, exhaustive testing that proves conclusively that the system works or reveals every single bug. The problem is that many managers and even some developers *do think* we can completely, exhaustively test software.

I have heard managers say things like, "Oh, how hard can it be? Anyone can test. Just make sure everything works before we ship it."

I have heard developers say things like, "Of course my units work fine. I ran unit tests and tested everything that could break."

Maybe you've heard statements like this too.

I used to ignore those statements or dismiss them as outsiders' blissful ignorance of the difficulties of my job. I found that testers ignore such statements only at their peril. Statements such as these indicate a fundamental misunderstanding of what testing can accomplish. That means people have expectations of you, the test professional, that you cannot possibly meet. When you don't

---

[1] For more on the important management issue of testing economics and return on investment, see my other two books, *Managing the Testing Process* and *Critical Testing Processes*.

meet those expectations, people might conclude that you're incompetent. Therefore, one of the first steps to testing success is the alignment of realistic expectations about testing across the project team.

NOTE One of the reviewers of this book, Judy McKay, mentioned, "We have to be sure that we don't compound this misperception that testing can prove the absence of defects or can discover all defects by publishing testing metrics with statements like '100 percent test coverage [achieved].' Just because we ran 100 percent of our test cases doesn't mean that we've covered 100 percent of what the code could do. We need to be sure our information is accurate, supportable, and understandable."

The following sections investigate what testing is, and isn't, as well as what it can realistically do for you.

Five Phases of a Tester's Mental Life

One of the three founders of modern software testing, Boris Beizer, identified five phases of a tester's mental life:

- **Phase 0:** There's no difference between testing and debugging. Other than in support of debugging, testing has no purpose.

- **Phase 1:** The purpose of testing is to show that the software works.

- **Phase 2:** The purpose of testing is to show that the software doesn't work.

- **Phase 3:** The purpose of testing is not to prove anything, but to reduce the perceived risk of the software not working to an acceptable value.

- **Phase 4:** Testing is not an act. It is a mental discipline that results in low-risk software without much testing effort.

The first two phases can be thought of as myths of individuals and organizations with immature testing practices and processes. [2]

This leads you to the practical testing reality in phase 2. Some testers stop here. In some organizations, that's fine. If all your peers and managers expect from you is that you find lots of important bugs, and find them quickly and cheaply, then this book can teach you how to do that.

However, you can also progress to phase 3. In this phase, testing is part of an overall strategy of risk management. Testing is risk focused. Testing produces risk-related information. This book can teach you how to do that too.

---

[2] See Boris Beizer's *Software Testing Techniques* for a more thorough description of the phases and his conclusions about them.

Phase 4 represents more of an organizational mindset than a tester's mindset. Once testing — and the implications of testing — become pervasive throughout the organization, everyone will start to act in a way that reduces bugs before a single test is run. [3]

So, what phase do you find yourself in right now, and why? In which phase do your peers and managers expect to find you, and why? In which phase does your organization need you to be, and why?

Other Founding Views on Testing

Another founder of the testing profession, Bill Hetzel, wrote, "Testing is any activity aimed at evaluating an attribute or capability of a program or system and determining that it meets its required results."[4]

This definition, while perhaps implying the dated concept of "proving that the system works," does include the useful concept of evaluating system attributes and capabilities. Indeed, tests *do* evaluate some facet of the system, under some set of conditions, and check system behavior against expected results. If you substitute the word *whether* — as in "determining *whether* [the system] meets its required results" — you can say Hetzel hit the nail on the head — such is the act of testing.

This leads to an obvious question, though: How do you know whether the system behaved as required? The collection of tools, techniques, and documents that testers use — together with the tester's judgment — to make this decision is referred to as the *test oracle*. The name comes from oracles in ancient Greek history (most famously the Oracle of Delphi), supposedly able to foretell the future. Calling the technique used to predict and/or check the expected result an oracle is a nice way of hinting at how hard this often is. This book revisits the challenges of test oracles in various chapters.

The first founder of the testing profession, Glenford Myers, wrote, "Testing is the process of executing a program with the intent of finding errors." Myers was onto something with his definition too. The mind tends to see what it expects to see. People who think they can achieve something often do. A good tester intends to and expects to find bugs because a good tester recognizes that all programs have bugs. [5]

Those of us who have carried on the work started by Myers, Hetzel, and Beizer have continued to refine their ideas on what software testing is all about. Mark Fewster and Dorothy Graham described testing as building confidence where the system under test works and locating bugs so that we can fix them. This definition bring us to the "why test?" question. We would want to

---

[3] This brings us to topics more properly related to test management again, so I'll refer you to my two books, *Managing the Testing Process* and *Critical Testing Processes*.

[4] See Bill Hetzel's *Complete Guide to Software Testing*.

[5] See Glenford Myers's *The Art of Software Testing*.

ship a system only when we were confident that the important stuff worked. We'd need to fix as many bugs as necessary — and then some, I'd hope — to get to that point. [6]

Testing as a Form of Quality Risk Management

So, now I've cited some people whose thinking on testing has influenced mine. Through my study of risk and risk management, I've come to think about system development, maintenance, deployment, and acceptance projects as dealing with four main variables:

- **Features:** Will the system provide the right capabilities?
- **Schedule:** Will you deploy or release the system soon enough?
- **Budget:** Will the overall effort or project make financial sense?
- **Quality:** Will the system you create satisfy the users, customers, and other stakeholders?

Because the answers to these questions are not clear in advance — that is, there are risks that might lead to answers you wouldn't like — you need some way to manage those risks. One or more risks in any of these areas can, if unmanaged, lead to undesirable outcomes that sink the project. Any attempt to reduce the risk in one category always affects the other categories, usually by increasing risk in one or more of them. If the project team properly manages and balances these risks, the project has a strong chance of succeeding.

So, as a test professional, you should give the management team insight into the fourth risk category, quality. You do that by producing and delivering assessments of quality and other quality-related information in terms management can understand and act upon.

Sometimes, that information leads to actions to improve the quality of the system. The management prioritizes the bugs you've found. The development team fixes the high-priority bugs. Sometimes, though, that information can lead to actions that trade risks in one category for risks in other categories. For example, if you can't get a feature bug free enough to be good enough for release, you might push that feature into a subsequent release.

So What Is the Test Team All About?

How do you summarize the purpose of the test team? Here's a generic statement that you can tailor for any of the organizations you may work in and with:

> *To effectively and efficiently provide timely, accurate, and useful testing services and quality information that helps the project team manage the risks to system quality.*

---

[6] See Mark Fewster and Dorothy Graham's *Software Test Automation.*

This statement is very similar to what a newspaper publisher wants to achieve. A publisher wants their newspaper to provide timely, accurate, and useful information to their readers.

As with newspaper articles and newspapers themselves, credibility is key for testers. This book focuses on effective ways to produce timely, accurate, and useful information. However, you must always remind yourself that how you produce the information is only the first half of the battle. You also must credibly provide that information. So effectiveness of communication is important, and details and presentation matter.[7]

What Does "Quality" Mean to You?

If you want to assess quality, communicate about levels of quality, and help management understand and manage quality, then you need a working definition for quality.

There are a number of different definitions for quality out there. I happen to like J. M. Juran's definition:

> *Fitness for use. Features [that] are decisive as to product performance and as to "product satisfaction"…. The word 'quality' also refers to freedom from deficiencies…[that] result in complaints, claims, returns, rework and other damage. Those collectively are forms of "product dissatisfaction."*[8]

To some extent, Juran's wording is a bit clunky and oblique. Fitness for use *by whom*? Who is being satisfied or dissatisfied here? Project sponsors, customers, users, and other stakeholders. Juran's definition of quality centers on the needs and demands, the desires and the preferences of the people who pay for, use, and are affected by our systems.

Contrast this with Phil Crosby's definition of quality. Crosby defined quality as conformance to requirements *as specified*, nothing more, nothing less. The problem for software testers is that they often receive flawed requirements specifications — or none at all.[9]

I suggest that, on most projects, testers should be free to call a behavior a "bug" when they suspect that, due to that behavior, the system might dissatisfy a sponsor, customer, user, or other stakeholder. I like Juran's definition because it makes it clear that we can do that, especially in the absence of clear requirements specifications. Even with them, testers, thinking skeptically, should recognize that those specifications are as likely to be wrong as the system implementation itself.

---

[7] See *Critical Testing Processes* for a detailed description of the issues relating to test results reporting.

[8] See J. M. Juran's book *Juran on Planning for Quality*.

[9] See Phil Crosby's book *Quality Is Free*.

Now certainly there are cases, such as contract development, where requirements specifications draw a contractual distinction between an enhancement request and a bug. However, for most IT and mass-market software, does the average project sponsor, user, or customer care about such distinctions? No. They simply want their software to show a preponderance of satisfying behaviors and a relative absence of dissatisfying behaviors. That's quality to them. Test professionals need to know how to assess quality. This book shows you the places to look for bugs and the tools to root bugs out.

Triangle Test Exercise

In this exercise, you get your first chance in this book to build a test case. Even if you think of yourself as an experienced tester, you might want to give it a try. It's amazing how few people — even people who have been testing for years — get this exercise right.

Exercise: The Triangle Test

Suppose you're told to test a very simple program. This program accepts three integers as inputs or arguments. These integers represent the lengths of a triangle's sides. The program prints "Equilateral" (three equal sides), "Isosceles" (two equal sides), or "Scalene" (no equal sides), as shown in Figure 2-1. [1]

Your assignment is to write an effective and efficient set of test cases. By effective, I mean that the set of tests finds common bugs. By efficient, I mean that the set of tests finds those bugs with a reasonable amount of effort. By test case, I mean tester action, data, and expected result. Here the action is usually to input some data, but it might be other actions as well.

A template is provided for your solution. I suggest you format your solution to look the same as the template. I suggest 30 minutes as a time limit. When you're done, continue through the rest of this chapter to see my answers.

---

[1] This classic exercise — which serves as a Rorschach test for test professionals in many ways — was created by Glenford Myers and is found in his book, *The Art of Software Testing*.

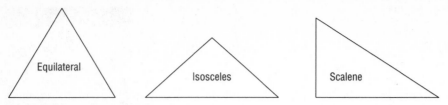

Figure 2-1:   Three types of triangles

Your Solution for the Triangle Test

TESTER ACTION AND DATA	EXPECTED RESULT

TESTER ACTION AND DATA	EXPECTED RESULT

Author's Triangle Test Solution

This exercise is a famous one, found in the first book on software testing, Glenford Myers's *The Art of Software Testing*. In it, Myers gives this seemingly trivial example and then shows many possible solutions to it.

To come up with my solution, shown in Table 2-1, I used a combination of equivalence partitioning and boundary value analysis. I'll cover both equivalence partitioning and boundary value analysis in later chapters.

My solution focuses on testing functionality and the user interface only. A later chapter introduces a number of other risks to system quality that might concern you.

Note that my solution is only one of a large set of possible correct answers. Some generic rules for determining a good set of tests are found in Myers's book, and you'll look at those rules later in this book. Myers also provides solutions for this exercise. Because he wrote his book in the days of green-screen mainframe programs, he did not have to cover some of the user interface tests that are included in my solution.

Table 2-1   Solution for the Triangle Test

TESTER ACTION AND DATA	EXPECTED RESULT
Erroneous input partition	
One test case each with a, b, or c a non-number	An error message
One test case each with a, b, or c a real number	An error message

Continued

Table 2-1 *(continued)*

TESTER ACTION AND DATA	EXPECTED RESULT
Scalene triangle partition	
2, 3, 4	Scalene
maxint-2, maxint-1, maxint (*maxint* = largest legal integer)	Scalene
1, 2, 3	An error message
5, 3, 2	An error message
1, 2, 4	An error message
-2, 3, 4	An error message
0, 1, 2	An error message
maxint-1, maxint, maxint+1	An error message
Isosceles triangle partition	
2, 2, 1	Isosceles
9, 5, 5	Isosceles
maxint, maxint-1, maxint	Isosceles
1, 2, 1	An error message
2, 5, 2	An error message
3, 1, 1	An error message
2, -2, 1	An error message
2, 2, 0	An error message
maxint, maxint+1, maxint	An error message
Equilateral triangle partition	
1, 1, 1	Equilateral
maxint, maxint, maxint	Equilateral
maxint+1, maxint+1, maxint+1	An error message
1, 1, -1	An error message
0, 0, 0	An error message
User interface tests	
Overflow each input buffer for a, b, and c	An error message

TESTER ACTION AND DATA	EXPECTED RESULT
Try a leading space for a, b, and c	An error message or ignore the space
Try a trailing space for a, b, and c	An error message or ignore the space
Leave a, b, or c (one at a time) blank	An error message

So, how did you do? What did my solution test that you didn't? What did you test that my solution didn't?[2]

If you missed a few of these, don't feel bad. By the end of this book, you'll be able to identify not only all the tests in my solution, but also tests in other risk areas.

However, even once you've completed this book, you might find you need to consult books and notes to come up with a complete set of tests. I had to reread Myers's discussion of the exercise to finalize my solution, and even so, reviewers of this book have pointed out many additional tests that they would try that I didn't mention.

This points out an important theme in this book. Doing test design and implementation without reference materials often leads to gaps in testing. Doing test design and implementation under the tight, often stressful time constraints that exist during the test execution makes such gaps even more likely, even for experienced testers. This underscores the need for careful analysis, design, and implementation of tests up front, which can be combined during test execution with reactive techniques (discussed in Chapter 20) to find even more bugs.

---

[2] One of the reviewers, Judy McKay, mentioned a number of additional questions she would want addressed by the tests: "Did you worry about order dependence in the input values? Maybe it reacts differently to a negative number if it's in the first position versus the second position versus the third position versus all positions. Maybe we could check the requirements. Did you worry about certain special characters being allowed or disallowed? What if it correctly recognizes that a '*' is a special character but thinks a '/' is acceptable? Did you test for all possible special characters, in all positions? Capital letters? Zeros? Nulls?" The possibilities are really almost endless, aren't they? Risk analysis, a topic we'll cover later in this book, helps us recognize when we've covered enough.

## CHAPTER 3

Aligning Testing with the Project

In this chapter, I cover the important concept of fitting testing into its project context. In Chapter 6 I will cover how to make sure you test the right quality characteristics to the right extent. In another chapter, I'll give you some ideas on how to choose the right test strategies. Both are critical to testing success.

However, failing to fit testing to the project is as dangerous as testing the wrong attributes of the system or using the wrong test strategies. So in this chapter, I'll discuss how projects need the services of a skilled test professional such as you.

Why Do Organizations Test?

Why are we here? I don't pose this question in a philosophical sense, but in a practical one.

When I work on projects, I expect to be paid. Someone probably pays you to test their system, or you're learning about testing to get a job in the field. Since testing does not generate money by itself, some organization is paying for testing to happen. Testing doesn't happen for its own sake, out of intellectual curiosity or to serve some noble purpose. Rather, testing happens because it serves needs and provides benefits as part of a project or operation.

Different organizations have different needs and benefits that they are looking for from your work, such as:

- Improved reputation for quality
- Lower post-release maintenance costs
- Smoother release cycles
- Increased confidence
- Protection from lawsuits
- Reduced risk of lost missions or even lives

These are needs and benefits that can be reworded in the negative and expressed as a risk. For example, a buggy customer release creates the risk of increased post-release maintenance costs.

Perspectives on Testing

You might be thinking, "Hmm, none of that stuff sounds like what I do as a tester. I look for bugs and try to figure out what works — and what doesn't work — within the parameters of my tests." Those are indeed the main tactics of testing, but most senior managers and executives don't think a lot about such matters.

Senior managers and executives think about more strategic, long-term issues. So, if you want to communicate to senior managers and executives about testing, you have to communicate strategically.

You communicate about testing strategically when you talk about how testing helps them manage risks. You can talk about how testing reduces the likelihood of the organization having to bear unanticipated future costs. This perspective is something like insurance, but without actuarial certainty or the promise of coverage for losses.[1]

Why should you care about communicating to senior managers and executives? Because they authorize the budgets that make our work possible!

Testing in Context

Much of the time, good testing groups deliver their value in the form of timely, accurate assessments of quality presented to the project team and managers in a credible, comprehensible way. For that to happen, the test subproject has to fit in the overall development or maintenance project. Otherwise, we're unlikely to generate timely, accurate information — much less be credible and

---

[1] Further ideas on communicating with senior managers and executives in terms they care about can be found in my books on test management, *Managing the Testing Process* and *Critical Testing Processes*, and on the Library page of our company website, www.rexblackconsulting.com, in the "Investing in Testing" article series and in the slides for my keynote speeches, "Four Ways Testing Adds Value," and "Investing in Testing."

comprehensible presenters of it — since we don't understand and make our work consistent with what's going on in the project.

Common Test Phases and Objectives

One common way of fitting testing activities into a project is to break the overall testing effort into a sequence of phases or levels. These levels are often organized by the sequence in which portions of the system become ready to test. Each phase then serves a high-level test objective.

The first phase or level is often called unit, component, or subsystem test. Here, you test portions of the system as they are created, looking for bugs in the individual pieces of the system under test before these pieces are integrated.

In the second phase or level of testing, often called integration (and less frequently, string) test, you test collections of interoperating or communicating units, subsystems, or components, looking for bugs in the relationships and interfaces between pairs and groups of these pieces of the system under test as the pieces come together.

In the third phase or level of testing, often called system test, you test the entire system, looking for bugs in the overall and particular behaviors, functions, and responses of the system under test as a whole.

In the fourth phase or level of testing, often called acceptance or pilot test, you generally are no longer looking for bugs. Rather, the objective is to demonstrate that the product is ready for deployment or release.

What is important in these levels is not so much the names or that all are present. Rather, you want to make sure that the right amount of testing is done as early as possible to prevent bugs from cropping up later, when they'll do more damage to the project. Proper definition of entry and exit criteria in test plans ensures smooth transitions between the phases or levels. Test planning also attends to the hand-offs between responsible parties that are essential to effective and efficient testing.[2]

Testing Throughout the Organization

When I mentioned hand-offs between responsible parties, I was hinting that one group does not necessarily perform all the testing tasks. Let me explain how that works, and why you might want to do that.

To read Figure 3-1, start at the bottom. The second half of the project timeline — omitting the requirements, design, and implementation of the system — shows time moving forward as you move right on the figure.

---

[2] Test planning is covered in detail in my books *Managing the Testing Process* and *Critical Testing Processes*, as well as *Software Testing: A Guide to the TMap Approach*, a book by Martin Pol, Ruud Teunissen, and Erik van Veenendaal.

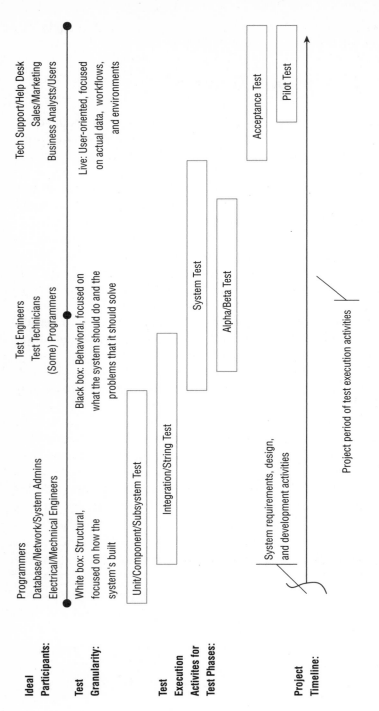

Figure 3-1: Test execution phases and participants in the project life cycle

Above the project timeline, you see the test phases mentioned previously, shown sequenced in time. Different approaches to managing projects allow different amounts of overlap between these phases, in some cases phases are missing entirely, and in some cases more phases are present. However, this figure shows a not-unusual project that happens to include all the test phases in a deliberate sequence.

Above the test phases, I have shown an annotated spectrum of test granularity. By *test granularity*, I mean the level of detail focused upon by particular categories of test techniques. White-box testing focuses on the implementation details, the code, data structures, classes, and other low-level elements of the system. It is the finest-grained category of test techniques. Black-box testing focuses on the quality risks, the requirements, and the high-level design. It is a coarser-grained category. Live testing focuses on the typical usage of the system. It is the coarsest-grained category. In later chapters of this book, you'll learn more about each category of test technique.

This figure shows that, as you move from unit testing to system testing to acceptance testing, the category of test techniques that predominates moves from fine-grained to coarse-grained.

Finally, above the spectrum of test granularity, you see the ideal participants. Unit testing and other finer-grained kinds of tests, like early integration tests, generally involve insight into how the system is built. So, the people who are building the system usually have the right skills. As you get into coarser-grained tests like later integration tests and system tests, the participants need to apply specific testing skills, like the ones you are learning in this book. Finally, once tests require the understanding of exactly how the system is used, those people who are closest to the users — or *are* users — are the ideal testers.

This figure is but one example of a sequence of test phases. What's important is selecting the right phases based on the objectives you want to achieve. For each test phase, the test manager should define the proper entry and exit criteria. These criteria should be followed as the project proceeds. They can be waived after careful consideration and through mutual stakeholder agreement, especially if needs change. It's problematic, though, if they're waived as a panicked reaction to schedule pressure. These are the keys to fitting a each test phase and a deliberate testing effort into a project.

I mentioned different approaches to managing projects. These are sometimes referred to as system life cycle models. Let's consider a few of these models now and how they affect your testing.

The V Model

The granddaddy of all system life cycle models is the waterfall model, where you start at a high level and define requirements, then fall to a lower lever of detail and create a high-level design, then fall to a lower level for low-level design, then fall to a lower level for implementation, then test. A refinement of this model that focuses on testing, called the V model, is shown in Figure 3-2.

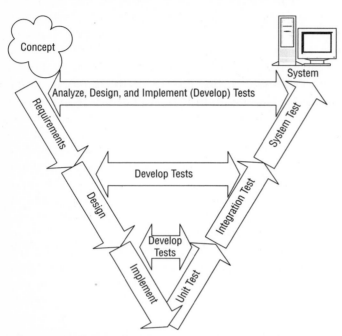

Figure 3-2:   The V model for system development

Here, the testing work in the waterfall is bent upward, to illustrate that early levels like unit test focus on low-level details, but later levels like system test are driven by high-level considerations.

The crossbars show the test analysis, design, and implementation tasks. Notice how these are driven by the project deliverables that are appropriate to each level of testing. For example, requirements specifications, being important descriptors of system behavior, are inputs to the system test level, which is primarily a behavioral, black-box level of testing. The arrowheads facing back into the requirements, design, and implementation processes indicate that test analysis, design, and implementation often locate bugs that can be removed early in the project, before test execution starts. This is an important theme of the book, which we'll revisit in later chapters.

While this model is intuitive and in many cases familiar to testers, developers, and managers, it has some weak spots. For one, it is usually schedule- and budget-driven. That is, when plans are flawed and money runs out, it's usually testing that is cut back, since most of the testing happens at the end. For large projects, the chances of perfect planning 6, 12, or even 18 months or longer in advance are very low. That said, this model beats chaos.

Some simple steps can help keep V model projects from becoming a testing disaster at the end. First, start test planning, analysis, design, and development early in the project so you can take advantage of early bug detection and removal. Second, be sure to plan test execution periods that include multiple cycles to allow time to fix bugs and retest the new builds. Finally, consider slipping features to a later release rather than slipping test phase entry dates or entering a test phase before the system is ready. The chances of getting lucky and having everything come nicely together during system test are very low. The "project catastrophe during system test" phenomenon is something that has been written about extensively.[3]

Figure 3-3 shows how a project-schedule view of a well-run V model project might look. Selected test-related development tasks are shown in gray. The testing tasks are shown in black.

Evolutionary and Incremental Models

To cope with some of the challenges of the V model, many projects have adopted evolutionary and incremental models, such as shown in Figure 3-4. In this case, the system is analyzed, designed, developed, and tested in clearly defined increments. At any point after the first increment is tested, the project team can deliver at least a portion of the planned functionality.

While the terms *evolutionary model* and *incremental model* are often used interchangeably, purists would say that an incremental model is being followed when the set of features can be defined up front. An evolutionary model is being followed when the set of features evolves over time.

Of course, you'd want the features to come together in a series of increments where the first increment is the core functionality. Each subsequent increment should add functionality that is not as important as that already added. Through this prioritization scheme, whatever the team delivers will be the most important functionality.

The approaches vary in terms of formality from Extreme Programming at the lightweight side to Rapid Application Development. Such models don't solve all our testing problems. It's still a temptation to ship a system with buggy features, though those should be the least-important features. Also, on projects applying the evolving agile methodologies, the role of testing is still evolving as well.[4]

---

[3] The first mention of which I'm aware is in Fred Brooks's classic book *The Mythical Man-Month*, which is must reading for every software and system engineer.

[4] See, for example, Lisa Crispin and Tip House's book, *Testing Extreme Programming*, for their experiences and viewpoints.

ID	Task Name	Start Date	End Date	Duration	2007			2008				
					Oct	Nov	Dec	Jan	Feb	Mar	Apr	
1	Capture Product Requirements and Write Project Plan	10/1/2007	10/26/2007	20d								
2	Analyze Quality Risks and Write Test Plan	10/1/2007	10/26/2007	20d								
3	Product Architecture and Design Specifications	10/29/2007	11/23/2007	20d								
4	Test System Architecture and Design Specifications	10/29/2007	11/23/2007	20d								
5	Develop Product	11/26/2007	1/18/2008	40d								
6	Develop Test System	11/26/2007	1/18/2008	40d								
7	Debug Product Units	12/2/2007	1/25/2008	40d								
8	Debug Test System	12/2/2007	1/25/2008	40d								
9	Unit Test Execution	12/5/2007	1/29/2008	40d								
10	Integration Test Execution	12/5/2007	1/29/2008	40d								
11	System Test Execution	1/30/2008	3/25/2008	40d								
12	Acceptance Test Execution	3/26/2008	4/8/2008	10d								

Figure 3-3: A Gantt-chart view of a V model project

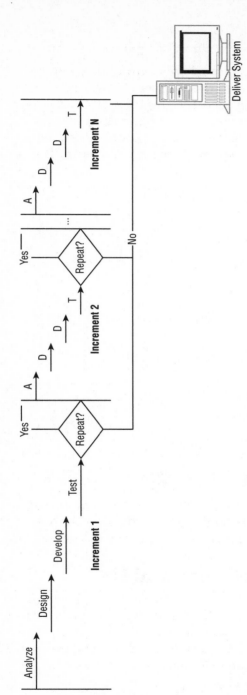

Figure 3-4: An incremental development life cycle

The Spiral Model

The spiral model is useful when the project team has no way of precisely specifying the system to be built in advance but must deliver the right set of features in the end. You can discover the needed features by prototyping. The developers build an initial prototype, then you start testing it. At that point, testing, redesign, and prototyping may well be continuous until the feature set is finalized. At that point, a more traditional set of tests might be run. This is shown in Figure 3-5.

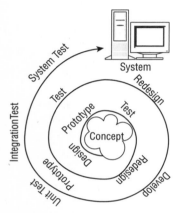

Figure 3-5:   A spiral model of system development

This is very different from the waterfall. In the waterfall, once you start testing, you are close to finished. In the spiral, the first prototype might enter testing very soon in the project, but you are still a long way from done.

You must be careful not to deliver the early prototypes to the users as finished products. Sometimes, the management pressure to do so is intense. In such a case, your risk analysis should help point out significant test gaps.

Regrettably Common Model: Code and Fix

Code and fix is a sarcastic name for beginning development of the system with no real idea of what you're building. Rather than building a prototype for early testing — and possible disposal — you set out to build the final product. To the extent that there's any process, it can look something like this:

1. Programmers write and debug code. Often, there's no unit testing, or at least none worth the name of testing.

2. Once the compiler produces an executable, the code is deemed ready for testing and released to an informal test team. These are often junior programmers or people who want to be programmers, can't land a job as a programmer, and have no professional skills as a tester.

3. Even with amateur testing, the testers often find many bugs. In a rush, these bugs are sometimes fixed live on the test environment by programmers, with the fixes not subsequently checked into the code repository. So testers find the same bug more than once. Sometimes customers find bugs that testers found and programmers fixed.

4. All of the preceding steps are repeated at the same time, with little coordination.

The process continues until the money, time, or patience of the project team are exhausted. At this point, the system is released. Or the project is cancelled. Sometimes, the company goes out of business after thrashing around like this for some time.

This approach often grows out of the typical startup experience, which I sometimes call "two dudes in the garage." Steve Jobs and Steve Wozniak, the men who built Apple, were two dudes who started Apple in a garage in Silicon Valley. Likewise, Bill Gates and a small team of programmers built Microsoft from similarly humble origins.

Both Apple and Microsoft learned over time, though, that what works for two dudes in garage doesn't work for project teams of dozens or even hundreds of people, especially when those teams are geographically distributed. When I encounter code-and-fix approaches in larger organizations, it's often the result of complete organizational ignorance of the negative effects that this kind of chaos has on their ability to deliver quality products on time and within budget.

Sometimes, though, people see software engineering realities as some kind of process prison to be escaped or a hoax being played on the feebleminded. In either case, "we're different," "we're more creative than that," "we have XYZ technology," "we're user driven," and other rationalizations are often used as excuses to continue to apply a model the company has outgrown.

Testing Maintenance Releases

New development is glamorous, but maintenance releases pay the bills. In my experience talking to audiences about maintenance releases, almost everyone has worked on at least one such project. Many software engineers have done nothing but work on adding features to or fixing bugs in existing code.

Many of the considerations discussed so far apply to the new features, but for bug fixes especially, regression of existing features is the big risk for maintenance releases. In Chapter 4, we'll look at various strategies you can use to manage the regression risk. The most widely touted strategy, full automation of your entire test set, is but one way to go. Less-frequent releases with broader test coverage for each release as well as intelligent selection of a subset of your tests are also options.

Another testing consideration arises when an organization tries to put a major release worth of features into a short maintenance release cycle. This creates the same kind of test squeeze I talked about in the context of V-model development. There is a strong temptation for project managers to allocate 100 percent of the development time to creating new features, which is never realistic. Who will fix the backlog of bugs? Who will fix the new bugs that are being introduced? Do the developers actually spend 100 percent of their time coding?

Finally, time to develop new tests is often scarce. This can result in an excessive reliance on the regression test suite, leaving new features inadequately tested and causing the regression tests to become outdated. This problem is especially acute when changes that were relatively simple to implement have serious and far-reaching test consequences.

System Integration

More and more projects involve more integration of custom or commercial off-the-shelf subsystems than in-house development or enhancement of software. While this might seem to reduce the overall risk, each integrated subsystem can bring with it significantly increased risks to system quality. Figure 3-6 shows how.

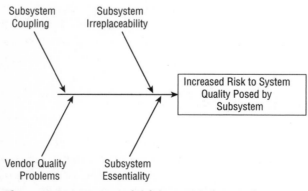

Figure 3-6: Sources of risk in system integration

One factor that increases risks is coupling, which creates a strong interaction with the system — or consequence to the system — when the subsystem fails. Another factor that increases risks is irreplaceability, when there are few similar subsystems available. To the extent that the subsystem creates quality problems, you are stuck with them. Another factor that increases risks is essentiality, where some key feature or features of the system will be unavailable if the subsystem does not work properly. Another factor that increases risks is vendor quality problems and slow turnaround on bug fixes. If there is a high likelihood of the vendor sending you a bad subsystem, the level of risk to the quality of the entire system is higher.

"Okay," you might say, "I see that there are sources of risk to system quality, but how can I mitigate those risks?" I have seen and used various options.

One is to integrate, track, and manage the vendor testing of their subsystem as part of an overall, distributed test effort for the system. This involves up-front planning, along with having sufficient clout with the vendor or vendors to insist that they consider their test teams and test efforts subordinate to and contained within yours. When I have used this approach, it has worked well.

Another option is simply to trust the vendor subsystem testing to deliver a working subsystem to you. This approach may sound silly and naive expressed in such words. However, project teams do this all the time. My suggestion is that you do so with your eyes open, understanding the risks you are accepting and allocating schedule time to deal with issues.

Another option is to decide to fix the subsystem vendor's testing or quality problems. On one project, my client hired me to do exactly that for a vendor. It worked out nicely. Again, though, your organization must have the clout to insist that you be allowed to go in and straighten out what's broken in their testing process and that there is time allocated to fix what you find. And don't you have your own problems to attend to? As such, this is an ideal job for a test consultant.

A final option, especially if you assume or find yourself confronted by proof of incompetent testing by the vendor, is to disregard their testing, assume the subsystem is coming to you untested, and retest the subsystem. I've had to do this, essentially, on one project when the vendor sold my client an IMAP mail server package that was seriously buggy.

Both of the last two options have heavy political implications. The vendor is unlikely to accept your assertion that their testing is incompetent and will likely attack your credibility. Since someone made the choice to use that vendor — and it may have been an expensive choice — that person will likely also side with the vendor against your assertion. You'll need to bring data to the discussion. Better yet, see if you can influence the contract negotiations up front to include proof of testing along with acceptance testing by your team prior to payment. It's amazing how motivational that can be for vendors!

Even the best-tested and highest-quality subsystems might not work well in the particular environment you intend to use them in. So, plan on integration and system testing the integrated subsystem yourself.

Hardware/Software Development

In addition to new or integrated software, some projects include custom hardware development or integration. This can involve brand-new hardware or hardware that is built in a unique way from off-the-shelf components.

The presence of new or unique hardware creates some interesting test complications. For one, if the software testers are required to test the hardware, you'll find out quickly that different skills are required. For another, the need to test the software subsystems on the hardware means that, while both hardware and software are under development, insufficient engineering prototypes might be available for test use. This needs to be worked out during the planning stage.

During the hardware design stage, you might want to work with the engineers to see if you can get the hardware made more testable. In other words, see if you can have internal states — especially error states — made visible using simple tools or techniques. Also, see if test automation and logging harnesses can be built into the hardware. Simulators or emulators may be needed. On an Internet appliance, we had a hidden serial port set up so that we could enable logging of various important actions through that port.

Don't make the assumption that testing the software on the hardware will sufficiently test the hardware. It won't. Ensure that competent hardware testing is done. There are various independent test labs that can handle this for you if your hardware vendor didn't.

That said, projects that involve new or unique hardware are fun. Don't shy away from them. Through thoughtful advance planning, hiring of an appropriate test team, and careful execution, these issues can be managed. Enjoy your chance to see something physical take shape as your project progresses.

The Test Process

So far, I've been talking about the various software development and maintenance processes. Figure 3-7 shows a simple process diagram that can help you think about the testing process.[5]

---

[5] The testing process, how to recognize when it is working well, how to handle challenges to it, and how to improve it, are all topics I cover in *Critical Testing Processes*. Figure 3-7 is reproduced from that book and used with permission of the publisher.

Your role as a tester might focus on some of these activities and processes, not all. That depends on how your roles have been defined and what services you provide. However, to be effective and efficient, you'll need to understand how the test process works and how it fits into the overall project.

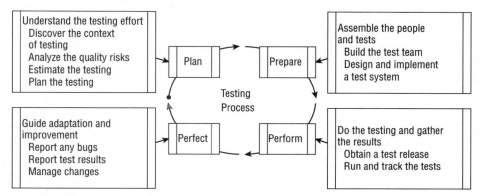

Figure 3-7:   A way to think about the testing process

Understanding Test Strategies, Tactics, and Design

In this chapter, I discuss how we as testers can link business and project testing needs to specific testing approaches. What are the test strategies, the general principles and ideas, for implementing a test effort? What are the test tactics, the techniques, processes, and approaches, available for specific tests? How can we design tests that suit our strategies, tactics, and needs?

Aligning Mission, Strategies, and Tactics

In Figure 4-1, you see a graphical representation of the perfect test effort. The following items are perfectly aligned:

- Test mission: How the test activities benefit the project.
- Test strategies: The guiding principles and ideas for the test activities.
- Test tactics: Techniques, processes, and approaches applied to specific test tasks.
- The entire test effort is also perfectly aligned with its project context.

Now, in the real world, you never have perfect projects or perfect alignment. However, the better aligned these elements are, the more effective and efficient your test effort.

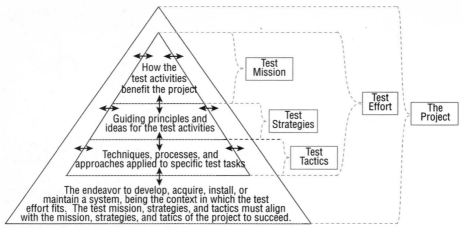

Figure 4-1:   Aligning test mission, strategies, and tactics

Many of the chapters so far have looked at the test mission and overall alignment between testing and the project. This chapter looks closely at test strategies and introduces test tactics and design.

There are many test strategies. I'll survey the most common ones. All of these strategies are in use by various test teams. Depending on the alignment of the strategies with the test mission and the project itself, any of these strategies can succeed — or fail. You don't have to choose a single strategy. While my dominant strategy in most cases is a risk-based analytical strategy, I blend and use multiple strategies.[1]

Analytical Test Strategies

Analytical test strategies start with analysis as a foundation.

With an *object-guided* strategy, you look at requirements, design, and implementation objects to determine testing focus. These objects can include requirements specifications, design specifications, UML diagrams, use cases, source code, database schemas, and entity-relationship diagrams. As you might guess, this approach relies on extensive documentation and breaks down when documentation is not available.

With a *risk-based* strategy, you use the informal or formal techniques that will be discussed in Chapter 6 on quality risk analysis to assess and prioritize quality risks. You can use various available sources of information, as with the object-guided strategy, but you should also draw on the insights of cross-functional project team members and other stakeholders. Adjust the tests and the extent of

---

[1] My list of test strategies grew out of an online discussion with Ross Collard, Kathy Iberle, and Cem Kaner. I thank them for their insights.

testing according to the risk priority levels. Unlike the object-guided variant, this approach can handle situations where there is little or no project documentation.

With a *fully-informed* strategy, you start with the object-guided or risk-based strategy but take the analysis further. Study the system, the usage profiles, the target configurations, and as much other data as you can find. Design, develop, and execute tests based on the broad, deep knowledge gained in analysis. This approach is great if you have lots of time to research the system.

The items being analyzed are sometimes called the *test basis*. The results of the analysis guide the entire test effort, often through some form of coverage analysis during test design, development, execution, and results reporting. These strategies tend to be thorough, good at mitigating quality risks and finding bugs. However, they do require an up-front investment of time.

Model-Based Test Strategies

Model-based test strategies develop models for how the system should behave or work.

With a *scenario-based* strategy, you test according to real-world scenarios. These should span the system's functionality. In the object-oriented world, a close relative is the *use-case-based* strategy, where you rely on object-oriented design documents known as use cases. These use cases are models of how users, customers, and other stakeholders use the system and how it should work under those conditions. You can translate these use cases into test cases.[2]

With a *domain-based* strategy, you analyze different domains of input data accepted by the system, data processing performed by the system, and output data delivered by the system. (Domains are classifications based on similarities inputs, processing, or outputs.) Based on these domains, you then pick the best test cases in each domain, determined by likelihood of bugs, prevalent usage, deployed environments, or all three.

With a model-based strategy, you design, develop, and execute tests to cover models you have built. To the extent that the model captures the essential aspects of the system, these strategies are useful. Of course, these strategies rely on the ability of the tester to develop good models. These strategies break down when the models cannot — or the tester does not — capture all of the essential or potentially problematic aspects of the system.

---

[2] Hans Buwalda has done some interesting work on scenario-based testing, which you can find in his article "Soap Opera Testing," found on www.stickyminds.com. For use cases, I created some material for Villanova University's (www.villanova.edu) online course "Mastering Business Analysis," and Ross Collard wrote two articles on translating use cases to test cases, which you can now find at www.stickyminds.com.

Methodical Test Strategies

Methodical test strategies rely on some relatively informal but orderly and predictable approach to figure out where to test.

With a *learning-based* strategy, you use checklists that you develop over time to guide your testing. You develop these checklists based on where you've found (or missed) bugs before, good ideas you've learned from others, or any other source.

With a *function-based* strategy, you identify and then test each and every function of the system, often one at a time. Similarly, with a *state-based* strategy, you identify and test every state and every possible state transition that can occur.

With a *quality-based* strategy, you use a quality hierarchy like ISO 9126 to identify and test the important "-ilities" for your system. For example, some groups in Hewlett-Packard use functionality, localization, usability, reliability, performance, and scalability. IBM uses capability, usability, performance, reliability, installability, maintainability, documentation, and operability.[3]

With a methodical test strategy, you follow these standard inventories of test objectives. These strategies can be quick and effective against systems that remain relatively stable or systems that are similar to ones tested before. Significant changes might render these strategies temporarily ineffective until you can adjust the test objectives to the new system or organizational realities.

Process-Oriented Test Strategies

Process-oriented test strategies take the methodical approach one step further by regulating the test process.

With a *standardized* test strategy, you follow official or recognized standards. For example, the IEEE 829 standard for test documentation, created by a volunteer standards committee of the nonprofit Institute for Electronics and Electrical Engineers, is used by some organizations to ensure regularity and completeness of all test documents. My book *Critical Testing Processes* describes 12 comprehensive, customizable, and lightweight processes for testing. Such standardization can help to make the test process transparent and comprehensible to programmers, managers, business analysts, and other non-testers. However, you must take care not to introduce excessive, wasteful, or obstructive levels of bureaucracy or paperwork.

One unofficial but increasingly popular test strategy, the *agile* test strategy, has arisen from the programming side of software engineering. Here, the testing

---

[3] For more on IBM's hierarchy of quality characteristics, see Stephen Kan's book *Metrics and Models in Software Quality Engineering, 2e.*

follows lightweight processes, mostly focused on technical risk (likely bugs). A heavy emphasis is placed on automated unit testing, customer acceptance testing, and being able to respond to late changes without excessive costs. These strategies are tailored for small teams on short projects with immediate access to the users. Large, long, geographically distributed, or high-risk projects are likely to find that the strategy does not scale.

The topic of automated unit testing brings us to a group of test strategies that rely heavily on automation. One such strategy is an *automated random* test strategy, where large amounts of random input data are sent to the system. Another such strategy is an *automated functional* test strategy, where you test system functionality using repeatable scripts. Either strategy might also involve an automated load, performance, or reliability testing element. These strategies rely on the ability to effectively automate most of the testing that needs to be done.[4]

Dynamic Test Strategies

Dynamic test strategies, like the agile test strategies, minimize up-front planning and test design, focusing on making the test execution period responsive to change and able to find as many bugs as possible.

With an *intuitive* test strategy, you test according to the collective experience, wisdom, and gut instincts of the test team. Discussions about what to test, anecdotal evidence from past projects, and oral tradition are prime drivers. With an *exploratory* test strategy, you simultaneously learn about the system's behavior and design while you run tests and find bugs. You continuously refine the test approach based on your test results, and refocus the further testing. With a *bug hunting* strategy, you use bug profiles, taxonomies (classifications), and hunches (bug assumptions) to focus testing where you think the bugs are.[5]

The hunting metaphor is a good one for all these strategies, which are more alike than different. I hunt and fish. I've learned one critical success factor for both sports: Hunt where the birds are and fish where the fish are. Likewise, these test strategies require that you be right about where you think the bugs are, often under conditions of schedule and personal pressure.

---

[4] If you intend to use automated testing, I highly recommend Dorothy Graham and Mark Fewster's book *Software Test Automation*.

[5] See James Whittaker's books *How to Break Software* and *How to Break Software Security* for a dynamic strategy for testing based on what he calls *attacks*. You can also refer to Elisabeth Hendrickson's website, www.qualitytree.com, for more on bug hunting test strategies. For exploratory testing, check James Bach's website, www.satisfice.com, but then check my website, www.rexblackconsulting.com, for my article "I Take It (Almost) All Back," which first appeared in *Better Software* magazine, for why exploratory testing is inadequate as a primary test strategy.

Dynamic test strategies value flexibility and finding bugs highly. They do not usually produce good information about coverage, systematically mitigate risks, or offer the opportunity to detect bugs early in the development life cycle. They are certainly much better than no testing at all and, when blended with analytical strategies, serve as an excellent check and balance that can catch gaps in the analytical-designed tests.

Philosophical Test Strategies

Philosophical test strategies start with a philosophy or belief about testing.

With an *exhaustive* test strategy, you assume that everything and anything can and will have bugs. You decide that the possibility of missing bugs is unacceptable and that management will support a considerable effort to find all the bugs. You attempt to test extensively across the functionality, the quality risks, the requirements, and whatever else you can find to cover. The essence of this strategy is captured in an old tester's joke, derived from the catchphrase on the back of U.S. currency: "In God we trust…all others we test."

With a *shotgun* test strategy, you also assume that everything and anything can and will be buggy. However, you accept that you cannot test everything. Since you lack any solid idea on where to find bugs, you test wherever and whatever comes to mind. You attempt to randomly distribute the test effort, like pellets from a shotgun, within the given resource and schedule boundaries.

With an *externally guided* test strategy, you accept not only that you cannot test everything, but also that you can't know where the bugs are. However, you trust that other people might have a good idea of where the bugs are. You ask for their guidance. You test according to their direction, including asking them to help you decide if the observed results are correct. Common guides include programmers, users, technical or customer support, help desk staff, business analysts, salespeople, and marketing staff.

If the underlying philosophies and beliefs behind these strategies are correct, they can be appropriate. For example, testing weapons systems like nuclear missile guidance software clearly requires an exhaustive strategy. However, when applied in inappropriate situations — and I'd guess that most projects are inappropriate for at least two if not all three of these strategies — they lead to dangerously misaligned test efforts.

At this point, I have surveyed what I believe are the primary test strategies in use in most organizations for new systems. However, many projects involve maintaining existing systems, which means that we also need to look at strategies for managing the risk of regression.

Regression

Regression is the misbehavior of a previously correct function, attribute, or feature. The word is also used to mean the discovery of a previously undiscovered bug while running a previously run test. Regression is generally associated with some change to the system, such as adding a feature or fixing a bug.

Regression falls into three basic types. The first is a local regression, where the change or bug fix creates a new bug. The second is an exposed regression, where the change or bug fix reveals an existing bug. The third is a remote regression, where a change or bug fix in one area breaks something in another area of the system. Of the three, the last is typically the hardest to detect, but any one of these regressions can slip past you if you're not careful.

Regression can affect new features. In Figure 4-2, you see a new development project that will produce *n* new features. The features are built, integrated, and tested one after another or in increments. Feature 3, it turns out, breaks something in feature 1.

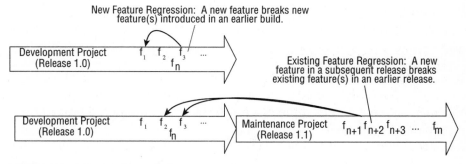

Figure 4-2: Types of regression

Regression can affect existing features. In the figure, you see a maintenance project that will add *m* new features in release 1.1. The features are added on top of the existing *n* features that were present in release 1.0. Feature $n+2$ breaks existing features 2 and 3.

Of the two effects, breaking existing features is typically worse. Users, customers, and other stakeholders come to rely on existing features in a system. When those features stop working, so do they. For new features, a user, customer, or other stakeholder might be disappointed not to receive the promised capability, but at least it was not a capability around which their daily work has become entwined.

Smart testers do not whistle past the graveyard of regression, assuming that it's no big deal. Smart testers have strategies that are effective against all the sources and effects of regressions. Let's look at five of them.

Regression Strategy 1: Repeat All Tests

Brute force is always an option. Brute force is usually the simplest approach intellectually. Simplicity is nice because we're more likely to screw up when we try to get too clever.

For regression risk mitigation, the brute force strategy is to repeat all of your tests. Suppose you've developed a set of tests that are well aligned with quality. You'll have done that if you've performed a solid quality risk analysis and received sufficient time and resources to cover all the critical quality risks. If you repeated all tests after the very last change to the code, you should find all the important regression bugs.

Realistically, automation is the only means to repeat all tests for large, complex systems. Automation is practical when you can design and implement automated tests where the high up-front test development costs are recouped, through frequent test repetition, by the low (ideally, close to zero) costs of executing and maintaining the tests. Test automation can occur at a graphical user interface (GUI), at an application programming interface (API), at a class function or method interface, at a service interface like those in a networked system with a service-oriented architecture, or at the command-line interface (CLI).

Regression Strategy 2: Repeat Some Tests

Even with effective automation, it is not always possible to repeat all tests. Often, full automation is impossible, impractical, or simply not supported by management. Perhaps only some of your tests are automated. Perhaps none are automated. Now what?

Well, you could select some subset of your overall set of tests to repeat. I'm familiar with three major techniques for selecting these tests.

The first is the use of traceability. Briefly, traceability is where tests are related to behavioral descriptions of the system like requirements specification elements, design specification elements, or quality risks. You can look at what requirement, design element, or quality risk is affected by the fix or change, trace back to the associated tests, and select those tests for reexecution.[6]

The second is the use of change analysis. In this case, you look at structural descriptions of the system to figure out how change effects could ripple through the system. Unless you have an in-depth understanding of programming and the system's design, you'll probably need help from programmers and designers.[7]

---

[6] I discuss traceability in *Managing the Testing Process, 2e.*

[7] Rick Craig discusses change analysis in *Systematic Software Testing.*

The third is the use of quality risk analysis. With traceability and change analysis, you are using technical risk — where bugs are likely to be found — to decide what to retest. However, you should also revisit your quality risk analysis to determine what areas have high business risk. Even if bugs are unlikely, areas with high business risk should be retested.

Since you're not rerunning every test, you are likely to miss regressions if they occur in unanticipated areas. So, you can use cross-functional tests to get a lot of accidental regression testing.

The analogy is clearing a minefield. The old-fashioned approach of clearing minefields by walking through the field looking for each mine one at a time has been superceded by the use of large earthmoving equipment fitted with heavy rollers and flails. These clear huge swaths of the minefield at once and are unlikely to miss anything.

Likewise, a cross-functional test touches lots of areas of the system at one time. The key assumption behind cross-functional tests is that you won't run into too many bugs. If you do, then you'll not get through any single test because you'll get blocked partway into your cross-functional voyage through the system.

I have a client that builds a large, complex, high-risk geological modeling package for industrial use. This client has a test set that is so large and complex that it takes a whole year — the length of its system test period — to run each test once, with only a small percentage of tests reexecuted to confirm bug fixes. The client relies on cross-functional tests to help mitigate its regression risk.

This client also uses code coverage to help assess the level of regression risk. Code coverage is a concept I'll explain further in the chapters on white-box testing. The premise of code coverage is that the greater the percentage of the program you have tested, the less likely it is that you'll miss bugs. Code coverage measurements allowed my client to make sure 100 percent of the statements in the program had been tested at least once in the one-year test period, which mitigated the risk of breaking existing features. Code coverage measurements also told the client that, thanks to cross-functional testing, in any given four-week period, between 50 and 70 percent of the statements in the program had been executed. This not only mitigated the risk of breaking existing features, but also the risk of breaking new features.

Three Other Regression Strategies

There are three other major regression-risk mitigation strategies that you should consider.

The first is to release more slowly. If you release an update every six months rather than every month, because the release is larger, it will be almost certainly more thoroughly tested. You'll have a chance to rerun a larger portion of your test set, and possibly even the whole test set, on bigger releases. Even if you don't repeat tests at all, if the changes and bug fixes are scattered around the whole system, you can use cross-functional testing to ensure that you've touched everything at least once.

The second of these strategies is to use customer or user testing. By this I mean beta testing for mass-market software. For in-house information technology projects, the analog is pilot, staged or phased, or parallel releases. Assuming you involve the right people in such tests, to the extent that regression has occurred but no user has detected it, it will likely involve minor regressions that few users or customers care about.

The third of these strategies allows you to cope with schedule pressure. It's not as if major, must-fix-immediately bugs will agree to not occur in the field, even with the best regression risk mitigation strategies. For these, you'll end up having to release poorly tested emergency patches. That naturally increases the regression risk. However, if you limit the patches to only those users who need them, roll all the patches into each major maintenance release, and ensure that all the patch users have installed the maintenance release once it comes out, the regression risk increase for your user base will be temporary.

I consider these three strategies to be useful together, ideally in conjunction with one of the other two regression strategies, full or partial retesting. I do not recommend these strategies by themselves, but based on the kinds of regression bugs I've encountered recently, it's clear to me that some large software organizations have no regression risk mitigation strategy at all.

Next, let's move on to a very brief overview of test design and implementation techniques. I'll then talk about general guidelines that can help you select the appropriate strategies and tactics for your testing effort.

Tactics: Categories of Testing Techniques

Being able to classify things is not the same as understanding them, but classifying can help to give you a structure to organize your understanding. With that in mind, here are the major types of test techniques you'll learn through study and hands-on exercises in the coming chapters.

The first major category of test techniques you'll study is static testing. This includes testing of the following kinds of project deliverables:

- Requirement specifications
- Design documents, including deliverables like UML diagrams, network architectures, system dataflow diagrams, and database schemas
- User and programmer documentation
- Source code
- System models

The second major category of test techniques you'll study is black-box (or behavioral) testing. We'll spend the most time on this category, covering the following types of tests:

- Equivalence classes and boundary conditions
- Use cases and scenario tests
- Live data and customer workflow tests
- Domain tests
- Orthogonal arrays
- Decision tables
- State models
- Exploratory

The third major category of test techniques you'll study is white-box (or structural) testing. This includes testing or using the following kinds of project deliverables:

- Control flows in procedural or object-oriented source code
- Data flows in procedural or object-oriented source code
- Interfaces (APIs), including class functions or methods
- Drivers, stubs, and mock objects
- Unit and component integration, including techniques like backbone integration

A well-run test program should use all the appropriate techniques, and a professional tester should be able to advise colleagues — including programmers and project managers, if they request such advice — on these techniques.

That advice might take the form of answers to questions about when particular techniques are useful, who's best able to implement the techniques, and what tools are available to support the techniques. Table 4-1 compares the techniques to answer those questions.

Table 4-1 Comparing Test Techniques

	STATIC	WHITE-BOX	BLACK BOX
What	Testing the system without actually running the system, based on project artifacts characteristics	Testing how the system works internally, how it's built, and its structural it solves	Testing what the system does, particularly its behaviors and the business problems

Continued

Table 4-1   *(continued)*

	STATIC	WHITE-BOX	BLACK BOX
Why	To identify the bugs before they're built (i.e., when they're cheap to fix) to isolate	To identify bugs in the functions, data structures, or interfaces when they're easy customers do	To identify bugs in system results, processing, and behaviors before
Who	All stakeholders	Typically developers	Typically testers
Phase	Usually during requirements and design specification and system development, though also upon any changes to the system definition	Predominant during unit, component, and integration testing, but useful for later phases, especially when automated unit test regression suites are available	Predominant during integration, system, and acceptance testing, but useful for early phases, to help build better unit and component test cases
Tools	Simulators, code analyzers, spelling and grammar checkers, graphics and diagramming, and spreadsheets	Profilers, coverage analyzers, harnesses, debuggers, data generators, and test case generators	Intrusive and non-intrusive GUI tools, load generators, performance tools, and data generators

Don't think of these techniques as rigid or inflexible, particularly not in the sense of creating rigid or inflexible organizational barriers. You can frequently share tools, data, and test cases created using one technique among various project participants. You should encourage cross-pollination of techniques with your colleagues.

Strategic and Tactical Considerations

In addition to the success and failure factors I mentioned when I discussed test strategies, some overarching considerations apply to choices of strategies and tactics.

This first consideration, of course, is resources. If you do not have the money, people (testers and other stakeholders), and time to put a particular strategy or tactic into action, it is obviously a bad choice.

You also must have available to you — or be able to quickly enough avail yourself of — an appropriate test environment. Some tests, especially security or performance tests, require an environment that closely resembles the production environment. This means not just physical availability, but also appropriate quality and technical support. A broken or misconfigured test environment will produce more bad information than good.

Likewise, certain kinds of tests require test tools. Do you have the tools you need, or can you buy them in time? Do you have skilled, trained, and experienced people on your team, or can you hire them in time? Do you have the time built into your schedule to allow for the creation and testing of test scripts, test data, and other test tool related deliverables?

Another key question pertains to the alignment of the test tactics, strategies, and mission with the project. What are the expectations and proclivities of users and other project stakeholders? What do they want and need in terms of coverage? How about accuracy of results? What kinds of reports do they expect from you? Are the stakeholders, the project team leaders, and the organizational leaders risk takers or are they risk averse? What spoken and actual value do they place on quality?

I also believe that, when choosing strategies and tactics, you should consider levels of risk. You need to consider the likelihood of various kinds of failures, definitely. But technical risk is not enough. You must also consider the business risks, the effects of the failures on customers, users, and stakeholders. There might also be legal and ethical concerns that apply, particularly in safety-critical, mission-critical, or government-services systems.

Various considerations related to the system under test apply, too. The current level of system quality will influence your choices. The application domain — the specific business problem being solved — makes some tactics and strategies more appropriate than others. The development, build, and integration processes can constrain your choices.

Finally, the stated and actual organizational mission of the test team will influence your tactical and strategic choices, along with the design of the existing test system.

I have now covered the topic of strategies and tactics. In subsequent chapters, you'll get more ideas about how to pick specific techniques within each category of test tactics. By the end of the book, you'll be able to select the appropriate test strategies and tactics for your testing effort. Let's finish this chapter with a quick look at some general principles and design concepts for building good test systems.

The Test System

In Figure 4-3, you see a view of the four major components of the test system and their relationship to each other:

- Test team: The test engineers, test technicians, and the test lead or manager, who bring their skills, experience, and hard work to bear in designing, implementing, and using the test components

- Testware: The test cases, the test data, the test tools, and the other stuff we build

- Test processes: The formal and informal, documented and undocumented ways in which the testing work is done

- Test environment: The hardware, software, network infrastructure, office and lab space, chairs, tables, phones, and all the other items that make up the testing workplace

To be effective and efficient testers, the test team needs the right test system. The best test team in the world can only achieve mediocre results with the wrong tools in hand.

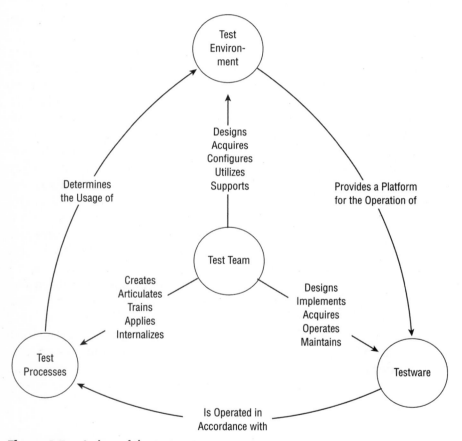

Figure 4-3:   A view of the test system

Designing, implementing, and using good test systems often involve consistent, coordinated high-level and low-level decisions. I refer to these decisions as the test system architecture and the test system engineering, respectively.

Test system architecture includes the design principles, the structure, and the chosen tools from which the system is built. It considers the relationships between the constituent pieces. Since the test system architecture should reflect the system under test now and as you see it evolving, the test system architecture is focused on building a test system you need for the current project and one that will serve you in the future, too. Test system engineering is the implementation of the test system architecture. It involves structured, organized test system development. Through good test system architecture and engineering, a good test team translates good test strategies and tactics into a good test system.

You can measure the quality of a test system in much the same ways as you might measure the quality of the system under test. Let's use the ISO 9126 structure of quality characteristics to look at this topic.

A test system must be functional. It should cover the critical quality risks. It should accurately model field usage and failures so your results are meaningful and understandable in context.

A test system must be reliable. You should be able to repeat your tests. When you run the exact same test against the exact same system under test, you should get the same results. The test system should be robust. Minor bugs and small changes in the test environment should not cause major failures and blockages in the tests. Furthermore, you should be able to use the test system flexibly, particular in terms of being able to run tests in various orders.

A test system must be usable by all those who will use it. This means that, in the hands of the testers and other users, the test system feels natural and powerful, with a clear purpose and operation. The learning curve for the test system should be short, given properly qualified staff. Especially for automated test systems, the test system should capture its results in consistently formatted and structured log files and rely on a sufficient but small set of tools for its construction.

A test system must be portable (at least, if the system under test is or ever will be). It should allow the testers to run tests on all supported platforms.

A test system must be efficient. Test execution should be quick. This implies again the need for test case order independence, as well as low coupling between tests.

A test system must be maintainable. It should grow with the system under test, including being able to support new platforms and new features. It should grow in terms of scale, too. It should exhibit consistent behavior and be built around consistent, understandable paradigms. That way, testers won't break it when they add to it.

Finally, some general observations. Document your test systems to the extent needed to help people understand them. If you are using automated tests, make sure to comment the scripts and use the same kind of structured programming techniques that your programmer peers should use. Keep your test systems clean, with a logical directory structure that is not cluttered up with junk files. Use best practices in release and configuration management to safeguard your test system components, and link their version numbers to the version numbers of the system under test. Finally, remember to test the test system, especially with static testing techniques like reviews!

These are general recommendations that do not apply to every test system. However, before dismissing any one of them as inapplicable for your test system, think carefully. This is a list I've developed through long years of experience, and it may have more applicability to your situation than immediately meets the eye.

Classic Principles for Test Design

In addition to my ideas, I recommend considering Glenford Myers's and Boris Beizer's ideas on test system design, too. I've derived this list from their books.[8]

A good test case should have an expected output or result. Otherwise, testing becomes what Beizer calls "kiddy pool," where whatever pocket the ball happens to end up in is declared the intended pocket.

Your tests should cover both valid, expected conditions and invalid, unexpected conditions. This principle perhaps seems almost too obvious for words, but it's amazing how often people don't adequately cover the error conditions. There are many reasons, including the fact that for many systems there are considerably more error conditions than non-error conditions.

You are most likely to find bugs when testing in those areas where you've already found the most bugs. This may surprise you, but this rule is borne out again and again. Bugs cluster due to the complexity of certain regions in the system, communication problems between programmers, programmer ability problems, and the gradual accumulation of too many hasty patches on a buggy area.[9]

You should consider a test case good when it is likely to detect a bug you haven't seen yet, and you should consider a test case successful when it does so. In other words, try to create tests that are likely to find a wide variety of bugs, and be happy when your tests do find bugs. I would generalize these statements to say that you should design test cases so that you can learn

---

[8] See Glenford Myers *The Art of Software Testing* and Boris Beizer's *Software Testing Techniques.*

[9] See, for example, Robert Sabourin's paper and presentation on bug clusters at
`www.amibug.com`.

something you didn't already know from each test case, and you should be happy when you do learn something from your tests. Furthermore, you should ideally learn the scariest, most dangerous facts first whenever possible. These outlooks help shape your work designing and creating tests.

Myers wrote that the test set should be the subset of all possible test cases with the highest probability of detecting errors. Of course, the set of all possible tests is infinite for any real-world system. Thus, there are infinite possible subsets too. Myers says that we should pick subsets based on the likelihood of bugs. I think Myers is half right. He considers only technical risk in this principle. I recommend considering business risk too. I find that the quality risk analysis technique discussed in Chapter 6 is a good guide to doing so.

Phases of Test Development

The exact phases and sequencing of your test system development tasks will vary. For example, some test strategies emphasize up-front analysis, while others emphasize "just in time" test planning and design. My preference is to do as much work as possible up front because I find I can discover lots of bugs in requirements and design specifications before they're expensive coding errors.

I find that a sequence of quality risk analysis followed by high-level test design and ending with low-level test design (or implementation) is often one that works well for me. Certainly, on a V model type project, this sequence fits into the horizontal arms of the V quite well. At each phase of test development, external inputs are used to create internal deliverables or testware. This sequence of phases, along with the inputs and outputs, are shown in Figure 4-4.

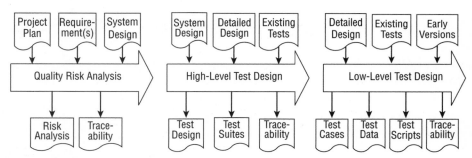

Figure 4-4: Phases of test development

Synopsis of Test Strategies, Tactics, and Design

So, to close this general discussion and get ready to move into specifics, I have some basic recommendations.

First, let the test mission drive the test strategies, let the test strategies drive the test tactics and techniques, and all along make sure that the test mission, strategies, and tactics match the needs of the project. And remember, those needs will likely change over the life of the project.

Be sure to test broadly enough. Cover all the important quality risks, not just functionality or whatever your tools can reach.

Be aware of real-world constraints of time and money and target your testing appropriately. Test extensively in areas of high risk. Reduce test coverage as the level of risk drops.

If you run into these constraints anyway, or if the constraints tighten later in the project, to find ways to save money or time, prune the test set intelligently. Use the smart, focused testing techniques discussed in this book to eliminate redundant or excessive tests. Let risk guide your test reduction activities, with the input of other project stakeholders.

PART

II

Risk-Based Testing

In this Part

Understanding Risks to System Quality

In this chapter, you'll survey a rogues' gallery of undesirable behaviors and outcomes that your system may exhibit. If present, these behaviors and outcomes can negatively affect various stakeholders' experiences of quality. The list of negatively affected stakeholders can include users, system administrators, customers, project sponsors, people who make decisions about your employment, and society in general. No matter who's affected, they won't be happy.

Some people with all sorts of unhealthy habits live to a ripe old age. Some incompetent system engineering teams violate every known best practice yet produce working systems. The undesirable outcomes and behaviors discussed in this section are potential outcomes, not certain results. So, these outcomes are referred to as risks to the quality of the system, or in short, *quality risks*.

This is a long chapter, so you might want to take a break or two as you work through it. If you're new to testing, this chapter will provide a foundation and motivation for much of what comes next. Beginning testers are encouraged to follow along with the entire chapter. For those of you who are experienced testers, if you've had trouble conveying the importance of testing or the effect of cutting back on test time, you might find some useful material here.

Categories of Quality Risks

Computer software, hardware, and systems can fail in the most amazing and various ways, can't they? I have seen many different bugs in my career of developing, using, administering, and testing software systems. Some bugs affect functionality. Some bugs are not functional problems but fall into other quality risk categories:

- Functionality
- Performance and reliability
- Stress, capacity, and volume
- States
- Transitions
- Installation and deinstallation
- Operations
- Maintenance and maintainability
- Regression
- Usability and user interface
- Data quality
- Errors and disaster handling and recovery
- Date and time handling
- Localization
- Configuration and compatibility
- Networked, internetworked, and distributed
- Standards and regulatory compliance
- Security
- Timing and coordination
- Documentation

You can't — and usually shouldn't try to — cover all possible quality risks in your test projects. In the next chapter, we'll talk about how to pick the risks you should mitigate. Chapter 4 takes a look at some categories of quality risks to stimulate your thinking about what to test and why to test it.

Functionality

The most obvious quality risk category is that of functionality. There's always a chance that the system does not provide some function it should.

The function can include a capability, feature, processing, input, or output. When I say the system *should* provide the function, I mean that the users, customers, or other stakeholders require or reasonably expect that function in the system. When I say the function isn't provided, I mean the function is missing entirely, is present but inaccessible to some or all users, or is impaired in some way that makes it less useful than the users could reasonably expect.

For example, if you're testing a calculator program, the lack of an *add* capability would fall into this category. So would a situation in which the *add* capability was implemented but the + key didn't cause the function to activate. The *add* capability might be implemented and accessible, but it might work only on integers, not real numbers. The add operation, when carried out, might give the wrong result, as in 2+2=5. Or there could be some strange side effect where the operation is handled but the result is not at all as expected, as in a divide function where 2 divided by 2 returned 1, but in Roman numeral format.

Parts IV and V cover black-box and white-box test design techniques that help you address risks in the area of functionality. As these test design techniques are covered, there will be a discussion about the kinds of functional and nonfunctional bugs they can find. Learning to pick the right technique for any particular potential bug is part of being a pragmatic tester.

Performance and Reliability

As e-commerce and other Internet applications have become more common, system developers, managers, and testers have become more aware of the importance of risks to quality in terms of performance and reliability. However, these risks were present — and important — even with the first computers.

In Figure 5-1, you see a graphical representation of three types of quality risks in the area of performance. The shaded area at the bottom of the figure represents the required performance, which is 1 second or less transaction processing time at a load of up to 1,000 transactions per minute.

Risks to system quality in the area of performance include the possibility that the system responds to input, produces output, or processes data too slowly under all levels of load. The straight dashed line shows this possibility. The system might perform fine up to some level of load but have an unacceptable nonlinearity in the performance curve, as shown by the steep curved dotted line. Finally, the system might perform within specifications during an initial test run, but subsequent tests—when the system is not rebooted between tests—might reveal an unacceptable performance degradation, as shown in the family of three gently curved lines.

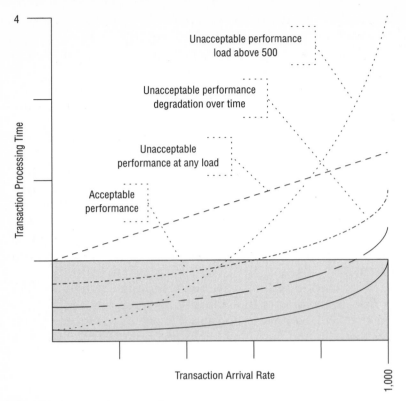

Figure 5-1: Performance bugs

The risk of performance degradation—and indeed, behavioral degradation of any sort—over time brings up the reliability category of risks to system quality. Reliability problems exist when the system fails to function normally each and every time. Such a reliability bug can exhibit itself as an intermittent functional problem. Sometimes, such bugs appear after a long period of runtime or after running under heavy load. I had such a problem with Windows 2000 while writing this book. Extended uptime between reboots usually resulted in characters in some applications taking on the wrong font or the wrong font size.

You might have seen another type of reliability bug, too, where the system functions normally when it functions but crashes or hangs unpredictably. Such bugs can occur after some long period of runtime or after running under heavy load. Alternatively, such bugs can be sporadic and hard to predict. I recently saw such a bug when a security patch caused reboots on a system every third or fourth time the system booted.

CROSS REFERENCE Chapters 10 and 11 cover the topics of functional and nonfunctional equivalence classes and boundary values. The techniques we discuss will help you find these kinds of bugs.

Stress, Capacity, and Volume

Reliability bugs are one kind of problem that often occurs when you load the system heavily. In general, there are various risks to system quality during operations under high stress, capacity, or volume conditions. Let's be a bit more specific.

Risks to system quality in the area of capacity include seeing functionality, performance, or reliability problems due to resource depletion. For example, the performance of operating systems often starts to degrade once the system consumes more than 80 percent of the available hard drive or memory space.

Risks to system quality in the area of volume include seeing functionality, performance, or reliability problems due to the rate of computational, data, and communication flows. For example, the performance of database management systems often starts to degrade when the database management system load exceeds 80 percent of the rated transactions per minute or the allowed number of simultaneous connections.

These kinds of risks to system quality tend to compound nonlinearly when combined, especially if you add inputs, data processing, or outputs that force an error-handling situation. I usually lump these combined quality risks together under the category of stress. When I was testing network operating system software early in my career as a test manager, my testers and I ran a stress test suite that filled the memory and disk space, saturated the CPU and network, and invoked commands, system calls, and standard libraries with legal and illegal parameters. This test had to run for 48 hours without serious system failure to pass. Such tests are sometimes called soak tests.

CROSS REFERENCE Chapters 11 and 12 cover the topics of functional and nonfunctional equivalence classes and boundary values. The techniques discussed help you find these kinds of bugs.

States

Another category of quality risks exists when the system goes to the wrong state or gets stuck in a state from which it can't escape.

In Figure 5-2, the system can accept two inputs. The first is any string. If that string is a number from 0 to 255, it will accept a second input, which must be an alphanumeric string. It gets stuck in the error state if the second input is nonalphanumeric.

This is a contrived example, but real-world examples are not hard to find. The Microsoft Windows operating system once had a classic stuck-state bug. If the system entered a "dangerously low on resources" state, it would display a prompt announcing the problem and offering the user the chance to kill processes in order to release resources and restore the system to stability. I never once found that killing processes resulted in anything other than wasted time. The end result, whether you killed no processes or all of them, was that you had to reboot the system and lose all unsaved data in the running applications.

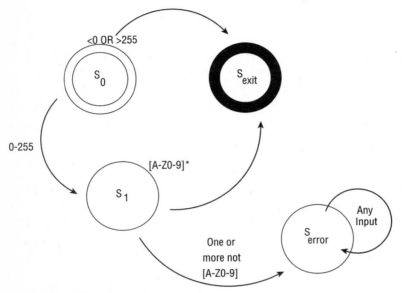

Figure 5-2: A simple state diagram

The state-transition diagram in Figure 5-2 represents a system with a bug. When you reach Part IV on black-box testing, you'll learn how to use state-transition diagrams to model correct system state behavior and how to cover such diagrams to find functional and nonfunctional bugs.

Transactions

Many systems exist to process discrete transactions in contrast to a theoretically unlimited and endless stream of data. For example, a word processor can handle an infinite variety of documents, but an automated teller machine processes only a small number of specific requests. For systems like an automated teller machine, one category of quality risk is that the system might reject or mishandle legal or reasonable transactions.

Here are two obvious examples. You try to withdraw one amount of money but receive another. The amount of money you receive differs from the amount shown on the receipt. Figure 5-3 shows a transaction flow for an ATM that dispenses both 10 and 20 dollar bills but won't handle a transaction to withdraw amounts divisible by 10 dollars.

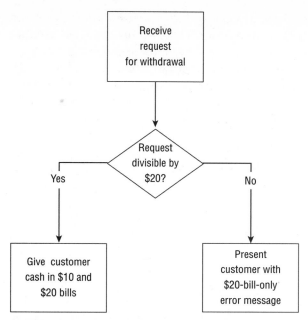

Figure 5-3: A buggy ATM transaction flow

CROSS REFERENCE Part IV covers boundary value analysis, equivalence partitioning, the more general technique of domain testing, and decision tables. These techniques will help you test for problems with transaction processing.

Installation and Deinstallation

Up until now, the discussion in this chapter has been about quality risk categories that arise with running systems. However, systems have to get up and running somehow; you often have to install applications on them, and not every application that you install on a system remains there forever.

Various things can go wrong when installing programs. These include situations in which the program won't install, especially with minimal, maximal, or unusual but supported options or configurations. Another kind of problem arises when the installation process causes damage to the system.

The latter kind of problem once was ubiquitous on Windows systems, with the appropriate nickname "DLL hell." Here, one program overwrote libraries used by another program during its installation process.

Deinstallation can also create problems. Sometimes, deinstallation does not completely remove files and undo changes. Sometimes, deinstallation removes too many files or "undoes" things the install didn't do, causing damage to the system. Sometimes, deinstallation properly removes the program but also removes the data, which should have been left.

Unfortunately, Windows certification testing has not resolved these problems entirely. It is still the case that one program can interfere with another during installation or deinstallation. In particular, many applications on Windows systems do not know how to adequately clean up after themselves when uninstalled, leaving residual files that might or might not be required for ongoing correct operation of the system. This slowly but surely chews up disk space, requiring a clean reinstall of the entire system at some point to reclaim the lost space.

CROSS REFERENCE Part IV covers boundary value analysis and equivalence class techniques that help you address these risks. You're also introduced to two techniques, orthogonal arrays and all-pairs testing, that prove useful when you try to figure out what installation and deinstallation configurations and variables to combine.

Operations

In addition to risks that jeopardize the quality of the system during normal and extreme processing and those that jeopardize the quality of the system during installation and deinstallation, there are risks associated with recurring operating activities.

These include activities carried out at the end of some operational period, such as closing out accounts at the end of the quarter or month. Problems can arise, especially with failure to archive inactive logical records in a safe and recoverable manner as well as archive data that should remain active. In addition, the timing of archiving and the calculation of when a period ends and a new period begins can fail.

For systems with databases, there can be regular requirements to compact or repair the databases. In addition, for such systems, operators often must back up data and configurations regularly along with verifying the restore process. There's a strong risk of side effects like performance problems related to backup or restore operations, the inaccessibility of some or all system functionality during backup or restore operations, and the failure of backup or restore operations under full system capacity conditions. Sometimes, operations activities happen automatically, in the background. For example, rollback logs for a database often need to be purged automatically to avoid major performance and reliability bugs. If the logs increase in size, they can become large, slowing processing, or even overflow storage boundaries and cause systems to crash.

CROSS REFERENCE Part IV covers decision tables, state transition diagrams, orthogonal arrays, and all-pairs tables along with other techniques that can prove useful if you need to test operations.

Maintenance and Maintainability

Other, somewhat-related risks to the quality of the system exist in the areas of maintenance and maintainability. When considering maintenance activities, it's possible that the update and patch install and deinstall processes won't work. Sometimes, users, operators, and administrators can't change configurations appropriately. This is especially true with dynamic reconfiguration activities like Plug and Play, hot plugging, and adding disk space.

In terms of maintainability, the classic risk here relates to the possibility of regression when changes are made. More subtle problems can occur. The system may prevent operators from upgrading databases, operating systems, and other cohabiting or interactive software. Sometimes, databases can grow monotonically, without any facility to archive or purge unneeded data or way to separate out unneeded data.

CROSS REFERENCE This chapter talked about installation and deinstallation, including configuration variables. Part IV discusses techniques like orthogonal arrays, boundary values, and decision tables that will help you design tests for these risks. Regression test strategies were also covered in Chapter 4.

Regression

Chapter 4 covers the topic of regression and regression testing in some detail, but let me speak briefly about this risk while you're surveying the broad galaxy of quality risks that afflict software.

By regression, I mean that a previously working feature, function, capability, or behavior fails following a change. The problem in system testing is that software/hardware systems, being digital, tend to be discrete rather than continuous in their failure modes.

What I mean by that can be illustrated by analogy. If you pop a single rivet out of a steel beam in a bridge, you weaken the bridge. That weakening is typically slight and can be calculated mathematically. Bridge-builders can cope with imprecision and unforeseen consequences by so-called "overengineering." Civil engineers might overengineer a bridge to withstand up to 200 percent of its expected loads. Civil engineers use scale models to accurately and realistically test proposed changes in materials and design along with foreseeable failures like the loss of a few rivets. Furthermore, suppose you drive your car up to a bridge and see that it has lost a rivet or two. This might make you concerned. However, if you see a large truck safely pass over the bridge, you'll probably be confident that, because the bridge supported the weight of the truck, it can support your car.

All of this predictability, calculability, and scalability arises because of the continuous nature of engineering materials and the systems like bridges that are built with them. Digital systems, consisting of discrete zeros and ones, do not exhibit such behaviors.

The effects of changes — even small, localized, isolated changes — are not always small, localized, or isolated. How many times have you heard a statement like, "How could that have happened? I only changed one line of code."

A small change, even one line of code, can affect the behavior of the rest of the system.[1] A small change can trigger an inappropriate decision, leading the program down the wrong path. A small change can cause incompatible data to enter shared data sets, including dynamic dataflows and static databases, resulting in bugs that exhibit their effects a long way from their origin. Side effects of changes can impair or even break cohabiting, interacting, or underlying software. The adding of yet another feature can lead to systemic performance and capacity issues.

CROSS REFERENCE In Chapter 6, you'll learn a set of powerful techniques that will help you manage these risks to system quality due to regression.

Usability and User Interface

One special category of quality risks relates to the usefulness and usability of the system by the intended user or operator. In some cases, systems present cumbersome interfaces that do not follow normal or expected workflows, leading to user frustration, confusion, and mistakes. In other cases, functionality, while present in the system, is practically inaccessible to the user or operator. Systems can be inappropriately difficult for the users to learn, leading to mistakes, inefficiency, and possibly abandonment. Finally, users and operators can find instructional, help, and error messages misleading, confusing, or misspelled.

Usability and user interface testing is a special field of study. If this is a high-priority risk category for your system, then I encourage you to learn more about it. You can start by reading some books on usability.[2] In this book, you learn the skills, attitudes, and outlooks that can help you get started identifying user interface and usability problems.

CROSS REFERENCE You learn to tell if something is a high-risk category for your system in Chapter 6.

---

[1] See Peter Neumann's book *Computer-Related Risks* for the story of massive toll-free phone service interruption resulting from a one-character typographical error in a program change that was not properly regression tested.

[2] Good examples include Donald Norman's *The Invisible Computer,* Jakob Nielsen's *Usability Engineering,* and Jeff Rubin's *Handbook of Usability Testing.*

Data Quality

Many systems exist primarily to do interesting things with data. Inputs are processed, transformed, and stored. Databases are queried, records linked through foreign keys, and integrity constraints enforced. Outputs are displayed, printed, and transmitted to other system.

So, data quality poses a major category of quality risks for many systems. The system might corrupt or lose data. The system might store bad or nonsense data in a database without integrity constraints. Databases shared across multiple systems can allow data that is valid for one system to be accessed by another system that does not know how to handle it, resulting in failures that are removed in time and feature space from the source of the problem.

Let me give you some quick examples, one irritating, some scary.

As a traveling consultant, I spend lots of time preparing expense reports after my lengthy business trips. I once used an expense-reporting package that ran on Windows 95. (I've been doing this traveling-consultant job for a while.) This expense-reporting program worked fine — except that it damaged the expense file when Windows crashed while the program had the file open. Sometimes the damage involved a single data element, like a lunch charge. I could fix those problems. More often, though, the corruption was invisible, in the form of damaged file indices. The application continued to work with the file for some time. During this period, the application gave no outward sign of problems, nor did the application give me a chance to correct the problems. However, after the corruption compounded over a few file open/update/save/close cycles, the application would start to crash every time the file was opened. There was no way for me to repair the files.

Now for the scary examples. I read an article in the mid-1990s about data quality problems in health care. The article quoted error rates in the 25 percent range per patient for hospital databases. That's okay if you're talking about losing track of how many syringes and bandages were used for a patient. But suppose you're talking about drug allergies? If you think that the situation is improved, in 2006 I read an article talking about banks and insurance companies that cited the identical error rate.

As with usability and user interface testing, data quality is a special field of study. If data quality is a high-priority risk category for your system — and you'll learn how to tell if it is in the next chapter — then I encourage you to learn more about the topic. Some helpful books have been written on the topic of data quality.[3]

CROSS REFERENCE In a later chapter, you'll learn about using decision tables and customer data for testing, which will help you get started with data quality testing.

---

[3] For example, Larry English's *Improving Data Warehouse and Business Information Quality*.

Error and Disaster Handling and Recovery

If life — and all the users and other systems your systems interact with — were perfect, you wouldn't worry about handling errors. However, systems invariably have to handle invalid inputs, connection failures, operating system crashes, corrupted files, and so forth. Many systems also have to handle more infrequent but more serious problems like earthquakes, fires, floods, and terrorism.

Now, you can't expect systems to proceed as if nothing had happened in these circumstances. The risk to system quality is that the system might handle these problems poorly. Users making input errors might receive unhelpful messages, like "Fatal Error: 0x35AF" or my own favorite from the Unix cpio program, "Out of sync: get help."

Sometimes, systems experience a disproportional loss of functionality due to an error. For example, if a word processor can't find the default printer, you wouldn't expect it to be unable to print to another printer or edit a file. Yet such errors happen.

Error conditions can result in loss of data. Sometimes you're lucky and the only data lost is the current screen, form, or record being input or edited. Sometimes, though, data corruption is extensive and not necessarily confined to the current application. Registry key corruption on Windows systems is an example of an error damaging the entire family of applications running on the Windows system.

Further complicating these situations, it is sometimes difficult to restore the system to working state after a badly handled error condition. In some cases, the system, in the course of succumbing to the error, damages configuration files or static data stores in a way that's hard to fix later. The data quality bug in the expense-reporting package I mentioned earlier is an example of this kind of misbehavior.

In some cases, you get all of these undesirable behaviors. While I was writing this very section of this chapter, Microsoft Word corrupted this file. First, I received an utterly inscrutable message, which included some hexadecimal error code, and then I received something perplexing about not being able to read a memory address, also given in hexadecimal. The application crashed and lost my most recent changes. I rebooted the system a few times, but Word continued to crash every time I tried to save this file. Furthermore, after Word crashed, if I tried to open PowerPoint or Acrobat format files, all the fonts were missing from the system and none of the text was visible. In order to get the system back in a working state, I had to save this file in rich-text format, then reconvert it back into Word format. The reason for the initial damage to this file remains a complete mystery to me.

NOTE If I'd had the time to really track this problem down, I could have written a thorough bug report on it and submitted it to Microsoft. Being in the middle of trying to get real work done, I didn't. Some ideas on how to write good bug reports can be found on the Library page of my website, `www.rexblackconsulting.com`, in the article "The Fine Art of Writing a Good Bug Report."

CROSS REFERENCE Chapters 10 and 11 discuss equivalence class partitioning and boundary value analysis. These will help you understand how to create error conditions.

Date and Time Handling

In addition to having to handle common errors, many systems must also handle dates. This has created significant information technology problems, including the infamous "Y2K bugs" that consumed huge proportions of company and government IT budgets in the late 1990s and contributed to the depression in the high-technology sector in the early 2000s. In addition to having to handle a once-in-a-hundred-lifetimes type of event like a new millennium, systems must frequently handle events like leap years.

NOTE Do you know the rule for calculating leap year? Are you sure? A year is a leap year in the Common Era calendar if it is divisible by four, unless it's divisible by 100, which is why 1900 was not a leap year and 2100 won't be one either. However, a year divisible by 100 *is* a leap year if it is also divisible by 400, which is why 2000 was a leap year.

Many systems must deal with expiration dates. Licenses expire. Credit cards expire. Insurance policies expire. After some period of time, the right of a bank to disqualify a borrower based on derogatory credit report entries (such as bankruptcies) can also expire. Failure to handle such expiry events properly can expose a company to serious financial and legal risks.

In addition to date-related and date-math-related risks, systems that deal with time zones are subject to time-related and time-math-related risks. These can interact with dates too. What are the current time differences between where you live and the following cities: Phoenix, Arizona; Tel Aviv, Israel; New Delhi, India?

Events that recur based on date or time have various complications and risks associated with them too. Are there weekly, monthly, quarterly, or yearly processing and reports that must be done? What might happen to an event that runs at 2:30 A.M. every single night? On which dates do the 12 most important holidays where you live fall next year? If you find these questions hard to answer, chances are your programmers do too.

DATA HANDLING FAUX PAS

Let me add a human element to the risk of date handling too. One reviewer, Michael Bolton, told me a wistful story about computer systems and automated data processing. While serving as the executor for his father's estate, he found a promotional insert from a credit card company in a letter that had arrived after his father's death. The letter, addressed to "The Estate of David Bolton," included the offer to "become a customer of our *new* credit card and get free oil changes for life."

CROSS REFERENCE Chapters 10 and 11 help you devise clever tests that root out date- and time-related bugs.

Localization

Localization refers to the ability of a system to support local customs, languages, norms, and laws. There are two broad categories of quality risks related to localization. One category relates to the user interface, and the other to operations. Let's start with the user interface issues.

Of course, if the system does not support the character sets used by the local language, you have a localization problem. Languages that use the Roman alphabet, such as English, German, and Spanish, have single-byte character sets. Some languages that use other alphabets, such as Russian and Hebrew, have single-byte character sets too.

Some languages — for example, those that use ideograms — have more extensive alphabets and need multibyte character sets. Examples include Japanese and Chinese.

Of course, whatever character set the messages are presented in, they must also be presented in the appropriate language translation. As anyone who speaks multiple languages can tell you, this is more complicated than a mechanical, word-for-word mapping. In addition to grammatical differences, you have cultural, ethnic, and religious taboos. Translators must take slang words, double meanings, and vulgarity into account.

Localization also has operational implications. For example, time zones and time formats vary based on locale. Does the time change in the summer? (In the United States, this is called daylight savings times, but it goes by different names around the world.) If so, when does adjusted time begin and end? Are dates written "month day year" (as in the United States) or in the more logical "day month year" format (as in much of the rest of the world)?

The locale affects the calendar in use. For example, when is year zero? Is it the Common Era, based on the birth of Jesus? Or perhaps, as in Taiwan, based on the date when Sun Yat-sen founded the Republic? Are lunar calendars, such as those used in Israel and the Muslim world, needed to calculate holidays and birthdays?

For financial applications, of course, the locale affects the currency. Does your system work in dollars, pounds, yen, euros, or shekels? If in dollars, are we talking about U.S. dollars, Australian dollars, New Zealand dollars, or Canadian dollars? What is the effect of exchange rate fluctuations?

CROSS REFERENCE Because localization is a specialized field of testing, this book doesn't go into it in much depth. However, during quality risk analysis — which is discussed in Chapter 6 — you should take care to include localization risks when appropriate.

Configuration and Compatibility

Another family of risks to system quality lives in the areas of configuration and compatibility. Different users configure both the hardware and software of systems differently. A family of systems may support various hardware configurations. Some systems support configuration changes after installation, such as adding disk space, memory space, or other storage or upgrading or adding processors or other boards. Each program on a system or even in a network of systems can conceivably interact. Both obvious and subtle interactions can occur between programs, operating systems, and databases sharing the same or networked hardware.

CROSS REFERENCE Often, the number of potential combinations of configurations is huge. In Chapter 18, you learn about orthogonal arrays and all-pairs tables. These are effective techniques for sufficient testing of factor and configuration interactions and compatibility. Domain analysis, the subject of Chapter 16, can be useful when the factors are known to interact in specific ways.

Networked, Internetworked, and Distributed

Speaking of networked systems, special risks to system quality exist here as well. Network latency can cause bugs. So can security and resource sharing. For systems that interact across metropolitan area networks, wide area networks, and the Internet, these risks increase significantly because packets might travel through multiple systems, switches, gateways, and firewalls before arriving at their destination. If the network or internetworked application is distributed across a wide area of locations, you must add in the risks associated with dates, times, and localization.

CROSS REFERENCE In Chapter 25, you learn techniques for dealing with these significant risks as early on in the life cycle as possible.

Standards and Regulatory Compliance

More risks to the quality of the system exist in the areas of standards and regulations. A system can work properly but be excluded from the market by failing to meet standards, either effectively (no one will buy it) or legally (the government won't let anyone buy it or sell it).

In terms of industry standards, the "Designed for Windows" logo and ANSI compliance are common examples. Government standards and regulations affect encryption (in terms of export from the United States), language support (in terms of sales in certain Canadian provinces), and measures and currency (in the European Union).

CROSS REFERENCE Chapters 6 and 7 cover the topic of risk analysis.

If standards and regulatory noncompliance are significant risks for your system, you'll want to identify them in the risk analysis. Next, you'll need to study the applicable standards and regulations that affect your system.[4] You might end up working with one or more external test labs to gain formal compliance status in this area. Be sure to pick a reputable partner.

Security

With the growth of the Internet, awareness of the risks associated with security has increased. However, not a week goes by that you don't read about some serious penetration or near penetration of some critical piece of infrastructure. While writing this chapter, I read of a country where people applying for security clearances did so online, using a nonsecured web page, and those applications were then processed almost entirely over the Internet. Apparently, X-raying shoes in airports is seen as an effective substitute for being careful about who is trusted with sensitive, classified data.

Security risks are legion. They include viruses and worms, criminals breaking into servers, vandals causing denial of service attacks, email and Internet communications being bugged and intercepted, and more. Criminals can break into your systems through computers, phones, and even through gullible people.

---

[4] You might consider Amy Zuckerman's *International Standards Desk Reference* as a resource.

Even people who are aware of security risks often make bad assumptions about how to reduce those risks. Some people assume that encryption (HTTPS) on web servers solves security problems. Some people assume merely buying a firewall prevents people from breaking into your network. Some people trust unskilled network or system administrators to deal with security problems.

Security testing is another specialized field of test expertise. You might want to read some books and online resources about the topic if it's important to you.[5] However, my recommendation to those new to security testing is to identify security risks during risk analysis, and then let professional security testers handle the testing.

Timing and Coordination

As we finish this chapter, let me mention a couple other risks to system quality. One is timing and coordination.

When you have communicating components, or shared components, timing and coordination between those components is a concern. For example, with an e-commerce system, how long should the system wait between events like mouse-clicks and submitted screens? At what point can it safely conclude that the customer has abandoned the transaction? As another example, consider the automated teller machine. What happens when the central computer times out or the network goes down? What if that happens in the midst of a transaction? For a last example, if we're testing an inventory system, what happens when two salespeople try to sell the same item at the same time?

CROSS REFERENCE Part IV, which includes chapters about black-box testing, discusses how to design tests using typical usage scenarios, state transition diagrams, and customer data. You can use these techniques to expose bugs that live in these quality risks.

Documentation

Finally, let me briefly mention the quality risks related to documentation. While little attention is paid to documentation — technical writers were among the first people laid off during the high-tech depression of the early 2000s — for many people the quality of the documentation significantly affects their impressions of the quality of the system.

Documentation quality problems include being technically incorrect, of course, especially the examples. The user can find the documentation insulting

---

[5] For example, check out the Risks Digest online at `//catless.ncl.ac.uk/Risks` or Steve Splaine's *Testing Web Security* or James Whittaker's *How to Break Software Security*.

or offensive, teeming with grammatical or spelling errors, or afflicted with distracting cosmetic or formatting problems.

Documentation refers not only to hard copy, but also to electronic documentation. Help screens, installation instructions, error messages, and wizards are forms of documentation.

CROSS REFERENCE All of the black-box test techniques in Part IV are useful in testing documentation.

Can You Think of Other Quality Risks?

Whew! Take a deep breath. You've just finished a long chapter.

"But wait," you might say, "I can't be finished. I can think of at least four or five other quality risk categories that I've seen or heard about."

Yes, and so could I. But isn't this list already too long? What if you tried to cover all the dozens of quality risks discussed in this chapter? Could you test them all? Would they fit into the budget and schedule context of the project? Would you end up wasting time and effort on unimportant problems? Surely any attempt to test this whole set of quality risks would be neither effective nor efficient by our definitions!

So, what shall we do? Chapter 6 gives you some ideas on how to trim the infinite number of things you could test into a finite list of risks you should mitigate.

Aligning Testing with Quality Risks

In this chapter, I introduce a powerful technique for targeting your test efforts. I call this technique *quality risk analysis*. I'm going to show you three approaches for quality risk analysis: one informal, one based on an industry-standard software requirements structuring practice, and the third based on a quality management system.

I use quality risk analysis to guide the project team through finding specific quality risks (groups of similar potential bugs) that live within the quality risk categories you met in the last chapter. Once those risks are discovered, the team assigns levels of priority to each quality risk based on likelihood and impact. These levels of priority serve to focus the testing effort. We should spend a lot of testing effort where the risk level is highest, less where it's a bit lower, even less where it's lower still, and ultimately, little if any effort where the risk is marginal.

Let's see how, starting with an overview of the quality risk analysis process and its goals.

Prioritize Risks to System Quality

Don't be mystified by the phrase "quality risk analysis." It's a simple concept: Test where the odds favor the highest benefit. Finding likely bugs is beneficial. Finding dangerous bugs is beneficial. The more likely or dangerous any particular group of potential bugs is, the more time and money you should invest in looking for them. Quality risk analysis makes testing a form of risk management.

Where do you find information about potential bugs? If you have them, requirements and design specifications are good inputs. Sales, marketing, and project sponsor documents should give hints about what's most important. Stand these documents on their heads by changing information about what the system should do into information about what it shouldn't do and you're off to a good start.

Check out bug tracking and field failure data from past releases or similar projects. Read trade magazines, test-related publications, books on software risk and testing, and online discussion groups. From these sources, you're likely to find out a lot about what the system could — or does — do wrong.

These sources of information give you a laundry list of potential bugs, but not all bugs have the same importance. To understand the relative importance of potential bugs, you have to ask yourself questions like the following:

- What matters to my customers, users, and other stakeholders?
- What bugs would cause the most trouble?
- What bugs are most likely, particularly under real-world circumstances, in actual operation?

You must consider customer and user requirements and usage, the system design and implementation, and the supported system configurations to get to the answers to these questions.

Once you have decided on relative priorities of potential groups of bugs, you have a framework that allows you to focus testing on the important risks to system quality. For those groups of bugs you need to test, you can base the extent of testing on the level of risk. You can also decide what level of risk you can ignore, allowing you to eliminate some areas from the scope of testing.

Okay, so that's quality risk analysis in brief. Let's get a bit more specific.

Testing, Customer Usage, and System Configurations

Ultimately, all the risks to system quality add up to the possibility that the users, customers, and other stakeholders will be dissatisfied. So, to mitigate that risk, you must test in such a way that you experience the quality of the system through the eyes of the users, customers, and stakeholders before they receive the system. You must build a test system — a collection of test data, test cases, test procedures, test tools, and so forth — that gives you this experience. In other words, you need a high-fidelity test system that gives you as a tester an experience of quality that truthfully reproduces the users' experiences of quality.

What you want to avoid is testing in such a way as to fail to understand the users', customers', and other stakeholders' experiences of quality. In other words, you want to avoid a low-fidelity test system that gives you as a tester an inaccurate experience of quality, one that does not reflect the user's. When I work as a test engineer or test manager, quality risk analysis is how I lay the foundation for a high-fidelity test system.

It's also important that quality risk analysis identify not only *what* users and customers do with the system, but the environments *in which* they do it and *how* they go about doing it. This is particularly critical when trying to test for nonfunctional risks. Why?

Many bugs are shy, especially during testing. They reveal themselves only during security, performance, stress, volume, data quality, and reliability testing, and then only if you get the conditions just right.

Why worry about shy bugs? These bugs are sometimes catastrophic. Shy bugs I've seen over the years have caused symptoms like server crashes, sudden loss of performance, and database lockups and corruption. Sometimes these bugs were a lot less shy in the real world than they were in the test lab.

So, I've found that tests for these bugs are most effective when I run them in fieldlike environments and configurations. Trying to explore many nonfunctional quality risks like security, performance, and reliability in less-complex settings often doesn't work. You can't extrapolate the results from simple configurations to more complex configurations many times since software is not linear.

The extent of the field and production environments' complexity can be daunting. I've worked with test configurations that involved dozens of interconnected servers, hundreds of clients, and a wide variety of local area network, wide area network, and phone system connections. In an in-house IT setting, the company can lock down the desktop, server, network, and other configurations, but in the Internet and shrink-wrapped software worlds, myriad possible configurations exist.

When confronted with diverse environments, you'll need to use representative sets of configurations, like typical IBM mainframe, client/server, or web configurations. The chosen configurations will be better at finding bugs if they live at the upper and lower boundaries of supported memory, CPU, disk space, and other parameters.

I'll talk about boundary values analysis, orthogonal arrays, and all-pairs tables, techniques that can help with configuration testing, in later chapters. For the moment, though, keep in mind that quality risk analysis must examine these risks.

How can you, as a tester, find out what the users and customers do or what configurations they use? As I mentioned earlier, requirements and design specifications, marketing and sales materials, bug and field failure data, all of these sources of information will help. However, I know from experience that an isolated effort by the test team to analyze the quality risks does not work. We simply don't know enough.

If you want to understand real-world usage and configurations, you'll need to involve others. The sales, marketing, and business analysts know the target users and customers. The technical support or help desk staff know the current users and customers. Project and senior management know the overall direction of the business and the system. Users groups, test newsgroups, peers, and publications have anecdotes and some data.

These risk analysis participants have their advantages and disadvantages. The sales, marketing, and business analysts know the users and customers. They want to deliver quality. However, they often don't have a lot of detailed technical information to offer. Sometimes, they only have experience with specific customers.

Technical support or help desk staff know the current customers — or at least the ones with problems. They are motivated to help you perform good testing since they know they'll suffer if you don't. However, the data they have is often incomplete. They typically know a lot about failing scenarios and configurations but not so much about working ones.

Project and senior management understand the product road maps and the strategic directions. However, like sales, marketing, and business analysts, they might not have a lot of detailed information.

If available, users groups will know the product, but nondisclosure and privacy issues may prevent open dialog with them. Similarly, you might have test newsgroups, peers, and publications who could help. These folks should understand the test issues, but of course they might work for competitors!

Any one perspective is a weak basis for quality risks analysis, but a cross-functional risk analysis team that includes these perspectives works well.

Approaches for Quality Risks Analysis

Once you've identified the key stakeholders — the people whose perspectives you need to understand all the important quality risks and their relative levels — you can use various approaches to perform the actual analysis.

The simplest way is an informal approach. You can start with the classic quality risk categories, such as those we went over in the previous chapter. You can augment that list with other sources, like historical bug data from your system. You might also consider books and other resources that include lists of common bugs.[1]

---

[1] For example, my own *Managing the Testing Process* and Peter Neuman's *Computer-Related Risks*.

For each category of quality risks, brainstorm with the cross-functional risk analysis team. What types of bugs might fall into this category that could afflict your system? For example, suppose you're considering performance for an e-commerce application. You might come up with the following risks:

- Failure to respond to a user input within half a second
- Failure to finish updating the screen within five seconds
- Failure to complete the check-out procedure within one minute

Once the team has listed the specific risks in each category, it's time to go back and prioritize them. I'll return to some approaches to doing that in a moment. First, though, let me mention two formal techniques for risk analysis.

The first is based on the International Standards Organization standard 9126. This standard provides a structure for examining the level of quality in the system. In the ISO 9126 standard, the standards committee identified six main quality characteristics for systems:

- Functionality
- Reliability
- Usability
- Efficiency
- Maintainability
- Portability

Within each characteristic, the committee identified some subcharacteristics. Not all subcharacteristics apply to each system.

To use ISO 9126 as a risk analysis approach, identify the subcharacteristics that apply for your system. At that point, you can proceed as with the informal approach, identifying specific risks to system quality within each subcharacteristic. The key differences are that you're using an industry-standard structure for your risk analysis and that you have a three-level hierarchy (quality characteristic, quality subcharacteristic, quality risk) rather than a two-level hierarchy (quality risk category, specific quality risk).

The most formal technique that I've used is called Failure Mode and Effect Analysis.[2] You can use either a quality risk category list or the ISO 9126 characteristics and subcharacteristics as a starting point. Some people also use subsystems as a starting point. However, I don't recommend subsystems as a basis for risk analysis because many bugs, especially at the system test level, are systemic rather than localized.

---

[2] See D.H. Stamatis's book, *Failure Mode and Effect Analysis,* for more information on this technique.

Within each grouping — whether categories, subcharacteristics, or subsystems — the risk analysis team then identifies specific quality risks again. In the Failure Mode and Effect Analysis approach, these specific quality risks are called failure modes, which is a straightforward name and a good way to think about specific quality risks.

The team then tries to anticipate the effects of each failure on the user, the customer, other stakeholders, or even society. Prioritization occurs based on an assessment of the severity, priority, and likelihood of each effect. A numeric scale — say 1 through 5 or 1 through 10 — is used for each of these three factors. The three factors are then multiplied together to calculate a risk priority number, which is an aggregate risk metric.

The common thread tying these techniques together is cross-functional teams brainstorming the risks and then assigning relative priorities. These priorities will serve to guide the extent of testing performed against each risk.

Let's now look at the process — and a way to document it — a bit more closely, using informal quality risk analysis.

Informal Quality Risk Analysis

In Table 6-1, you see a template that can be used to capture the quality risk analysis. As I explain this table, I'll clarify the key concepts of quality risk analysis.

Table 6-1   Quality Risk Analysis Table

QUALITY RISK	TECH. RISK	BUS. RISK	RISK PRI. #	EXTENT OF TESTING	TRACKING
Risk Category 1					
Risk 1					
Risk 2					
Risk n					

In the first column you list the quality risks identified by the cross-functional team. This table shows a two-level hierarchy, where you have risk categories and, within each category, specific risks. You could use this same template for an ISO 9126–structured analysis. You'd have a three-level hierarchy in that case.

In addition to helping jog your memory about types of bugs to remember, the categories or characteristics and subcharacteristics, serve to structure the analysis and the documentation. However, you needn't try to identify all the bugs within one category before moving on to the next. If you and your quality risk analysis team members find it more productive to brainstorm risks without regard to category and then put the risks into the categories as a subsequent step, that's fine, too.

Don't worry too much about which category a given risk falls into either. As long as it appears somewhere on the list, you won't forget to prioritize it — which is the important part.

If you're using an approach where you have requirements and/or design specifications as inputs for your risk analysis, as you identify risks you should also, using the last column in the table, capture the specification elements to which each risk relates.

As a simple approach to prioritizing risks, you can say that there are two recognizable and independent contributors to the level of risk for any given bug.

First is the technical level of risk. This is primarily the likelihood that a type of bug might exist. To assess the technical level of risk, include system architects, designers, and senior programmers in your risk analysis process.

Second is the business level of risk. This is primarily the impact that a type of bug might have on the users, customers, or other stakeholders. To assess the business level of risk, involve business analysts, product and project managers and sponsors, customer support or help desk staff, and other people who are "close to the customers."

Keeping matters simple, you can rate both business and technical risk on the same scale:

1. Very high
2. High
3. Medium
4. Low
5. Very low

You can use a different scale if you'd like. What matters is that you are able to distinguish between different levels in the scale and use those value consistently. I usually don't use a 10-point scale anymore because I can't distinguish between a 9 and a 10 or a 2 and a 3 on such a scale.

Having rated the two contributors to the level of risk, you'll now want to aggregate them to produce a single quality risk priority rating. One way to do this is to multiply them. Another way is to add them. You can also use a weighting factor if you decide that one contributor is more important than the others.

Keeping it simple, suppose you multiply the two risk factors with no weighting. You then have a risk priority number from 1 to 25 for each risk. If you use the descending 1 to 5 scale given earlier for each, that means that a risk priority number of 1 is most important and 25 is least important.

You can then use this risk priority number to determine the appropriate extent of testing for each specific risk. You can group risks with similar risk priority numbers into categories that will receive approximately the same amount of testing effort. Here's an example:

- Risks rated from 1 to 5 receive extensive (or comprehensive) testing.
- Risks rated from 6 to 10 receive broad testing.
- Risks rated from 11 to 15 receive cursory testing.
- Risks rated from 16 to 20 will be tested if the opportunity arises.
- Risks rated from 21 to 25 will have bugs reported against them, if discovered, but will not be tested.

Let me explain each of these extent-of-testing categories a bit further. To make them clear, let's suppose that you're talking about testing the file-import facilities for an application like Microsoft Word.

Extensive testing means testing that is both broad and deep. If you're testing Word, you know that it can open not only files in the latest Word format, but also files in previous Word formats as well as files in other formats like WordPerfect, text, spreadsheets, and so forth. Within each supported file type, there are a number of objects that might exist, such as headings, paragraphs of text, headers and footers, tables of contents, footnotes and endnotes, and pictures. Extensive testing would imply testing each supported file type, with every supported object type for that file type.

Broad testing means trying to span the functional capabilities but not trying every variation. In the Word example, that means trying each supported file type but not every supported kind of object in each supported file type.

Cursory testing is a sampling approach. In the Word example, that would mean some of the supported file types and some of the supported objects in those file types but not every file type nor every object gets tested. There is a clear commitment to do some level of testing with cursory testing though.

That's not the case with opportunity testing. Opportunity testing means that, if you end up testing somewhere else and you have an opportunity to test against a risk rated as deserving opportunity testing, you'll spend some minimum amount of time — that is, you'll take the opportunity — to test this risk. In the Word example, you might say that, since you'll be testing file-open operations, you'll look for opportunities to open files other than those in the latest Word format.

The level of resource commitment is even lower with the report-bugs extent of testing. Here, if you happen to see a bug related to the risk, you'll spend the time to report it. However, you won't invest any time in testing for this risk. In the Word example, if while doing some exploratory testing with non-Word files you come across a bug in the area of file importing, then you will report it. (Of course, since the report-bug extent of testing is associated with very low risk, the fact that you found bugs in this area might call into question your risk analysis and trigger a reanalysis.)

Now, you might notice a few interesting facts about this risk prioritization approach. Some of these facts might trouble you. Let me point them out, along with possible solutions.

First, notice that the risk levels from 1 to 5 that I'm placing on business and technical risks aren't really numbers. They represent categories. I am then using those numbers — which aren't numbers — to calculate another number. I then translate this number into a new category, the extent of testing. If it bothers you that I'm performing mathematical operations on entities that aren't numbers, then you can use a different approach. You can use a lookup table approach to translate the two risk factors into an extent of testing without any math. If you do so, though, notice that the same table can be modeled with a mathematical formula, which is why I don't worry about this fact too much.

Second, the categorization I showed earlier with the risk priority number is biased toward extensive testing. There are many combinations of business and technical risks that can result in extensive testing, but only one that can result in the report-bugs-only extent of testing. That bias is appropriate for some systems and not for others. Feel free to adjust the translation of risk priority numbers to the extent of testing as appropriate.

Finally, this approach can feel very rigid. It isn't meant to be, though. If you feel that a particular risk deserves a greater or lesser extent of testing than the numbers might indicate, change the extent of testing. The risk priority number is a guide. It is not a magic crystal ball.

Tips for Risk Analysis

Now that I've covered the basic approach and considerations for risk analysis, you're just about ready to put the technique to work. However, let me give you some tips.

First, the cross-functional team is essential. Ideally, have everyone in the room at once for a brainstorming session. One of the benefits of quality risk analysis is that it can build consensus around what is going to be tested — and how much — and what is not going to be tested. However, that project-team-wide consensus can be built only when everyone is involved.

When you use the team approach to quality risk analysis, I suggest developing the list of risks first, then assigning the risk levels as a second pass-through. This is best because the risks are relative to each other; that is, a given risk is higher or lower not in a vacuum but as compared to all the other risks.

Sometimes you'll have trouble getting people to commit to the long sessions required to hold a quality risk analysis meeting. In that case, it can shorten the meeting if you put together a draft quality risk analysis first (using requirements and design specifications) and then have a review meeting with the whole team. Supplying a draft can work, but make sure people actually participate in the review, adding more items and adjusting the risk levels. Otherwise, the quality risk analysis will represent only your thinking. Quality risk analysis works only when the perspectives of all the important stakeholders in quality and testing participate.

It's also a good idea to have the team update and review the quality risk analysis at key points in the project. For example, if you're following a traditional waterfall/V model project methodology, you can prepare the quality risk analysis during the requirements phase, update it once the design specification is prepared, review the technical risk when the implementation is complete, and update the technical and business risk ratings as the unit, integration, and system test phases begin. That will allow you to fine-tune the focus of the testing as you get more and better information.

One problem almost everyone has when they first start using quality risk analysis is that they get too detailed. Testers seem to want to jump straight into test case design because that's the fun part. However, quality risk analysis must stay at a higher level. You should only separate risk items when it's necessary to distinguish between different levels of risk. If the document gets too long, with every possible test condition listed as a risk, then the document will be hard to use and people will get lost in the "can't see the forest for the trees" complexity.

Finally, another common mistake that people make with risk-based testing is considering only technical risk (more frequently) or only business risk (less frequently). True quality risk analysis involves analyzing both technical *and* business risk. Again, technical risk is the likelihood of the potential problem and, to a lesser extent, the impact of the potential problem on the system. Business risk is the likelihood of the potential problem occurring in real-world usage or environments and the impact of the potential problem on the user, customers, and other stakeholders.

Challenges of Risk Analysis

As I mentioned, one important benefit of quality risk analysis is that you can build consensus across the team on the level of risk associated with each potential problem and the appropriate amount of testing to perform. However, you might find it challenging to obtain this consensus.

One challenge to consensus is when people don't agree on the level of risk due to a lack of knowledge. For example, a marketing person might say that the level of risk related to a security bug is low. However, a programmer might explain that, since the system is written in C++, it is technically possible for a hacker to exploit buffer overflows. This quick education on the sources of technical risk usually solves such problems.

The trickier challenge with consensus occurs when two participants in the quality risk analysis meeting are defending the interests of different constituencies. For example, suppose you have two salespeople in the meeting, each of whom has a customer who has a critical feature that will be built for this release. Each salesperson will insist that their customer's critical feature is the most important and must be thoroughly tested.

What to do? You'll need to be able to involve a senior manager to settle the dispute. Serious political problems could arise for you, the tester or test manager, should you decide to unilaterally determine the level of testing for each feature.

Another challenge is to avoid priority inflation. You might find, as you go through the quality risk analysis, that people want to assign risk priority number 1 to every risk. After all, any one bug might be the bug that dooms the system!

In the absence of any other considerations, we would all like to test everything extensively. That's not connected to reality.

The reality is that every project involves trade-offs. I said that the quality risk levels are relative to each other. Quality is also relative to other considerations in the project. So, if you find that people are rating everything as a priority 1 ask them what they would give up. Would they be willing to spend an extra thousand dollars to thoroughly test this risk? Ten thousand dollars? A million dollars? How about slipping the release date by a week to ensure thorough testing of this risk? A month? Six months? How about dropping the feature entirely if it couldn't be thoroughly tested?

If the answer is, "Not a dollar more, not a day later, and the feature stays in whether it's thoroughly tested or not," then you're not dealing with a priority 1 quality risk.

Another strategy for dealing with risk inflation is to include a column in the quality risk analysis table that estimates the cost associated with a given specific risk receiving the proposed extent of testing. This can be approximate. The key is to balance the extent of testing against the cost.

Yet another challenge in risk analysis is that people aren't very good at making rational decisions about risk. For example, I know intelligent people who worry about air travel but not driving. This is not rational because the risk of being killed in a car accident is 100 times greater than the risk of being killed in a plane wreck. Using historical bug and field failure data from past projects can help people make more rational risk decisions, but keep in mind that your quality risk analysis will be a rough and somewhat irrational estimate at first. This is why updating and reviewing your quality risk analysis at regular points in the project, based on new information, is so important.

The time investment is another challenge to quality risks analysis. It can take a lot of time, especially the group-brainstorm approach. (However, the group-brainstorm approach produces the most thorough, accurate quality risk analysis.) Don't overextend your team. Pick an approach that will work the first time. Once people see the benefit of quality risk analysis, you'll be in a better position to advocate a larger investment of time on the next project.

Finally, let me point out that categorization is not quantification. The numbers I assign to the risk levels represent categories. Even though I'm using numerical scales for risks, these aren't really numbers. Be careful of treating them like real numbers.

Quality Risk
Analysis Exercise

Let's put what you've learned about quality risk analysis to work for our hypothetical Omninet project. In this exercise, you'll analyze the quality risks for Omninet. Assume that you are doing this analysis during the requirements specification phase of the project. Use only the Omninet Marketing Requirements Document (MRD), which is included in Appendix A.

I recommend that you apply the informal quality risks analysis technique, unless you know ISO 9126 or Failure Mode and Effect Analysis or want to try them. To make this exercise even more lifelike and more valuable, see if you can work as a small team with some other people. In such a team, have each person take a different perspective, such as programmer, tester, marketer, business analyst, project manager, and others.

In the previous chapter, I provided an informal template. I'd suggest that you use that, and use a list of quality risk categories like the one from Chapter 5. I suggest 120 minutes as a time limit. When you're done, keep reading this chapter to see my solution.

As discussed in Chapter 6, first identify the risks, then prioritize them. Once you have an aggregate priority, use that priority to guide the extent of testing in each risk area. To briefly recap, I suggest you use five levels of extent:

- Extensive testing: Test the entire risk area with many variations.
- Broad testing: Test the entire risk area but with few variations.
- Cursory testing: Test a sample of the risk area, exploring it briefly.

- Opportunity testing: Test the risk area only if some other test brings you to the area.

- Report bugs: If you see problems in this risk area, report them, but don't do anything more.

As you work through the Marketing Requirements Document and discover the risks associated with each area, you should retain tracing information between the section of the MRD and the associated risks. You'll use this information in later exercises.

My Solution

My solution to the Omninet quality risk analysis exercise is shown in Table 7-1.

Table 7-1   My Omninet Quality Risk Analysis

QUALITY RISK	TECH. RISK	BUS. RISK	RISK PRI. #	EXTENT OF TESTING	TRACKING
Functionality					
Customers unable to access Web (at all).	5	1	5	Extensive	3.1
Time accounting (blocks, limits) not handled properly.	4	2	8	Broad	3.1.2, 3.1.7
Time keeping too fast (cheat user) or too slow (cheat Omninet).	4	3	12	Cursory	3.1.2, 3.1.7
Valid payment rejected/ invalid payment accepted.	5	2	10	Broad	3.1.2
Expiration process mishandled.	3	2	6	Broad	3.1.2
Specified alternate browsers not supported.	4	4	16	Opportunity	3.1.3
Inappropriate content not blocked properly.	1	1	1	Extensive	3.1.6
Appropriate content blocked improperly.	1	1	1	Extensive	3.1.6
Firewall/antivirus software does not block worms, virii, etc.	1	1	1	Extensive	3.1.6
User logout fails.	5	2	10	Opportunity	3.1.7

QUALITY RISK	TECH. RISK	BUS. RISK	RISK PRI. #	EXTENT OF TESTING	TRACKING
User logout (before or at expiration) results in refund.	3	2	6	Opportunity	3.1.7
Localization					
Kiosk not configured in primary local language.	5	2	10	Broad	3.1.5
Not all languages supported by the browser or OS accessible.	3	5	15	Cursory	3.1.5
Offensive site blocking not appropriately localized.	1	2	2	Extensive	3.1.5, 3.1.6
Local currencies not properly handled.	5	2	10	Broad	3.1.2
Local time zones cause update, reliability problems.	3	2	6	Broad	3.1.5
Usability and User Interface					
Welcome screen not inviting.	1	1	1	Extensive	3.1.1
Payment screens/process discourage/drive away potential customers.	1	1	1	Extensive	3.1.2
Expiration screens/process discourage/drive away repeat customers.	1	1	1	Extensive	3.1.2
Language selection process confusing, unusable.	1	2	2	Extensive	3.1.5
Confidentiality not preserved.	2	2	4	Extensive	3.1.8
Browser does not exit at end of session.	5	2	10	Broad	3.1.8
Browser does not restart after exiting at end of session.	4	2	8	Broad	3.18
Call center agents unable to access/control current sessions.	2	2	4	Extensive	3.1, 3.2.2
Call center agents unable to access information about past sessions.	3	2	6	Extensive	3.1, 3.2.2

Continued

Table 7-1   *(continued)*

QUALITY RISK	TECH. RISK	BUS. RISK	RISK PRI. #	EXTENT OF TESTING	TRACKING
Kiosk does not report status (hourly/at all) to call center.	3	2	6	Broad	3.2.2
Call center cannot connect to kiosk to gather status.	3	2	6	Broad	3.2.2
Call center agent unable to modify user session.	2	5	10	Cursory	3.2.4
Call center agent able to give away more than 60 minutes of time.	3	3	9	Broad	3.2.4
Call center agent unable to terminate session.	2	1	2	Extensive	3.2.5
Termination refund excessive/insufficient.	2	3	6	Broad	3.2.5
Localization					
Kiosk not configured in primary local language.	5	2	10	Broad	3.1.5
Not all languages supported by the browser or OS accessible.	3	5	15	Cursory	3.1.5
Offensive site blocking not appropriately localized.	1	2	2	Extensive	3.1.5, 3.1.6
Local currencies not properly handled.	5	2	10	Broad	3.1.2
Local time zones cause update, reliability problems.	3	2	6	Broad	3.1.5
Usability and User Interface					
Welcome screen not inviting.	1	1	1	Extensive	3.1.1
Payment screens/process discourage/drive away potential customers.	1	1	1	Extensive	3.1.2
Expiration screens/process discourage/drive away repeat customers.	1	1	1	Extensive	3.1.2
Language selection process confusing, unusable.	1	2	2	Extensive	3.1.5

QUALITY RISK	TECH. RISK	BUS. RISK	RISK PRI. #	EXTENT OF TESTING	TRACKING
Termination message inappropriate.	3	2	6	Broad	3.2.5
Color schemas, fonts, etc. not appropriate/accessible.	1	1	1	Broad	3.1
Reliability					
Server farm unable to support 1,000 kiosks.	1	1	1	Extensive	2
Kiosk sessions crash during use.	1	1	1	Extensive	3.1
Kiosks too frequently unable to access the Web.	1	1	1	Extensive	3.1
Dial-up (PSTN) kiosk sometimes establishes <= 50 KBPS connection.	1	2	2	Extensive	3.1.4
Cable/DSL kiosk sometimes establishes <= 128 KBPS connection.	4	2	8	Broad	3.1.4
Call center agent access/control/termination sometimes fails.	2	3	6	Broad	3.2.1–3.2.5
Call center availability too low.	3	1	3	Extensive	3.2
Internet gateway servers availability too low.	3	1	3	Extensive	3.1
Termination message inappropriate.	3	2	6	Broad	3.2.5
Color schemas, fonts, etc. not appropriate/accessible.	1	1	1	Broad	3.1
Reliability					
Server farm unable to support 1,000 kiosks.	1	1	1	Extensive	2
Kiosk sessions crash during use.	1	1	1	Extensive	3.1
Kiosks too frequently unable to access the Web.	1	1	1	Extensive	3.1

Continued

Table 7-1   *(continued)*

QUALITY RISK	TECH. RISK	BUS. RISK	RISK PRI. #	EXTENT OF TESTING	TRACKING
Dial-up (PSTN) kiosk sometimes establishes <= 50 KBPS connection.	1	2	2	Extensive	3.1.4
Cable/DSL kiosk sometimes establishes <= 128 KBPS connection.	4	2	8	Broad	3.1.4
Call center agent access/control/termination sometimes fails.	2	3	6	Broad	3.2.1–3.2.5
Call center availability too low.	3	1	3	Extensive	3.2
Internet gateway servers availability too low.	3	1	3	Extensive	3.1
Kiosks unable to recover from power failure, other external failure.	5	1	5	Broad	3.1
Web site/URL compatibility problems, some sites misdisplayed.	2	4	8	Opportunity	3.1
Intermittent valid payment rejection/invalid payment acceptance.	5	4	20	Report bugs	3.1.2
Performance					
Initial or expiration payment processing too slow.	5	2	10	Cursory	3.1.2
Dial-up (PSTN) kiosk never establishes > 50 KBPS connection.	5	2	10	Broad	3.1.4
Cable/DSL kiosk never establishes > 128 KBPS connection.	5	2	10	Broad	3.1.4
Call center agent access/control/termination too slow (after the fact).	2	1	2	Extensive	3.2.1–3.2.5
Update/session performance problems.	4	3	12	Cursory	3.2.1

QUALITY RISK	TECH. RISK	BUS. RISK	RISK PRI. #	EXTENT OF TESTING	TRACKING
Supportability					
Firewall/antivirus software not updated regularly.	5	3	15	Cursory	3.1.6
Software updates do not occur automatically.	4	1	4	Extensive	3.2.1
Software updates never succeed.	4	1	4	Extensive	3.2.1
Software updates fail too frequently.	5	1	5	Extensive	3.2.1
Kiosk remains connected after checking for/ performing update.	5	4	20	Opportunity	3.2.1
Kiosk retry-on-overload process fails (no disconnect/ no reconnect).	3	1	3	Extensive	3.2.1
Agents can't push updates to kiosks.	3	1	3	Extensive	3.2.1

Comments on My Solution

I found that working directly from the requirements specification made identifying the risks straightforward. You *can* perform risk analyses without specifications of any kind. I have, successfully. However, it's easier when you have something in writing, even an imperfect document like the Omninet Marketing Requirements Document.

For some risks, I deviated the extent of testing from what the aggregate risk priority number would suggest. For example, I assigned opportunity testing for "user logout fails," which had a risk priority number of 10. Why? Because it's a simple programming task, most likely, and you can easily integrate testing it into some other tests.

Can you spot the other risks for which I deviated the extent of testing? Can you figure out why? It's probably best to document those decisions and the underlying assumptions. Without an explanation like the one in the preceding paragraph, it's hard to know my reasoning.

Notice that the relationship between the quality risks and the requirements specification elements is many-to-many. One requirement can relate to multiple risks. That's okay. One risk can relate to multiple requirements. That's okay, too, in small numbers. If you find that you have too many requirements associated with one risk, though, you probably aren't being specific enough. For example, "system doesn't work" would relate to any requirement, but it doesn't help you figure out where to focus your testing.

As I prioritized risks, I found that some items I had included as two risks collapsed into one risk. For example, "call center agents unable to access/control current sessions," was originally two line items, one related to access, one to control. When I saw they had the same risk priority numbers, I combined them. Take advantage of such discoveries to keep your risk analysis charts as short as possible.

Because I did this analysis alone, I'm sure I missed some important risks. Cross-functional teams working together don't tend to miss nearly as many risks.

I probably also got the priority numbers wrong in many cases. Of course, technical and business priority both depend quite a bit on the technical and business context of the project. Working on a hypothetical project like this, it's hard to say whether the priorities are right or wrong.

Looking at the priorities and the extent of testing, you can see how the mapping from aggregate priority to extent of testing that I used here results in a bias toward extensive testing. Again, feel free to adopt other mapping schemes to change the bias toward broad or even cursory testing if appropriate.

A Funny Thing Happened to Me on the Way to the Quality Risks...

I came up with the following list of bugs, assumptions, comments, and questions related to the Marketing Requirements Document while doing this risk analysis:

- Not all the acronyms defined in section 1.1 are actually used in the document. This is confusing because I'm not sure why I needed to know about them.

- It would be helpful to have those screen prototypes mentioned in section 1.2 for the risk analysis.

- In section 2, it mentions the "financial third quarter," but of what year?

- In section 3.1.3, the user is to be offered a choice of browsers. Shouldn't this section say they are allowed to switch to another alternate browser? I would assume that the entire kiosk program would be a browser-based application running on some sort of local web server (such as IIS or Apache), which would mean that, except during boot periods or as a result of a fatal error, the kiosk software would always run within a browser. This function would seem to provide for swapping to another alternate browser.

- If section 3.1.3 should be changed as specified in the previous paragraph , then the lack of specification of alternate-versus-default browsers for all supported kiosks operating systems is an omission in the requirements, or at the very least should be addressed in the design specification.

- Referring to section 3.1.2, what happens if the timer expires while the user is purchasing an additional block of time? Does the user's session terminate, taking with it all the session data (as described in section 3.1.7)?

- Following on the previous comment and again referring to section 3.1.2, what *is* a reasonable time-out period for the initial or additional-time payment process? What happens when the user changes his mind and walks away from the kiosk?

- Following this thread further and again referring to section 3.1.2, does a credit/debit card customer have to reswipe her card to buy additional time? If not, consider the risks associated with a customer walking away without terminating her session.

- Regarding section 3.1.4, the "primary local language" could vary from one side of town to another. For example, in San Antonio, Texas, where I live, about half the population is Hispanic and Spanish is a primary language for many people in certain neighborhoods. Demographic studies of the actual kiosk location — rather than just census data for a town or region — would have to drive this decision to avoid underutilized kiosks.

- Again regarding section 3.1.4, I identified "language selection process confusing, unusable" as a risk. Here's an example. I have a phone that a client lets me use while I'm in Israel. The software on the phone supports multiple languages, including English. However, while the phone is in Hebrew mode, the only way to find the English mode selection is — you guessed it — in Hebrew. Since I speak only a little Hebrew, I had to ask a Hebrew-speaking colleague to reconfigure the phone.

- Regarding section 3.2.1, I identified "software updates fail too frequently," but of course we'd have to define — either in the design specification ideally or at least in the test cases themselves — what "too frequently" would mean. Clearly 100 percent reliability of the update process is unreasonable, but what is a reasonable rate of failure?

- Regarding section 3.2.2, call center agents will have access to sensitive customer information like credit card numbers, URLs visited, and so on. This is not test risk, but rather a business risk: How do we ensure that these people do not misuse this information? Perhaps the system should disallow screen captures, file saves, and email from the call center agent desktops? If so, then that *would* have test implications.

- Regarding section 3.2, I identified "call center availability too low," but we'd have to define — either in the design specification ideally or at least in the test cases themselves — what low availability would mean. Clearly 100 percent availability of the call center is unreasonable, but what is a reasonable amount of yearly downtime?

- Regarding section 3.1, I identified "Internet gateway servers availability too low," but we'd have to define — either in the design specification ideally or at least in the test cases themselves — what low availability would mean. Clearly 100 percent availability of the Internet gateway servers is unreasonable, but what is a reasonable amount of yearly downtime?

- Regarding section 3.1, I identified "kiosks too frequently unable to access the Web," but we'd have to define — in the design specification ideally or at least in the test cases themselves — what "too frequently" would mean. Clearly 100 percent availability of the kiosks is unreasonable, but what is a reasonable amount of yearly downtime?

- Regarding sections 3.2.1 through 3.2.4, I identified "call center agent access/control/termination too slow (after the fact)" as a risk. What I mean is that, by the time the call center agent learns about, tries to affect, or tries to end some sort of antisocial usage of the kiosk or software-related kiosk misbehavior (such as infection by worm), the damage has already been done. This requires some further careful thinking on the part of system designers, ideally security experts.

- Regarding section 3.1.5 and 3.1.6, I identified a risk as "offensive site blocking not appropriately localized." Local customs, religions, and so on influence what is offensive. Designers and programmers must be careful to take this into account.

- Regarding section 3.1, should a kiosk go into a power-saving mode when the public space (in which it resides) is closed? If so, then there are test implications.

- I didn't go into a lot of detail regarding section 3.1.2, payment processing. There are many things that could go wrong here. I'm assuming that the designers would be smart and use a commercial off-the-shelf payment subsystem, such as those found at parking kiosks and car washes. That's worth bringing up with them, just to be sure.

- You probably noticed that my list of risks is high level. Again, I don't decompose (split) risks unless I can identify different levels of risks in the two or more decomposed risks that I can name. If I can't, then decomposing risks means launching (prematurely) into test design. However, when working from a more detailed document like a design specification, I would be more specific. At that point in the project, that level of specificity would be appropriate.

What bugs did you find in the requirements? It's a nice side benefit of quality risk analysis that it serves as a structured form of requirements review. You'll see in a later chapter how beneficial that can be.

Bonus Exercise

Want some more practice? Working in an environment where documentation is hard to come by? Here's another quality risk analysis you can try, this time without any formal requirements specification.

Again, by yourself, in pairs, or as a small team, analyze quality risks for a calculator program such as the one included with Windows. Again, use the informal technique, or if you'd like to try, ISO 9126 or Failure Mode and Effect Analysis.

I have provided a template with a few categories. Again, don't feel compelled to fill the template! You can use an even simpler approach for prioritization, assigning a single aggregate priority number that takes into account both likelihood and impact. Then, use priority to guide the extent of testing in each risk area. I suggest you try the following simple extent of testing mapping:

- Extensive testing: Cover the risk area both broadly and deeply.
- Balanced testing: Balance the extent of testing against schedule constraints, performing broad testing.
- Opportunity testing: Leverage other testing to check these risk areas if possible.
- Report bugs: Do no testing against this risk, but report related bugs if you see them.
- None: Ignore this risk area, even if bugs are observed.

I suggest that you spend 60 minutes or less on this exercise.
Ready? Get started!

Template

QUALITY RISK CATEGORY/SPECIFIC RISK	PRIORITY	EXTENT OF TESTING
Functionality		
User Interface		

QUALITY RISK CATEGORY/SPECIFIC RISK	PRIORITY	EXTENT OF TESTING
Localization		
Data Quality		
Usability		
Capacity and Performance		

Continued

(continued)

QUALITY RISK CATEGORY/SPECIFIC RISK	PRIORITY	EXTENT OF TESTING
States		
Install, Uninstall, and Maintenance		

QUALITY RISK CATEGORY/SPECIFIC RISK	PRIORITY	EXTENT OF TESTING

Configuration and Compatibility

Regression

My Solution

My solution to the calculator quality risks analysis exercise is shown in Table 7-2.

Table 7-2   Calculator Quality Risk Analysis

QUALITY RISK CATEGORY/SPECIFIC RISK	PRIORITY	EXTENT OF TESTING
Functionality		
Add, subtract, multiply, divide	1	Extensive
Memory operations	2	Balanced
Statistical operations	2	Balanced
Binary, octal, hexadecimal operations	2	Balanced
Trig and other advanced functions	2	Balanced
Angle unit handling	3	Opportunity
Constants (pi, e)	3	Opportunity
User Interface		
Copy and paste	1	Extensive
Active keys based on mode	3	Opportunity
Maximum and minimum values	3	Opportunity
Legal and illegal values	3	Opportunity
Mode switching	2	Balanced
Help screens and error messages	2	Balanced
Data editing and formatting	2	Balanced
Localization		
Decimal point, thousands separator	2	Balanced
Help screens and error messages	2	Balanced
Menus and screens	2	Balanced
Data Quality		
Rounding and representation errors	1	Extensive
Usability		
Clumsy, insulting, obscene interface	4	Report bugs
Capacity and Performance		
Crashing under memory load	1	Extensive

QUALITY RISK CATEGORY/SPECIFIC RISK	PRIORITY	EXTENT OF TESTING
Slow due to load, complex operations	1	Extensive
Crash with large statistical data sets	2	Balanced
Crashing after continuous use	3	Opportunity
States		
Continuation after error or help	3	Opportunity
Continuation after normal use	3	Opportunity
Install, Uninstall, and Maintenance		
Setup to remove, install fails	3	Opportunity
Applying service packs, patches	3	Opportunity
Configuration and Compatibility		
Minimum memory, CPU problems	3	Opportunity
Multi-CPU support	3	Opportunity
Regression		
Failure of new releases	2	Balanced
Interaction with other programs	4	Report bugs

Comments on My Solution

You probably noticed that I didn't bother to include some risk areas that I considered low priority:

- Documentation: Does anyone read the calculator part of the Windows manual?
- Timing and coordination: Not applicable, as far as I can tell.
- Security: I'm assuming there is no secret data handled by the calculator.
- Standards: I'm not aware of any standards that apply, other than the rules of math.
- Networking: I'm assuming that we're using the Windows desktop calculator.

- Date and time handling: Not applicable, as far as I can tell.

- Operations: Not applicable, as far as I can tell.

Of course, for other applications these risk areas could be important, even critical.

Bonus Example: Grays and Blues Quality Risk Analysis

To finish this chapter, I'll show you a very simple example quality risk analysis. This analysis is for a hypothetical video game. Here's the scenario.

Assume that you are the test manager or a test lead. You and your fellow testers are going to be testing a video game called Grays and Blues. This is a first-person United States Civil War action game for PCs and arcade systems. It has the usual features of such games, though it is set in a period and involves weapons that are not typical of such games. (This game and its weapon-selection features will be the topic of a later exercise.)

Suppose that you have assembled the key stakeholders in testing and quality to perform an informal quality risk analysis.

This analysis is even simpler than the one described earlier in that it uses a simple five-point scale to rate the overall risk priority for each risk. On this five-point scale, I've assigned the following extent-of-testing mapping:

1. Extensive: This has the same meaning as discussed in the previous module.

2. Balanced: This is a test approach where the extent of testing done would be limited based on some preset time constraint. You would balance breadth and depth of testing of the feature against the time allowed.

3. Opportunity: This has the same meaning as discussed in the previous module.

4. Report bugs: This also has the same meaning as discussed in the previous module.

5. None: This states explicitly that those risks not specifically mentioned will be ignored, even if we see bugs in these areas.

Study the analysis shown in Table 7-3 for a moment. I'm not presenting it as right or wrong, but simply as food for thought.

Table 7-3 Grays and Blues Quality Risk Analysis

QUALITY RISK CATEGORTY	QUALITY RISK SUB CATEGORY	PRIORITY	TESTING LEVEL
Functionality	Acquisition and use of stuff	1	Extensive
	Terrain and levels	1	Extensive
	Movement and actions	1	Extensive
	Hints and backdoors	2	Balanced
	Injury and recovery	2	Balanced
	Multiplayer	2	Balanced
User Interface/ Usability	Realism of rendering	1	Extensive
	Smoothness during action	2	Balanced
	Obviousness	3	Opportunity
States/Transactions	Arcade payment	2	Balanced
	Extended play	2	Balanced
	Level progress	2	Balanced
	Inventory	2	Balanced
Data Quality	Saving names and scores	3	Opportunity
Load, Capacity, and Volume	Networked multiplayer	2	Balanced
	Other applications	3	Opportunity
Reliability	Play to end with no fatal error	1	Extensive
Error Handling	Multiplayers drop off	2	Balanced
	Host system crash	3	Opportunity
Localization	Canada	2	Balanced
	Europe	3	Opportunity
Compatibility	PC configurations	3	Opportunity
	Video cards and game peripherals	1	Extensive
	Arcade configurations	3	Opportunity
Installation	Windows	3	Opportunity
	Linux	3	Opportunity

Continued

Table 7-3 *(Continued)*

QUALITY RISK CATEGORTY	QUALITY RISK SUB CATEGORY	PRIORITY	TESTING LEVEL
	Mac	3	Opportunity
	Arcade configurations	3	Opportunity
Documentation and Packaging	Any	4	Report bugs
Others	All others	5	None

Now that you've read the example, I'd like you to think about three issues:

▪ What are some items that you think are missing from this list? Why?

▪ What prioritizations are incorrect? Why?

▪ What do you think about that concept of some risks being explicitly ignored? Why?

What's important here is not the answer to the first of the two questions in each preceding list items, but your answer to the second question. Those answers give you some clues into your thinking about testing.

PART

III

Static Testing

In this Part

Reviews and
Other Static Tests

In this chapter, I'm going to cover static testing, the most notable form of which is the review. Static testing, done properly, is the most efficient category of testing in terms of the financial and schedule benefits yielded for the money and time invested.

Static testing is commonly defined as the testing of the system under test without execution, but that defines what static testing *isn't*, not what it *is*. Let's take a closer look at static testing.

Testing Requirements and Designs

Most broadly, you can think of static testing as the evaluation of representations of the system under test. The system under test is a collection of hardware, executable software, data, networking connections, and other tangible and intangible items. Representations of the system under test include requirements and design specifications. Representations of the system under test also include the source code itself, both in terms of high-level languages and database metadata.

The most common forms of static testing are reviews, walk-throughs, and inspections, all of which I'll refer to generally as reviews. Reviews frequently focus on requirements specifications, design specifications, and source code. These activities vary on a spectrum from informal to very formal.

However, representations of the system under test include dataflow diagrams, entity-relationship diagrams, and other document models of the system, and you can review those too. A diagram of a complex system can often reveal problems that can hide in words. An ugly diagram can reveal lots of bugs. A prototype is a representation of the system under test, as are spreadsheets and simulations. These representations are often executable as well as reviewable.

Another representation of the system under test is the test cases and data. The test analysis and test design processes often transform one set of representations of the system — say, requirements and design specifications — into another. That transformation is a form of structured review. As such, the test analysis and design processes often reveal problems in these other representations. We'll see that added benefit arise during later chapters.

Reviews Costs and Benefits

Not all organizations use static testing. Many organizations overestimate the costs and underestimate the benefits. Most forms of static testing do indeed have costs. At the very least, there is the time required to perform the reviews. In more formalized approaches, static testing costs also include the effort required to gather and analyze review metrics as well as the cost of implementing process improvement opportunities discovered through the metrics.

However, these costs are usually outweighed by the benefits when static testing is done properly. The efficient and quick removal of bugs during reviews shortens the overall development or maintenance schedule. Particularly, since the number of bugs delivered to the testing process is one of the primary determinants of the time required to properly complete testing, reviews lead to shorter testing periods and lower testing costs. Less time spent debugging code — which is purely wasted time — means higher developer productivity.

Reviews can be more effective at removing bugs than testing. In addition, the multistage quality improvement that occurs when reviews and testing are both used results in improved quality of the system delivered to the customers and users. This improved quality decreases downstream maintenance costs. The section "Reviews as a Way to Improve the Process, Improve the System, and Reduce Costs" later in this chapter provides a quantified demonstration of these perhaps-controversial assertions.

So, the costs may be significant, but the costs are outweighed by the benefits. Reviews of all kinds are proven, high-return-on-investment techniques for improving quality and reducing costs.

Types of Reviews

As I mentioned, reviews come in various types. These vary from informal to highly formal.

In an informal review, there is no real process or structure. The review can take the form of hallway chats, buddy tests, or pair programming. Much of the static testing that I've seen took this form. Such static tests are useful, cheap, and popular.

A more formalized review type is the peer review. This can include documented and defined processes for detecting and removing bugs. For example, the organization might provide standard checklists for each type of review. Some people adopt rules for peer reviews that allow the participation of peers and technical experts but not managers.

Slightly more formalized is the walkthrough. Here, the author of the item under review walks the peers and technical experts through the document or code.

The most formal type of review is the inspection. A trained moderator leads the inspection team through the item being inspected. The moderator is someone other than the author. Each member of the inspection team has a role. The process follows clear rules. Checklists serve as bug-finding tools. Entry criteria determine when an item is ready for inspection. Exit criteria determine when the inspection is complete. Metrics are gathered on the numbers and types of bugs found.

Reviews for Verification and Validation

Whatever form of review you chose, it can help you reach a number of goals. One goal is verification and validation of the system.

In Figure 8-1, you see the V model introduced in Chapter 3. I've added a phase exit review meeting at the end of each phase. These review meetings are shown as diamonds. The dotted arrows outside the *V* indicate verification tasks in each exit review meeting. The dashed arrows inside the *V* indicate validation tasks in each exit review meeting.

Verification involves looking for bugs in the deliverables for each phase. The question you're trying to answer is, Are we building the system right? In other words, have you done everything properly, have you created the right documentation, have you reviewed each document to ensure they are of acceptable quality, and so forth?

Validation involves looking for bugs in the system based on the deliverables for each phase. The question you're trying to answer is, Are we building the right system? In other words, does the system you're building, when measured against the requirements, have quality from the users', customers', and other stakeholders' perspectives?

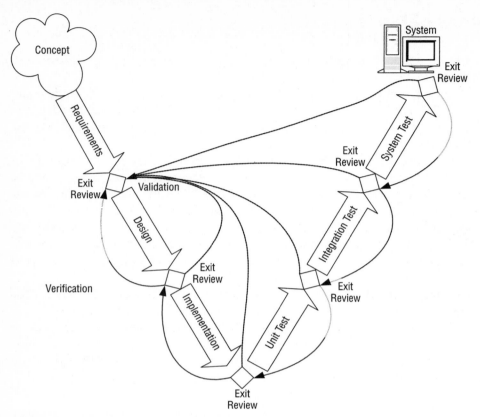

Figure 8-1: Verification and validation during phase exit reviews

This use of reviews at major project milestones ensures that the project is on course for success and following the plan. If you detect deviations, you can course-correct in time. While this example involves the V model, you can use exit reviews for any structured life cycle.

Reviews as a Way to Improve the Process, Improve the System, and Reduce Costs

Exit reviews at the end of one phase allow you to make major adjustments, but reviews also help adjust each step of the process, and each deliverable in the process, as you go along. This reduces costs, which I'll illustrate. In Figure 8-2, I've used the V model to keep the diagram as simple as possible, but similar results would apply for other models.

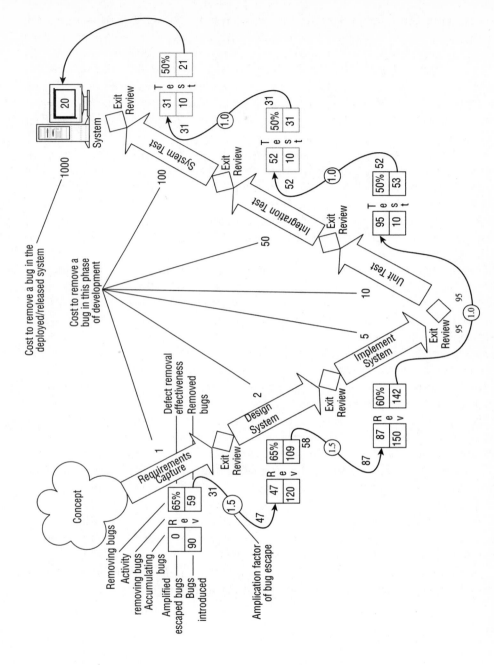

Figure 8-2: Savings, quality improvement, and process improvement through reviews

Bugs found in later phases cost more than bugs found in earlier ones. So, starting with the inside of the *V*, you can see the average increase in the relative cost of fixing a given bug (or defect) in each phase. The relative costs are 1, 2, 5, 10, 50, 100, and 1,000, depending on whether the bug is found in requirements, design, code, unit testing, integration testing, system testing, or postrelease, respectively. These relative costs are not necessarily correct for your organization, but the multiplicative increase in cost from one phase to another is typical.

Reviews and testing are the two activities used to remove bugs. You can apply reviews in early phases, and testing predominates in later phases. The tables shown outside of the *V*, next to each phase, show the results of these bug-removal activities. *Rev* abbreviates the review processes. *Test* abbreviates the testing processes. In each table, the left-side column has to do with bugs accumulating or being added to the system. The right-side column has to do with bugs being removed from the system.

The upper-left cell shows the amplified, escaped bugs from the previous phase. The amplification factor is shown in the circle on the arrow that connects the table with the previous table. This shows that each bug that escapes from requirements to design or from design to code will turn into one-and-a-half bugs in the next phase.

The lower-left cell shows the number of bugs introduced in each phase. In requirements and design phases, these bugs are defects in the specifications. In the implementation and testing phases, these bugs are in the code. Bugs introduced during test phases are regression bugs.

The upper-right cell shows the percentage of bugs removed by reviews or testing in each phrase. The percentage of bugs removed in each bug-removal activity is called the defect removal effectiveness. This percentage is also sometimes called the defect removal efficiency, but that is incorrect. This percentage does not measure efficiency because it is not normalized by a metric of cost, time, or effort.

The lower-right cell shows the number of bugs removed by the activity. These bugs would be bugs introduced during the current phase as well as bugs that accumulated from previous phases.[1]

Spend a minute tracing bugs from the upper-left side of the *V* down to the lower middle of the *V* and then back up to the upper-right side.

---

[1] The bug counts in these figures are hypothetical, but the proportions are based on industry reports. I conservatively derived the amplification factor for escaped bugs from Roger Pressman's book *Software Engineering*. I derived the proportion of the hypothetical number of bugs introduced in each phase from Capers Jones's book *Estimating Software Costs*. Jones's book also provided the basis for the defect removal effectiveness figures.

Now, answer three questions:

1. How much money did the project team spend removing bugs if we assume that the average bug found and removed in the requirements phase costs $1?

2. How much money did the project team save by using reviews as a bug-removal activity during the requirements, design, and implementation phases as compared to letting those bugs escape into the testing phases?

3. How much *could* the project team save if they analyzed the findings of their reviews; used that analysis to implement requirements, design, and implementation process improvements; and thus reduced by 50 percent the number of bugs introduced in each phase?

Questions 1 and 2, taken together, give you a sense of the money saved by reviews. Comparing the bugs delivered to the customers in questions 1 and 2 also gives you a sense of the quality differences between systems developed with reviews and without them. Question 3 demonstrates the process-improvement potential of reviews.

Here's a hint: Use a spreadsheet and you can answer these three questions in a half hour or less. The answers are shown on the next page.

---

² For details, see nssdc.gsfc.nasa.gov/database/MasterCatalog?sc=1998-073A.

Answers to the Three Questions about Static Testing

Phase	QUESTION 1 Bugs			QUESTION 2 Bugs			QUESTION 3 Bugs		
	Present	Removed	Cost	Present	Removed	Cost	Present	Removed	Cost
Requirements	90	59	59	90	0	0	45	29	29
Design	167	109	218	255	0	0	84	55	110
Implementation	237	142	710	533	0	0	119	71	355
Unit Test	105	53	530	543	272	2,720	53	27	270
Integration Test	62	31	1,550	281	141	7,050	31	16	800
System Test	41	21	2,100	150	75	7,500	20	10	1,000
Deployed/Released	20	20	20,000	75	75	75,000	10	10	10,000

Reviews as a Way to Achieve Consensus and Understanding

Another goal of reviews is to achieve a common consensus and understanding of key requirements and design elements across all the stakeholders and contributors. Missing details (incompleteness) and fuzzy statements (ambiguity) can hide the real meaning of the requirements and design specifications. By achieving consensus and understanding before you build the system — and by reconfirming that consensus and understanding throughout the project, especially at key milestones like phase exit reviews — you reduce the likelihood of discovering serious problems during integration, system, or acceptance test — or worse.

The United States space program offers a classic example of a problem that could easily have been solved by reviews. One of the probes sent to Mars in the 1990s was lost after a navigational failure on arrival at Mars. Analysis of the failure revealed that one of the software subsystems involved in navigation used English units. Another used metric units.[2]

Software engineering professionals have recognized the value of requirements and design reviews for well over a quarter century, which is about half the time that human beings have been doing software engineering. In 1975, a book by Fred Brooks based on his experiences in the 1960s and early 1970s at IBM came out. In it he wrote, "Long before any code exists, the specification must be handed to an outside testing group to be scrutinized for completeness and clarity. As [V.A.] Vyssotsky [of Bell Lab's Safeguard Project] says, the developers themselves cannot do this: 'They won't tell you they don't understand it; they will happily invent their way through the gaps and obscurities.'"[3]

Apparently the programmers at NASA happily invented their way through an unconscionable gap in the design. It's easy — and wrong — to blame the programmers though. The root of the problem lies in then-NASA Director Dan Golden's mantra: "Faster-better-cheaper." Such a statement orders an organization to take shortcuts. Two natural shortcuts are inadequate requirements and design specifications and reviews because they won't show up in the form of missing code. Such a statement is tantamount to insisting that code and fix is a great way to build high-risk, mission-critical software. Organizations and managers who ignore the lessons of the last 50 years of software engineering are playing Russian roulette with the quality of their systems.

---

[3] See *The Mythical Man Month* by Fred Brooks, Jr.

The Review Process, Roles, and Responsibilities

While the details of the review process depend on the specific review type used on the project, here's a generic process you can adapt to get started.

1. **Planning**. The estimation and planning required to include reviews in a project. Effectively, the project team is spending time and effort during requirements, design, and implementation phases to save a larger amount of time and effort in later phases and after release. The project plans must reflect this trade-off. If this is the first project where the organization will use reviews, management will need to provide training for the project team members. Make sure that people know the review process, the ground rules, the objectives, and how to contribute.

2. **Kick-off meeting**. A briefing to make sure that all the participants understand the process.

3. **Preparation**. One to two hours of reading and commenting on the item under review, done by each participant alone.

4. **Review meeting**. One to two hours of group discussion to go through the item under review and note issues and problems.

5. **Re-review**. Performed when needed for an item. If a review identifies too few bugs, you might conclude that inadequate preparation or review work took place. If a review identifies too many bugs, the author might need to do serious rework to fix these bugs, which means that new bugs are likely.

6. **Follow-up**. Following up on individual items to make sure that all issues were resolved. You might also follow up on the overall process to look for opportunities to improve the processes — including requirements and design specification, implementation, and reviews themselves. In some organizations, you also check to ensure that you found and removed the expected total number of bugs in each phase as covered in the phase exit review meetings.

The particular roles and responsibilities of each participant in the review process depend on the specific review type used. Here are some typical roles and responsibilities.

Moderator. Leads the review meeting.

Scribe or secretary. Takes notes, particularly gathering information on the bugs found in the item under review.

Author. Describes and explains the item under review. Also answers any questions about the item.

Reviewers. Find bugs in the item under review. They might be called inspectors if you're following an inspection process.

Project manager. Responsible for planning, arranging sufficient resources and training, supporting the process, and analyzing metrics derived from the reviews to discover opportunities for process improvement.

In some cases, one person may play multiple roles in this process. For example, in the walk-through approach, authors sometimes act as moderators. One of the reviewers can act as the secretary.

Deliverables and Ground Rules from Reviews

So, what should you expect from reviews?

Certainly, you should expect to see the reviews locate bugs. You should also want those bugs fixed. Remember, you can find bugs in requirements, design, code, test cases, bug reports, and many other items with a review.

If you take the time to gather information on bug counts, types, and so forth, you can get valuable metrics from reviews. You can use these metrics to build what are called defect removal models. These are mathematical models that predict the number of bugs you'll find on future projects. Such models often use parameters like system size, complexity, and so forth to predict bugs.

If you're a manager, be careful not to misuse these metrics. For example, using review metrics as part of the programmers' yearly performance evaluations will render the review process political and will make the metrics derived from it meaningless.

You can use metrics to make smart decisions about how to improve your processes. For example, you can use root cause analysis of the bugs found during reviews to change the requirements, design, and coding practices in your company. You can also institute a process of gathering feedback from testing to improve the review process. For example, for every bug found during testing, perform an analysis to see if that bug could have been found earlier during a review.

Whatever your role, remember that you are supposed to review the product, not the producer. You should comment, in a professional, supportive fashion, on the problems you find in the item under review. You should not comment on the abilities of the person who created the item. If reviews become personal and insulting, people will avoid participating and the process will again become political and meaningless.

As with any other meeting, you should set an agenda and stick to it. Everyone is busy. You should also limit debate. This is part of sticking to an agenda.

Another important part of sticking to the agenda is to focus on finding problems rather than fixing them. The author will take the secretary's notes on the problems and fix them later. You should assume that the author is competent to fix the problems in the item under review; that's why he was assigned to create that item in the first place.

Do have a secretary and do have that person take written notes. With written notes you can make sure that every issue raised was resolved. Without notes, some items will fall through the cracks.

Don't invite anyone who might be interested, but rather limit the number of participants to those who can really add something. Try to include as many viewpoints with as few people as possible.[4]

Make sure that those who are invited prepare by reading the item under review and noting problems. There are few bigger time-wasters on projects than meetings in which one person sits and asks questions that he could have gotten answers for before the meeting, especially if he could have gotten those answers by careful study. In addition, people who come to review meetings unprepared seldom find lots of bugs. One way to ensure that people come prepared is to make sure they submit notes before they arrive.

Checklists of typical kinds of problems found in each type of item reviewed can be helpful. You could have a requirements review checklist, a design review checklist, a code review checklist, a test plan review checklist, and so forth.

Make sure to allocate sufficient time and resources for the reviews. Reviews are proven to return hours of saved time for every hour spent, so rushing the process robs you of time later. However, try to avoid reviewing things in large chunks. Instead, make sure a review covers material you can comfortably review thoroughly in one or at most two hours.

Finally, make sure that you review the reviews. Sometimes, the review process can become a ritual, an item on a checklist, that might not be providing results. Keep doing the reviews, but make sure the reviews are working and continue to work.

Common Requirements and Design Bugs

There are four kinds of requirements and design problems that I have seen on every project in which I participated in requirements and design reviews.

First, I have always found ambiguities. So while preparing for a review meeting, I ask, "What *exactly* does each sentence, each picture, each section mean?" For example, suppose you had a requirement that said something like, "The system shall allow the user to send and receive Internet service provider (ISP) email." Well, what ISPs are supported? What's the maximum size email allowed? Are attachments allowed? If so, what kinds of attachments? How about non-U.S. English characters?

---

[4] In an article in *Software Quality Professional*, Volume 6, Issue 1 (December 2003), "Identifying Code-Inspection Improvements Using Statistical Black Belt Techniques," Jeff Holmes reported that studies at Motorola revealed that the ideal number of people for a code review was three people, including the author and two other experts.

Second, I have always found requirements and design specifications to be incomplete. So, I ask, "Okay, and then what happens?" For example, suppose you had a requirement that said something like, "Upon three invalid passwords, the system shall lock the user's account." So, how long should the account remain locked? How can the account be unlocked before that time? Who can unlock a locked account? If only the supervisor or administrator can unlock a locked account, don't we have a potential denial-of-service attack designed into the system?

Third, I have always found testability problems with requirements and design specifications. So I ask, "How can I check this element of the specification?" For example, suppose you had a requirement that said something like, "The system shall provide 100 percent availability." That's a nice capability to want to deliver to users, but you'll never know if you've delivered it. There's no known test technique to demonstrate perfect availability.

Fourth, look for ugliness, awkwardness, and fragility. I ask, "Do I see signs of excessive dependencies? How about the potential for errors to ripple through the system, magnifying along the way? Is the complexity of the design overwhelming?"

This is just a start. I'd encourage you to build a checklist, as I mentioned earlier, and include your own favorite requirements and design bugs.[5]

Reviewing (and Testing) Documentation

In addition to reviewing requirements and design specifications, my testers and I have often had to review user documentation. I've found the following common bugs in documentation.

Perhaps not the most common, but surely the most embarrassing documentation bug is when the instructions are incorrect or impossible. So I'm definitely going to look for this kind of bug.

More commonly, the documentation addresses the wrong audience. The writer uses words that are too simple or too technical. Remember, readers stumble over jargon and acronyms. Improper assumptions about user and reader knowledge make the meaning ambiguous. These kinds of bugs flourish in documentation written by amateur technical writers like programmers and most of our fellow testers. Less frequent but more serious choice-of-words problems include the use of patronizing, insulting, offensive, obscene, suggestive, and profane words and symbols. Try to see the documentation from the user's eyes.

---

[5] Karl Wiegers, in his excellent book *Software Requirements*, gives some other pointers on potential requirements problems.

Grammatical and spelling errors, along with cosmetic and formatting issues, round out my list. Even if the meaning is clear, these problems damage the perceived quality of your system. Users might laugh out loud at the manual or even email a favorite snippet of tortured wording to a friend.

Remember, documentation can be a contract with your customers. I've seen a situation in which a system created huge legal problems for the company by failing to conform to just one line on one page in a user's guide.

Since we're on the topic of documentation, let me jump ahead to dynamic testing for a moment and offer some suggestions for testing the documentation against the live system.

Make sure you have tried all the examples. If there are screen shots showing dialogs, make sure they actually look and behave as shown. Make sure you have verified all claims. For example, if the system is supposed to work over a dial-up Internet connection at 28.8 Kbps or better, try the system at 28.8 Kbps. For good measure, try the system at 26.2 Kbps. It's reasonable for users to expect such situations to be handled, and you should ensure that the system handles them.

For electronic documentation such as online help, be sure to try all the hyperlinks within the document, including links that launch other programs. For example, look at links like "mailto" links and links that cause the browser to access the Internet. Don't forget wizards and "What's This?" pointers, which are another, more dynamic form of electronic documentation.

In addition to online help, embedded within every program are prompts, messages, and so forth. These are also documentation. Get a listing of all these program messages, especially error messages. It's a good idea to try to force every possible message to appear, though this isn't always possible for every error message. At least review the messages to make sure they're reasonable and helpful.

Other Static Tests

To finish up this section on static testing, let me briefly mention that there are other forms of static tests. Most common of all static tests are code reviews and inspections. Increasingly, these activities are augmented and supported by automated code-analysis tools, such as Cpp-Test and J-Test by Parasoft and lint in the Unix world, or complexity analysis tools like BattleMap by McCabe.

Another form of static testing is to build models of the system using simulators and then run these simulations. For example, I've used a program called General Purpose System Simulator to model various kinds of queues and arrival rates in systems. For those blessed with big budgets, you can buy specialized performance modeling and operations research tools. If you don't have the time, budget, or skill to build executable simulations of the system, static models using spreadsheets can be helpful.

You can use multiple kinds of static and dynamic tests on one project. On an Internet appliance project, the system architect used a spreadsheet model to design the server farm. We then hired specialists to simulate the performance and load behavior of these servers. Finally, we ran performance and load tests. At each step, we compared the simulation or test results against the desired results and against each other, iterating, correcting, and refining as we went.

For these kinds of static tests, many professional testers do not have the requisite skills to participate. In addition, these are typically not within the purview of the test team, but rather are done by programmers or by specialists.

Review Exercise

It's time to apply the review concepts you've learned to the Omninet Marketing Requirements Document.

Reviews

In this exercise, you'll perform a requirements review (a static test) for Omninet by reviewing the Omninet Marketing Requirements Document. By yourself, in pairs, or in small teams, review version 0.3 of the Omninet Marketing Requirements Document. Identify problems with specific phrases and sections. Try to fix those problems by rewording the phrase, changing the sentence, adding new sentences, or even whole new paragraphs.

I have provided an informal template for this chapter. Don't feel compelled to fill in every blank in the template. I suggest 60 minutes as a time limit. That's a typical amount of recommended time to perform a review. To make the situation even more realistic, work by yourself for 60 minutes prior to a group review. When you're done, check out my solution in this chapter.

Your Solution

SECTION #	PROBLEMATIC PHRASE OR SECTION	REWORDED PHRASE OR SECTION

Continued

SECTION #	PROBLEMATIC PHRASE OR SECTION	REWORDED PHRASE OR SECTION

(continued)

SECTION #	PROBLEMATIC PHRASE OR SECTION	REWORDED PHRASE OR SECTION

SECTION #　PROBLEMATIC PHRASE OR SECTION　　　REWORDED PHRASE OR SECTION

My Solution

SECTION #	PROBLEMATIC PHRASE OR SECTION	REWORDED PHRASE OR SECTION
1.1	Not all the acronyms are used in the document. This is confusing, because I'm not sure why I needed to know about them.	Delete the unused acronyms, which are AS, cable, CC, CS, DBMS, DC, IE, Linux, PIN, WS, and WXP.
1.2	It would be helpful to have the screen prototypes.	Create separate screen prototype document.
2	The document mentions the "financial third quarter" but does not specify the year.	Change phrase to include the appropriate fiscal year.
3.1.1	Does it make sense for the Welcome screen to be displayed if the public space (in which the kiosk is located) is closed?	Add the paragraph "During installation, personnel shall customize each kiosk for its location such that, when the public space in which the kiosk is located is closed, the kiosk goes into a power-saving mode. (If a session is active when the public space closes, the kiosk shall wait for the session to compete before going into a power-saving mode.) The kiosk shall return to an active mode, with the Welcome screen displayed, when the public space in which the kiosk is located reopens."
3.1.1	How does the user navigate past the Welcome screen to the Payment screen?	Add the sentence "The user may navigate from the Welcome to the Payment screen by providing the kiosk with any input other than selection of the alternate browser (see section 3.1.3) or alternate language (see section 3.1.4) options."
3.1.2	What happens if the user declines to purchase more time when the timer expires?	Add the sentence "If the user declines to purchase more time, the kiosk shall return the user to the active session until the current block of time has expired."
3.1.2	Is timer-based session termination different from logout termination in terms of the session data cleanup? It shouldn't be, but the requirements do not say.	Add the sentence "The kiosk shall clean up all the session data (as described in section 3.1.8) upon any such timer-expiration-based session termination."

SECTION #	PROBLEMATIC PHRASE OR SECTION	REWORDED PHRASE OR SECTION
3.1.2	What happens if the user walks away from the kiosk during the initial payment process? What is a reasonable time-out period to return to the Welcome screen?	Add the paragraph "If during the initial payment sequence the user does not respond to any prompt (e.g., 'Please swipe card,' 'Please insert bills,' 'Please enter time block to purchase,' etc.) within 30 seconds, the kiosk shall terminate the payment screen, refund any currency received during this payment sequence, and return to the Welcome screen."
3.1.2	What happens if the timer expires while the user is purchasing an additional block of time? What is a reasonable time-out period for the additional-time payment process? What happens when the user changes his mind and walks away from the kiosk?	Add the sentence "If the current block of time expires while the user is purchasing an additional block of time, the kiosk shall give the user an additional notification and shall extend the timer for 15 seconds. If the extended timer expires before the user has completed the purchase, the kiosk shall terminate the user's session."
3.1.2	Do credit and debit card customers have to reswipe their cards to buy additional time? If not, consider the risks associated with a customer walking away without terminating her session.	Add the sentence "Credit and debit card customers must reswipe their cards to buy additional blocks of time."
3.1.2	It's not clear whether the 1-hour limit on purchases applies to additional blocks of time purchased after the 60-second-warning pop-up.	Add the sentences "The kiosk shall sell additional blocks of time in five (5) minute increments, up to one (1) hour for each session. No limitation shall apply to how many times a user can extend a session by buying new blocks of time upon timer expiration."
3.1.3	The choice of browsers is said to depend on the kiosk operating system, but the supported kiosk OSes are implied, not specified.	Add the sentence "To prevent a single operating-system-specific worm or virus epidemic from taking down the Omninet network, 50 percent of the kiosks shall be installed with Linux, while the other 50 percent of the kiosks shall be installed with Windows XP."

Continued

(continued)

SECTION #	PROBLEMATIC PHRASE OR SECTION	REWORDED PHRASE OR SECTION
3.1.3	The kiosk is to offer the user a choice of browsers, but shouldn't the requirement say "alternate browsers"? I would assume that the entire kiosk program would be a browser-based application running on some sort of local web server (e.g., IIS or Apache), which would mean that, except during boot periods or as a result of a fatal error, the kiosk software would always run within a browser. This function would seem to provide for swapping to another alternate browsers.	Change phrase to read "At the Welcome screen, each Omninet kiosk shall provide the user with a choice of alternate browser(s). These shall be the latest versions of Netscape, Opera, or Internet Explorer (available on Windows kiosks only)."
3.1.3	If the comment above is correct, then the lack of specification of alternate-versus-default browsers for all supported kiosks OSes is an omission in the requirements, or at the very least should be addressed in the design specification.	Add the phrase "Windows kiosks shall default to the latest version of the Internet Explorer browser. Linux kiosks shall default to the latest version of the Netscape browser."
3.1.4	The "primary local language" could vary from one side of town to another. For example, in San Antonio, Texas, where I live, about half the population is the potential customers visiting the actual kiosk site."Hispanic and Spanish is a primary language for many people in certain neighborhoods. Demographic studies of the actual kiosk location – rather than just census data for a town or region – would have to drive this decision to avoid underutilized kiosks.	Change the phrase to read, "primary local language based on the installed locale and the demographics of
3.1.4	"In locales where multiple languages are commonly used," will the user have the option to select his preferred language in his preferred language?	Add a second sentence to this paragraph, "The kiosk shall present each optional language to the user in that language (e.g., 'Para Español, tócate aquí,' rather than 'For Spanish, touch here')."
3.1.5	Local customs, religions, etc., influence what is offensive, but there's no recognition of this issue in this section.	Add the sentence "Content blocking shall be localized for each kiosk and shall take into account local customs and religions as well the ages of the expected users of the kiosk."

SECTION #	PROBLEMATIC PHRASE OR SECTION	REWORDED PHRASE OR SECTION
3.2	The references to the appropriate administrative screen prototypes are missing.	Add appropriate references in each subsection in 3.2.
3.2.1	The automatic updates are to happen at "2:00 A.M. local time," but this is an hour that happens twice one day a year and zero times one day a year in many locations where daylight savings or summer time clock changes occur.	Add the parenthetical phrase "(In the event of a locale- or calendar-based clock change [e.g., daylight savings time] that would interfere with this schedule, the kiosk shall nevertheless connect exactly once per day as close as possible to 2:00 A.M..)"
3.2.1	What is the maximum allowable time for an update?	Add the phrase "Update periods shall not exceed 30 minutes. In the event that any single update package would cause the update to exceed 30 minutes, that package shall be split into a collection of prioritized smaller update packages that the kiosks can download and install within this limit. The kiosks shall download and install those update packages serially, in priority order."
3.2.1	Is the kiosk available for use during updates? What if the kiosk is in use when a scheduled update is to begin?	Add the phrase "The kiosk shall remain available for use during updates. The kiosks shall not terminate active sessions if an update initiates during the session. During active user interaction with the Internet, the update process shall consume no more than half the kiosk bandwidth."
3.2.3	What are the business risk implications of call center agent access to the sensitive customer information like credit card numbers, URLs visited, and so forth?	Add the paragraph "To minimize the opportunities for call center agents to misuse access to sensitive customer information like credit card numbers, URLs visited, and so forth, call center agent desktops and servers shall disallow screen captures, copy-and-paste, file saves, email, or any other data transfer from the call center agent desktop or the call center servers to any other system except as necessary to fulfill specified functions."

Comments on My Solution

I could have found a number of other bugs — or possible bugs — with this document, but the time limit cut me off. I also found a number of bugs or potential bugs that probably needed to be resolved in a lower-level document, like the Omninet System Requirements Document.

If you paid careful attention to my quality risk analysis solution, you can see that the bugs I found in the Omninet Marketing Requirements Document during that analysis also showed up in my solution.

Want a bonus exercise? If so, review the Omninet System Requirements Document. Carefully look for ambiguities or discrepancies that arise between that document and the Omninet Marketing Requirements Document. Do you need to make any changes to the Omninet System Requirements Document specifically due to changes you made to the Omninet Marketing Requirements Document in order to fix bugs in the latter document?

Bonus Exercise: Reviewing Triangle Requirements Title Page

Want some more practice? Here's another requirements specification you can test.

Triangle Requirements Review Using Wiegers's List

Suppose you've received the following requirements specification for the triangle classification program mentioned in Chapter 2.

The program shall accept, in a user-friendly fashion, three integers representing the lengths of a triangle's sides. It shall quickly draw the triangle, then output "scalene" (no equal sides), "isosceles" (two equal sides), or "equilateral" (three equal sides).

In the Chapter 8, I referenced Wiegers's top 10 list of requirements problems, which I include here:

1. Omitting key requirements, including business, user, quality, functional, and nonfunctional requirements.

2. Inadequate customer involvement. Of course, we can't always talk to the customers, so you might need to rely on customer surrogates like sales, marketing, and technical support staff.

3. Vagueness and ambiguity, which in my experience are universal problems.

4. Unprioritized requirements, which is especially an issue if requirements conflict or if we want to build and test features in priority order.

5. Building functionality no one uses or needs (aka, "gold plating"). This is an urge many engineers find impossible to resist. A good design provides for future expandability, but good project managers make sure we provide only those functions needed now.

6. Analysis paralysis. How much more information do you need to make a final decision about whether to include a feature or not? What are the risks and costs associated with not making a decision *right now*?

7. Scope creep. Did you ever work on a project where the requirements were supposedly frozen only to hear someone say, "We just gotta add one more feature, capability, report, screen, etc., etc."? Remember, a missed project completion date is as likely to arise through dozens of small missed delivery dates as from one big missed delivery date.

8. Inadequate requirements change control processes. This can also apply to situations where people subvert the change control processes to slip in their "pet features" after requirements freeze.

9. Insufficient change impact analysis. If we do decide to make a late change to the requirements, what is the impact on the programming effort? How about testing? How about configuration management, technical publications, project management, and other supporting teams? Do the opportunities and benefits really outweigh the risks and costs when all the risks and costs are considered?

10. Inadequate version control. If you hear someone asking a question that means, "What's in the product?" you can be sure that version control for the requirements and design specifications is a problem.[1]

By yourself, in pairs, or as a small team, use Wiegers's top 10 list of requirements problems to identify as many problems as you can in this requirements specification. To keep it challenging, since this is a very small snippet of what would be a larger document, keep your review to 5 minutes or less. Then try to fix the problems you found in the requirements specification in 15 minutes.

If you do have the benefit of working through this book with others, trade your corrected requirements specification with another team, then review each other's requirements specifications. Again, limit the review period to 5 minutes.

---

[1] See Karl Wiegers's article "Avoiding the Top Ten Requirements Traps," available on www.stickyminds.com.

The Requirements Bugs You Found

PROBLEMATIC WORDING	WIEGERS' ISSUE NUMBER

PROBLEMATIC WORDING	WIEGERS' ISSUE NUMBER

Continued

(continued)

PROBLEMATIC WORDING	WIEGERS' ISSUE NUMBER

My Solution: Requirements Bugs

PROBLEMATIC WORDING	WIEGERS'S ISSUE NUMBER
Missing any discussion of how errors are handled	1. Omitting key requirement
What does "in a user-friendly fashion" mean?	3. Vague, ambiguous
How is the program to "accept" input? File? GUI? Command-line? Look and feel for UI?	3. Vague, ambiguous
What does it mean to "quickly draw" a triangle? How long is quickly?	3. Vague, ambiguous
Missing any discussion of supported platforms and interfaces, which does matter.	1. Omitting key requirement
Do we really need to draw the triangle?	5. Unneeded function
Without knowing the angles, can we really draw the triangle?	7. Scope creep
What is the priority of drawing the triangle versus returning the classifying information?	4. Unprioritized requirements
Where does the "output" (i.e., "scalene," etc.) end up? File? GUI? Character-based UI?	3. Vague, ambiguous
How does the program start and end?	1. Omitting key requirement
Other than vague usability and performance requirements, we only have functional requirements.	1. Omitting key requirements
We don't have any indication of the customers	2. No customer involvement or users.
Is there any documentation or help?	1. Omitting key requirements

IMPROVED WORDING	RESOLVED ISSUE NUMBER
High Priority Requirements	
Program shall run on the command line of Linux systems.	1. Provides key requirement
User shall start program by typing "triangle [-h] | a b c."	1. Provides key requirement
Program shall provide Linux script writers with a filter to classify triangles.	2. Identify customers
Triangles shall be classified as "scalene," "isosceles," "equilateral," or "not a triangle."	3. Unambiguous

Continued

(continued)

IMPROVED WORDING	RESOLVED ISSUE NUMBER
Standard Linux I/O redirection shall be used to direct I/O from/to files.	1. Provides key requirement
High Priority Requirements	
Program shall accept as input three integers (i.e., a b c), white-space (space, tab) separated.	3. Unambiguous
If integers are in file, each line shall contain exactly three integers separated by white space.	3. Unambiguous
Program shall return classification within 100 milliseconds of receiving input.	3. Unambiguous
If multiple triangles have been specified in a file, each classification will be on its own line.	3. Unambiguous
If the user specifies the "-h" flag, program shall display the "man" page for help.	1. Provides key requirement
If the user specifies the "-h" flag, program shall ignore any other inputs provided.	3. Unambiguous
If the program receives only valid triangle dimensions, exit with 0 status.	1. Provides key requirement
If the program receives non-integer dimensions, conclude processing, exit with 1 status.	1. Provides key requirement
If the program receives invalid triangle dimensions, conclude processing, exit with 2 status.	1. Provides key requirement
If the program encounters missing dimensions, exit immediately with 3 status.	1. Provides key requirement
Program shall accept up to 4MB of input.	1. Provides key requirement
Low Priority Requirements	
Extend program to accept "triangle a b c AB BC AC" where AB, BC, AC are angles.	1. Provides key requirement
Create website (HTML/GIF) showing triangles, one per page, while processing as before.	1. Provides key requirement
Start browser, pointed to web page illustration, once first drawing is done.	1. Provides key requirement
Show triangles as black lines on a white background, with dimensions and angles labeled.	1. Provides key requirement

Comments on My Solution

I've resolved some of the problems in the requirements document. However, my new version is not really a best-practices requirements document. For one thing, the requirements don't have identifiers, so we can't trace the tests back to requirements. For another thing, the document has no structure and merely jumps around from topic to topic.

The Omninet Marketing Requirements Document is much closer to what you'd find in an organization with a mature requirements process. However, I'd guess that many organizations provide their test teams with requirements documents much like the triangle requirements specification document I provided at the beginning of this bonus exercise.

It's hard to write good requirements, but bad requirements create many program bugs.[2] Given the time and money savings attributable to earlier bug detection — as seen in this chapter — it makes good sense to try to get this third or half of all bugs out of the system before we started dynamic testing.

---

[2] Boris Beizer, in his book *Software Testing Techniques*, estimates that 30 percent of all bugs are requirements or design specification bugs. Capers Jones, in *Estimating Software Costs*, puts the figures at around 20 percent requirements bugs and around 25 percent design bugs, which would mean that about 45 percent of the bugs in the system existed on paper somewhere before they existed in executable code.

PART

IV

Behavioral Testing

In this Part

Equivalence Classes and Boundary Values

In this chapter, I begin examining test design techniques, which will take up the rest of this book. I start with test design techniques that focus primarily on intended behaviors. These are sometimes called black-box test techniques because the focus is on the externally visible aspects of the system (the "box") rather than how the system works. I start this sequence of chapters with two prevalent techniques, equivalence class partitioning and its extension, boundary value analysis.

Before we get into the trees, let's explain the forest. When writing a program, a big part of the job is recognizing that the program will need to deal with various situations, some of which will require unique elements of the program to handle them correctly. There is always a risk that the programmer might fail to recognize a particular situation as unique and needing unique handling. Another risk is that the programmer recognizes that the situation is unique but might create unique elements of the program that handle the situation *incorrectly*. Equivalence partitioning helps you recognize and test these unique situations to make sure the programmer didn't make such mistakes.

Often, when considering these unique situations, you see that they have boundaries; that is, the smallest value that qualifies for handling under the rules of this situation and the largest value that qualifies for handling under the rules of this situation. The programmer must also understand these boundaries and create unique elements of the program that allow the program to correctly handle the boundaries and all points in between. So, there is yet another risk: that programmers might fail to recognize or properly define these boundaries. Boundary value analysis helps you recognize and test these boundaries to make sure the programmer didn't make this mistake either.

Equivalence Partitioning

Equivalence partitioning, or equivalence class partitioning, is a fancy name for a simple idea. You identify the inputs, outputs, behaviors, environments, or whatever factors you are interested in testing. You group the factors into classes that the system should handle equivalently. Thus you have *partitioned* the factors into *equivalent classes*, hence the name.

Based on the equivalence classes, you create tests where at least one option from each class is represented. When dealing with factors that are ranges, you might use boundary values to select the test or tests. (We'll get to that in more detail in a minute.) You can also use marketing information to favor classes and options within classes.

For example, suppose I were testing supported printers for an application. If I suspect hardware bugs, one factor I might be interested in is the physical interface. Some printers use parallel interfaces, some serial, some USB 1.1, some USB 2.0, some infrared, some FireWire, some SCSI, and so forth. I could test at least one printer for each option.

If I suspect driver bugs, another factor I might be interested in is the logical interface. Some printers use PostScript, some HPPL, some ASCII, and so forth. I could test at least one printer for each option.

If I suspect printing bugs in the application itself, a third factor I might be interested in is the image application; that is, how the ink actually gets on the paper. Some printers use laser jets, some ink jets, some bubble jets, some dot matrix, some line printers, some the old spinning ball letter quality, some draw with pens like plotters, and so forth. Again, I have to test at least one printer for each option.

Notice that any given printer has one option for each factor. I could test a parallel, PostScript, laser jet printer. I can minimize the number of printers I use for testing by covering a previously uncovered option for each factor each time I add another printer to the set of tested printers.

Boundary Value Analysis

Boundary values exist on equivalence classes when the options are in some sense ordered. In other words, options can be said to be *greater than* and *less than* other options. For such equivalence classes, we can identify some options for some of the factors that are particularly interesting as tests. These interesting options often occur near boundaries.

A boundary is a place where the system's expected behavior changes. A boundary exists at the point at which an input value goes from valid to invalid. A boundary exists where an output can overflow a display field. A boundary exists where internal processing limits are encountered.

In the case of numeric data, you see boundaries at high and low values. You see boundaries due to representation and format. In the chapters in Part V on structural (white-box) testing, you'll see internal processing boundaries where accumulator variables overflow.

In the case of character and character string data, you have the numeric boundaries — all data is represented as binary numbers inside the system, after all. However, you also find boundaries due to collating sequences or character sets, character size, and string length.

In the case of date values, you again have numeric boundaries, but in this case you have a field with numeric subfields whose values influence each other. Remember the big Year 2000 scare? Another such problem is coming when the Unix operating system hits a date-storage limit. In addition to calendar or year rollover problems, you have boundaries due to leap years and date formats.

Time values are similar to date values in that you have a field with subfields. Time fields roll over and are displayed with 12- and 24-hour clocks. You also have format considerations.

For currency values, you have the various issues associated with rounding and fractions when you handle them. These problems are especially important when systems convert from one currency to another.

Some factors don't have ordering of their options. Therefore, they don't have boundary values. However, they usually have equivalence classes, and you want to make sure each option is processed in the correct equivalence class. For pick lists, check boxes, and buttons, this is the typical case.

Because equivalence partitioning and boundary value analysis are such powerful and pervasive techniques, let's look closely at each of these examples.

Integer

Let's start with a simple example, the equivalence classes and boundary values for an integer field.

Suppose you're testing a point-of-sale system for a fast-food restaurant where clerks ask customers questions such as, How many items would you like to order? Here you have at least the two obvious equivalence classes: valid order quantity and invalid order quantity.

Within the valid equivalence class, you have the boundary values of lowest valid quantity and highest valid quantity. Typically, the minimum order amount is 1. The maximum order amount could be a bit harder to specify. If you rely on the representation of the integer in the system, then 127, 255, 32767,

65536, and so forth are potential values. If you're familiar with programming or the way in which computers represent numbers, you'll recognize those as integers that are powers of two and often related to the maximum integers for certain data types.[1]

However, at some point such a number becomes ridiculous. Should the system allow the clerk to submit a customer order for, say, 30,000 deep-fried chicken breast sandwiches? A nice side benefit of test design, as I mention elsewhere in this book, is that it leads you to ask "dumb questions" that are really smart questions, such as, How many bags of French fried potatoes *should* the system allow the clerk to enter as a legitimate order?

Let's suppose in this case that the maximum quantity is 99. So, the basic equivalence classes and boundary values are shown in Figure 10-1.

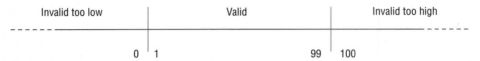

| Invalid too low | Valid | Invalid too high |

0   1   99   100

Figure 10-1: Integer equivalence partitions and boundary values

There might be two subclasses within the valid order quantity class, too. Perhaps you allow the clerk to embed a thousands separator, such as ',' in the United States or '.' in Europe. This makes sense only if you allow orders in thousands, as you would if you were selling ingots of pig iron or the like. So, 65536, 65,536, and 65.536 might all be valid integer inputs — and they might be maximums.

Of course, if you allow someone to submit an order of 65,536 pig iron ingots, why not 65,537? Relying on internal representation to create and enforce your boundaries, especially maximum boundaries, often is a sign of missing requirements, sloppy design, or buggy programming.

So, you have two invalid equivalence classes, quantity too low and quantity too high. You have boundary values at lowest valid quantity minus one and highest valid quantity plus one. Typically, zero is a boundary value for an order quantity. Selling one bag of French fries makes sense; selling zero bags of French fries doesn't.

However, if you're selling ingots of pig iron, then selling one ingot doesn't make sense. Perhaps you sell them in minimum quantities of 100. Alternatively, perhaps you sell them in lots of 100. If you only sell ingots in lots of 100, why would you allow the user to enter an order for 99 or 101 ingots? Why not just ask for the number of lots?

[1] If you are not a programmer or a person familiar with the internal workings of computers and you intend to pursue a career as a tester, I would encourage you to learn a bit more about the technology that makes all these systems go — and stop going. Charles Petzold's book *Code* is a good introduction to how computers work.

These are business decisions that have very real programming and testing implications. A good tester thinks about the business behavior that the system should exhibit — what's a reasonable user expectation — and designs tests to cover those behaviors.

Other invalid equivalence classes might exist if it's possible to enter the wrong thousands separators, decimal points, and negative numbers.

Perhaps you can think of other invalid equivalence classes? There's at least one other obvious one.

Real Numbers

For real (floating-point or decimal) numbers, the situation becomes a bit more complicated. All of the issues mentioned in the preceding section apply, along with a question about what the smallest distinguishable difference is between values. This smallest distinguishable difference is sometimes referred to as *epsilon* and sometimes represented by the Greek letter Σ.

Suppose you're testing a system that handles weather data. One possible use case is for the user to submit a request to display historical weather information, such as the average temperature in Duluth or Anchorage.

To identify the equivalence classes and their boundary values, you have to know what epsilon is for floating-point numbers. Suppose epsilon is one hundredth of a degree. Boundary values in the valid equivalence class for the temperature displayed field might include -99.99, -0.01, 0.00, 0.01, and 999.99. This is shown in Figure 10-2.

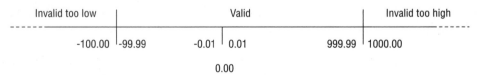

Figure 10-2: Real number equivalence partitions and boundary values

In this case, I split the valid equivalence class into three subclasses: greater than zero temperature, less than zero temperature, and zero temperature. This yielded boundary values at and near zero. Strange things can happen at zero. For example, what if a programmer forgets to check for zero values when doing division? Null values are sometimes treated as zero in calculations. If it's easy to check at and near zero in a data value, it's often worth doing.

As earlier, the valid equivalence class might divide into two subclasses: a period (.), the U.S.-style decimal digit separator, or a comma (,), the European style.

The invalid too low and invalid too high equivalence classes have boundary values like -100.0 and possibly 1000.0. There are also invalid equivalence classes like using the wrong thousands or decimal separators (if that's possible), entering too many digits for the epsilon, such as -99.999, or entering non-digits, such as ABC.

Again, applying insight and common sense into the testing can reveal interesting bugs. In this example, local variations in temperature probably make measuring and reporting temperatures for a city to two decimal points of precision meaningless at best. If the requirements or design specification calls for two decimal points of precision, then perhaps that's a bug in the specification. If the requirements or design specification is silent on the matter of precision of real number fields — perhaps among other matters — then did the programmer simply code through the ambiguities?

That can lead to behavior that's silly. In this case, reporting historical temperature data to two decimal points is displaying data with a level of precision that exceeds the accuracy of measurement and the meaningfulness of the data. If I tell you I have a pencil that's 6.727593 centimeters long, you'd laugh and ask me why I would need to know that, right? So, would it really make sense to know the average temperature to hundredths of a degree?

If I told you I had measured the pencil as exactly 6.727593 centimeters with a tape measure, you'd start to question my intelligence, at best. A tape measure is not accurate to millionths of a centimeter. Neither are a few weather stations in a city able to tell you to within hundredths of a degree the temperature in the entire city.

Finally, my example of the pencil might be triggering a question in your head. It's a reflex reaction every professional tester should have when looking at a numeric field: What are the units for that temperature field? Centigrade? Fahrenheit? Kelvin?

Why is it so important for testers to develop this reflex? As I mentioned in Chapters 8 and 9, the United States National Aeronautics and Space Administration lost a mission to Mars when two modules disagreed on the units of a numerical value. One module used English units, the other used metric units. Since those two modules had to interact properly during landing, that seemingly minor misunderstanding resulted in the total loss of a multimillion-dollar space mission. Even if your application isn't rocket science, units matter.

So, I have identified three possible bugs with this field in the course of designing tests:

- It displays data to a degree of precision that is useless to the user.
- It presents data to a degree of precision that probably exceeds the accuracy of the measurement.
- It doesn't specify the units.

Thinking about boundary values and equivalence classes is likely to help you find the first two possible bugs. The third possible bug is something that with practice will come to mind when you see numerical fields.

There are other possible bugs and potentially smart tests for this field. Can you think of some?

Character and String

Character and character string fields introduce even more possible complications into equivalence partitioning and boundary value analysis.

Suppose you're testing a secure application where the user is prompted, "Enter an alphanumeric password from 6 to 10 characters long." You might say, "Okay, there's the valid equivalence class, which is made valid by having the right number and kind of characters. There're two invalid equivalence classes based on the wrong kind of characters, at least one too low on the ASCII sequence and at least one too high on the ASCII sequence. There're two invalid equivalence classes based on the number of characters, too few and too many. So, there are four invalid equivalence classes if I put them together." This could be drawn as shown in Figure 10-3.

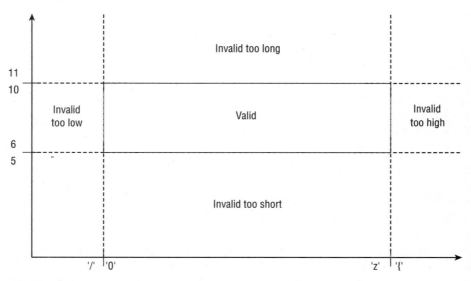

Figure 10-3: Character string equivalence partitions and boundary values

That reasoning could lead you to create 10 tests. The first 4 tests cover the valid class at the boundaries, '000000', 'zzzzzz', '0000000000', and 'zzzzzzzzz'. The next four tests cover the invalid too few characters and invalid too many characters classes, '00000', 'zzzzz', '00000000000', and 'zzzzzzzzzzz'. The last two tests cover the invalid too low on the ASCII sequence and invalid too high on the ASCII sequence classes, '//////' and '{{{{{{'. This is not the worst set of tests you could come up with, but there's room for improvement.

For one thing, this set of tests includes unnecessary tests based on a faulty assumption about likely bugs. In hardware testing, you use combinations of extreme conditions to learn interesting things about the system under test. Under both operating and shipping conditions, thermal tests (sometimes called *four-corners tests*) cover the four extreme combinations of temperature and humidity. Extremes of shock, vibration, temperature, and humidity are used in accelerated life tests.

In hardware testing, combining extremes is a smart test technique. Component failures occur when high temperature and high humidity act together. Components age and fail faster in extreme conditions due to a chemical phenomenon described by the Arrhenius equation.[2] Combined extremes works for certain kinds of software testing too. However, combined extremes usually don't make sense for functional testing of software. To understand why, let's briefly digress into principles of good system design.

A smart way to design systems is to separate the system architecture into layers, like the layers of a cake or the floors of a skyscraper. Each layer uses services or capabilities of the layer or layers below it while offering services or capabilities to the layer or layers above. Within each layer, components (functions or classes) handle logically related activities.

To return to our example, assuming a well-designed system, there would be one chunk of code to distinguish between valid and invalid characters for the password. Another chunk of code would check for valid password length.

The chunks that check for invalid characters and invalid length run sequentially. This means that one chunk of code or the other, but not both, would reject a password that is invalid in terms of both the length and the kind of characters.

If a password is accepted as having valid characters, having the maximum number of those characters doesn't matter. Either the number of characters to be checked is programmed properly or not — which still must be tested — but which characters you use for that test is immaterial. Therefore, you can eliminate one of the tests for invalid too many characters and one of the tests for invalid too few characters as well as two of the valid tests that are at the extremes in terms of both length and character types.

Another problem is that you are not really testing the check of valid characters very well. The '0' character has the smallest possible valid ASCII value of all legal alphanumeric characters, it's true. The 'z' character has the larger possible

---

[2] If you are involved in hardware testing or are simply curious about how this works, see Harry McLean's book *HALT, HASS & HASA Explained*.

valid ASCII value of all legal alphanumeric characters. However, the colon ':', the ampersand '&', the open brackets '[', and the back quote '`' are all nonalphanumeric characters that lie between those two values.

This is a common pitfall for equivalence partitioning and boundary values analysis. The 10 tests fail to recognize that what appears to be membership in a single class, the valid alphanumeric characters, really consists of membership in three classes, the decimal digits, the uppercase letters, and the lowercase letters. So, I really should add tests that cover these valid and invalid characters. Or better yet, I could simply add those characters to existing tests.

For the valid tests, you can change the passwords to include the valid characters that exist at these boundaries. A password like 09AZaz would be good. Think about it: A function is going to have to check the password character by character. So long as each character is good, you can hit each of the six boundaries formed in terms of valid characters with this one test.

You should also change the test that has 10 characters to include different characters. Something screwy like 51YBrMpc8x is good. The theory behind boundary value analysis says that these characters aren't likely to reveal bugs. However, I already tested the six boundaries with the previous test. What will I learn by testing those same six boundaries again?

In general, a good set of tests should have variety. Why? Because there are the bugs you look for and there are the bugs you forget to look for. A risk of using boundary value analysis is that you focus too much on two kinds of bugs — using the wrong comparison operator or setting some limiting value too high or too low by one — and forget that other kinds of bugs exist. For example, if the programmer used a *switch-case* block to divide input values into subsets, the most likely problems are not comparison operators but missing case labels. By making sure that your tests have sufficient variety, you increase your odds of stumbling across bugs that you forget to look for.

Unfortunately, this approach doesn't work for invalid tests. The reason is that, as soon as the system finds it's working with an invalid password, for purposes of efficiency and security, it will likely reject it. In other words, if I enter '/:@[`{', what I'll probably learn is that the system rejects the password and stops further checks as soon as it hits the '/' character. If I change the '/' to an 'e', say, then I'll get stopped at the ':'. And so on.

So, my tests for invalid boundaries should include an invalid character that is the only invalid character in an otherwise-valid password. Likewise, I need to have one test that consists only of valid characters but has one too few of them and one test that consists only of valid characters but has one too many of them.

There are two more equivalence classes that boundary value analysis can help you find. One is the no input class, the null string. The other class is the very much too long class. You can try a really long string, for example, hundreds or even thousands of characters.

It might sound like I'm contradicting myself with this advice, but I'm not. Certain programming languages — for example, C and C++ — make it easy to introduce array-related bugs that occur when an array has zero elements or way too many elements. The latter situation, way too many elements, is sometimes referred to as a buffer overflow bug. Such bugs are behind many of the security problems that plague the Internet.

Are there other tests? You bet. There are at least two areas to consider. First, who said that this system uses the ASCII character set? Perhaps it's a mainframe that uses EBCDIC? Second, what about systems in locales where the language isn't English? Is ñ, ö, or á allowed?

At this point, you might be getting concerned. There are clearly many tests that can be run for each different field. Do I need to rerun all of these tests for each field?

In a well-designed system of the kind mentioned earlier, the answer is no. In such a system, a component or some set of components in the user interface layer will handle input data validation. In that case, repeatedly running tests that try to stuff invalid data into input fields isn't a smart use of your limited time. Once you've tested that the program can recognize valid and an invalid characters, integers, real numbers, and so forth, rerunning such tests for each subsequent field is a waste.

However, testing the upper and lower limits of validity, special restrictions on characters (like the password restriction on alphanumeric characters), or the epsilon values for each of the fields does make sense. Programmers can forget that just because a function filtered out some invalid inputs, that doesn't mean that, in this context, an input the validation function allowed makes sense. That leads to bugs where systems accept nonsensical inputs like weather temperatures measured to two decimal points and orders for 65,000 bags of French fries.

Date

A date is a special kind of field with subfields that influence each other. This makes boundary value analysis tricky.

Suppose you're testing a travel package. It prompts the user to enter a requested departure date for an airline flight. The requested date can fit into two broad equivalence classes, valid and invalid. There are 12 valid months. Any input that specifies a month other than 1 through 12 is invalid. Of course, the format in which the user inputs the month might be character based, not numeric. Both formats might be allowed.

Given a valid month, do we have a valid day? Well, that depends on the month. There are at least 28 days in every month. February usually contains only 28 days, but based on the value of the year, 97 times in 400 years there are 29 days in February (remember that we discussed the rule for leap years in

Chapter 5). The other 11 months predictably contain either 30 or 31 days. The trick is remembering how many days are in each month. This equivalence partitioning and boundary value analysis is shown in Figure 10-4.

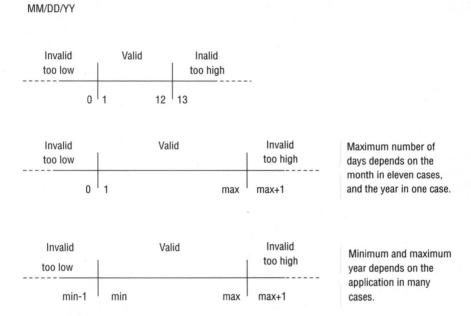

Figure 10-4: Date equivalence partitions and boundary values

You also have representational limits to consider. Through great expense and preparation, the software industry and indeed all industrialized society managed to head off a disaster by fixing systems that used two-digit year fields before January 1, 2000, arrived. Some operating systems use fixed-bit-size counters to count the number of seconds since some milestone occurred to keep track of time. Unix and Linux are examples. One of those bit sizes is 32 bits. One of those milestones is January 1, 1970. We might well run into another form of the Y2K bug all over again.

Another wrinkle to remember is that, in the U.S., dates are written in a month-day-year format. Frankly, that's illogical, because the least significant field should not come in the middle, after the median significant field and before the most significant field. If the more logical day-month-year format is used, then you have to look at the subfields differently.

In addition, while Europe and the Americas use the Common Era Gregorian calendar, where year one is the birth of Jesus, not all calendars work that way. In Taiwan, years are counted based on the founding of the Republic by Sun Yat-sen.

Jews and the State of Israel use a lunar calendar to determine the holidays. To bring the calendar back in line with the solar period, a leap month, Adar II, is inserted every so often. The rule for when Adar II happens is about as complicated as the rule for leap years in the Gregorian calendar. What's more complicated is to remember whether the holiday of Purim, which falls in the month of Adar, is in Adar I or Adar II.

Time

Compared to dates, times don't seem so bad at first. However, they have their quirks, which you must consider.

Suppose you're testing the travel application mentioned earlier. After entering a date, the user is supposed to enter the departure time for the flight. This seems easy. There are 60 seconds, 0 through 59, in each minute, and 60 minutes, 0 through 59, in each hour. There are 12 A.M. and 12 P.M. hours. So you could enter one too many seconds, minutes, or hours to create invalid times. You can enter valid time values just at the boundaries to create valid times, as shown in Figure 10-5.

However, that's not completely accurate. For one thing, there are format questions. If you're using a 12-hour, A.M. and P.M. format, then 13:00:00 is an invalid value. If you're using a 24-hour format, then 0:00:00 is a valid value.

For another thing, there are various kinds of daylight savings or summer times around the world. In the United States, under daylight savings time, when the clock moves ahead in the spring, the hour of 2:00:00 to 2:59:59 disappears. Later in the fall, that same hour happens twice. To make it more complicated, not every state in the United States observes daylight savings time. Summertime start and end dates vary in Europe, Israel, and other parts of Asia.

The problem of time is complicated enough that the developers of many software packages simply throw up their hands and leave it to you. For example, the Microsoft Outlook package saves time in local time. You can't specify a time zone for an appointment. This causes me a lot of grief when trying to set appointments, say, on the East Coast of the United States while I'm in Europe, Israel, or Asia. I have to try to figure out what the local time will be in that location to set the appointment time.

HH:MM:SS

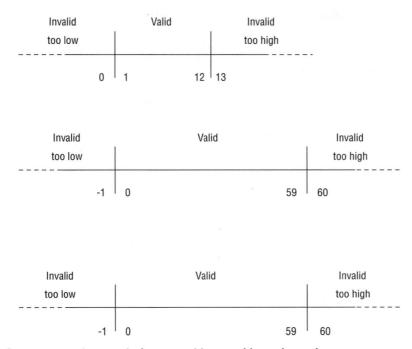

Figure 10-5: Time equivalence partitions and boundary values

Currency

Currency fields are typically fixed-decimal-point fields. As such, they are real numbers with a well-defined epsilon (smallest distinguishable difference), though they may be stored as integers.

Suppose you're testing an auction application. One prompt might tell the user, "Enter a bid price (under 1,000 dollars)." At first impression, boundary values in the valid bid price equivalence class include 999.99 and 0.01. Or is 0.01 actually in the invalid bid price equivalence class? If the only clue you have is the prompt, you might guess that bids must be entered to the nearest dollar. If so, this changes the nature of the field. You should get clarification on this matter if it's unclear.

You might also consider testing '999.', '999.00', '000.01', '.01', and '.010'. If fractions are supported, you might want to test something like '110 1/8'. If the system has a shared input validation component in the user interface layer, though, you only need to run such tests once. Again, a typical currency field is a valid real number that is then further restricted in terms of the decimal digits allowed and possibly the maximum value.

If the system allows the user to specify the currency, then you have another special set of boundary values in the valid bid price equivalence class, like '$999.99', '¥999.99', '£999.99', and '€999.99'. If changing currency is not allowed, these exact same values are smart tests but test the invalid bid price equivalence class.

If you can't get clarification on whether decimal digits or specifying the currency is allowed, here's a trick I've used. Test these values anyway. See what the system does. Report whatever it does as a bug and use the bug reporting process to resolve the ambiguity in specified behavior. That's not efficient, but it works. As a general technique for resolving questions about what is correct behavior, this approach works.

The boundary value in the invalid too high bid price class is '1000'. You could test with and without a thousands separator unless you've already checked support for thousands separators. The boundary value in the invalid too low bid price class is either '0.00' or '0', depending on whether cents are allowed. This is shown in Figure 10-6.

Figure 10-6: Currency equivalence partitions and boundary values

Other invalid class entries might include '110.111' (too many decimal points), '110.1 1/8' (mixed decimal points and fractions), '110 1/7' (usually not a legitimate fraction for currency fields).

Another concern is making sure that the fixed epsilon really is fixed. My colleagues and I tested a loan processing application once. The expected results were defined to the nearest cent for loan amounts, monthly payments, and other currency fields. Once we started running tests, we saw something odd. Sometimes the actual results matched the expected results. Sometimes they didn't. That's not what's odd. What's odd is that the mismatches were usually off by exactly one cent.

This odd bug became a frustrating bug. Sometimes the bug triage committee — the project management team that considered bugs — would say, "Yes, this is a bug, we must fix it." It would go away for a while; then it would come back somewhere else. Then the answer might be, "Well, no that's not a bug." Then business analysts would get involved and yes, it would be a bug again.

Money is something people tend to feel strongly about. So when defining tests, be careful to make sure that the epsilon value is well specified in advance. Then take advantage of that as a tester. Rounding errors happen. If real number variables are used to store and manipulate currency values, using very large currency values with cents — for example, $1,576,879.92 — as test values might well provoke them.

Beyond Functional Classes and Boundaries

So far, we've only looked at equivalence classes and boundary values for functional tests, especially of the user interface logic. However, you can also use equivalence classes and boundary value analysis for tests of quality risks other than functionality.

For example, suppose you have a capacity requirement that states in part, "…system shall handle 16MB data files…." Clearly this requirement creates valid and invalid classes of data files, with the boundary at 16 megabytes and 16 megabytes plus 1 byte.

Nonfunctional boundaries tend to be slightly softer than functional boundaries. In this example, the system might not fail at exactly 16 megabytes plus 1 byte. You might need to push it to 17, 18, maybe even 20 or 25 megabytes before the behavior starts to degrade.

What's important with any error handling tests, and especially nonfunctional boundary tests, is that the degradation of performance be graceful. For example, it's okay if the system rejects a data file as too big, presenting the user with a polite message to that effect. It's not okay if the system goes berserk and deletes the offending data file.

You can construct similar nonfunctional tests for volume, configuration, and other quality risks. If you have a volume requirement that states in part, "…system shall handle 150 transactions per second (TPS)…" then test at 150 and 151 transactions per second. If you have a configuration requirement that states in part, "…system shall run on Windows NT 4 or better…" then test at least one Windows NT 4 configuration.

By testing at combined boundaries, you create stress tests. If all the preceding requirements fragments describe the same system, then you might create a stress test that tests 150 transactions per second using 16MB files on Windows NT 4.

Boundary conditions abound in software systems. Bugs tend to congregate in such boundaries. So effective and efficient testers look for boundaries intuitively and often test there first.

Curious about those other smart tests for some of the fields I mentioned earlier? Here are some that come to mind for me. Test illegal character strings into numeric fields, like "ABC" into an integer. Test scientific notation, like 9.7E2, for real numbers. Test entering three valid dates on which it is impossible to fly to Yakutsk because there's no airline service to that city on those dates.

You might have come up with others, too. That's okay. There're an infinite number of tests you can run, and different assumptions about likely bugs can make many of those tests smart tests under certain circumstances. What's important is that you identify the bug assumptions you are making when you decide which tests to run and which tests not to run.

## CHAPTER 11

Equivalence Classes and Boundary Values Exercise

It's time to apply the equivalence class partitioning and boundary value analysis techniques to the Omninet project. Let's start with functional testing and then move on to nonfunctional test areas.

Functional Boundaries and Classes

You are testing an e-commerce system that sells Omninet knickknacks like baseball caps and jackets. The exercise is to create functional tests for the web page that accepts the orders. A screen prototype for the order-entry web page is shown in Figure 11-1.

The system accepts a five-digit numeric item ID number from 00000 to 99999. In the product catalog in the system database, these item IDs are sorted by price, with the cheapest items having the lower (closest to 00000) item ID numbers and the most expensive items having the higher (closest to 99999) item ID numbers. You don't have to worry about testing the sorting of data in the database, though, as you are not testing the data-entry process for the catalog.

The system accepts a quantity to be ordered, from 1 to 99. If the user enters a previously ordered item ID and a 0 quantity to be ordered, that item is removed from the shopping cart.

Based on these inputs, the system retrieves the item price, calculates the item total (quantity times item price), and adds the item total to the cart total. Due to limits on credit card orders that can be processed, the maximum cart total is $999.99.

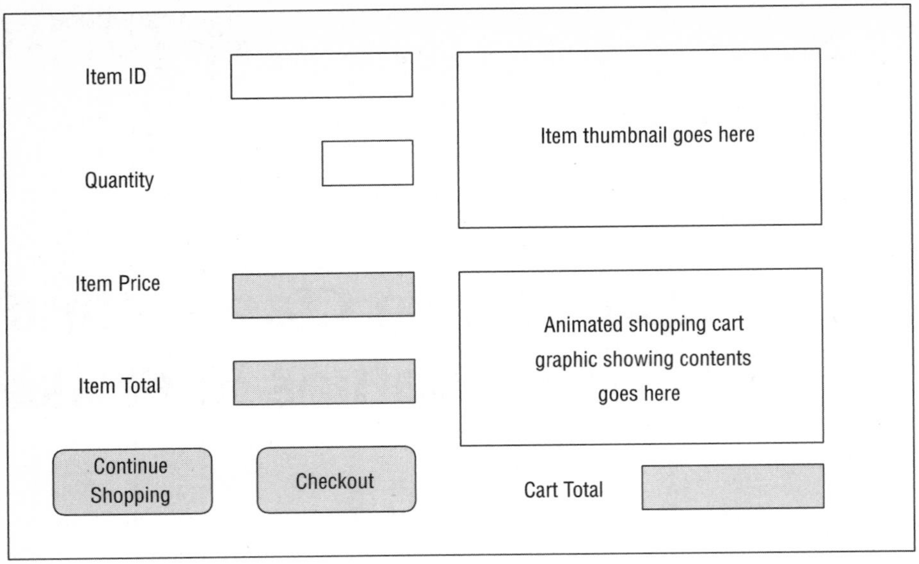

Figure 11-1: Omninet e-commerce order entry page screen template

Your job as a tester is to use boundary value analysis and equivalence class partitioning to create tests. I have provided an informal template for your test design in this exercise, which you can use. I suggest 60 minutes as a time limit for completing the work. When you're done, keep going in the chapter to see my solution.

First, draw the equivalence classes and boundary values for the item ID number on a blank piece of paper. Next, draw the equivalence classes and boundary values for the quantity ordered.

Now, use the template as a model for your own set of inputs, actions to take, and expected results. The equivalence classes and boundary values should be an inspiration to you, and you should cover them, but don't feel constrained by them. Similarly, if you think inputs, actions, and expected results other than those in the template should be checked, feel free to add them.

Test Number					
Inputs, Actions					
Item ID					
Quantity					
Expected Results					
Item Price (IP)					
Cart Contents					
Cart Total					

My Solution and Comments

I drew the equivalence classes and boundary values for the item ID number in two ways, as shown in Figure 11-2. There are two ways to think about this field. One is as an unsigned integer field with a minimum value of 0 and a maximum value of 99999. In that case, the number-line representation at the top of the figure makes sense. You'll want to test four item ID values: '-1', '0', '99999', and '100000'.

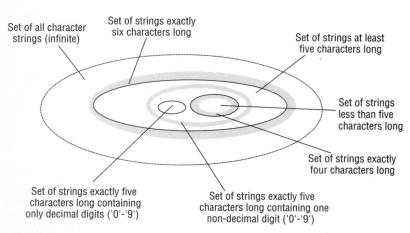

Figure 11-2: Equivalence classes and boundary values for the item ID

The other way to think about the field is as a character string that must be exactly five characters long and consist only of decimal digits. In that case, the set graph representation at the bottom of the figure makes sense. You'll want to test a really, really long string (for buffer overflow), a six-character string like '100000' (illegal for length only), two five-character strings like '31:75' and '27/86' (illegal for the non-digits that are almost a digit, ASCII-wise), a four character string like '9999' (illegal for length only), a zero-character string like the null string "" (usually an interesting character input), and two five-character strings like '00000' and '99999'.

Which representation is correct? Well, if you can ask the programmer how the field is implemented, you could test it according to what she tells you. However, it doesn't make it that much more difficult to assume that either might be correct and test it both ways. In that case, if the implementation changes, your tests will cover all the interesting cases.

I drew the equivalence classes and boundary values for the quantity ordered as shown in Figure 11-3. Notice how the zero value is sometimes valid and sometimes invalid, depending on whether the item ID has been previously entered.

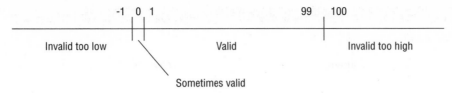

Figure 11-3: Equivalence classes and boundary values for the quantity ordered

The test inputs, actions, and expected results are shown in the following tables.

TEST NUMBER	1	2	3	4	5
Inputs, Actions					
Item ID	-1	0	00000	31:75	99999
Quantity	1	1	99	2	1
Next Action	Continue	Continue	Continue	Continue	Checkout
Expected Results					
Error Msg?	Yes	No	No	Yes	No
Item Price (IP)	Blank	Confirm	Confirm	Blank	Confirm
Item Total	Blank	1*IP	99*IP	Blank	1*IP
Cart Contents	Empty	00000×1	00000×100	00000×100	00000×100 99999×1
Cart Total	0.00	1*IP	+99*IP	=	+1*IP
Checkout	No	No	No	No	Yes

TEST NUMBER	6	7	8	9	10
Inputs, Actions					
Item ID	55555	27/86	12785	12785	63041
Quantity	9	3	16	0	1
Next Action	Checkout	Checkout	Continue	Checkout	Continue
Expected Results					
Error Msg?	No	Yes (2)	No	Yes	No
Item Price (IP)	Confirm	Blank	Confirm	Blank	Confirm
Item Total	9*IP	Blank	16*IP	Blank	1*IP
Cart Contents	55555×9	Empty	12785×16	Empty	63041×1
Cart Total	9*IP	0.00	16*IP	0.00	1*IP
Checkout	Yes	No	No	No	No

TEST NUMBER	11	12	13	14	15
Inputs, Actions					
Item ID	70152	63041	70152	100000	Really long
Quantity	5	0	2	1	17
Next Action	Continue	Continue	Checkout	Continue	Continue
Expected Results					
Error Msg?	No	No	No	Yes	Yes
Item Price (IP)	Confirm	Blank	Confirm	Blank	Blank
Item Total	5*IP	Blank	2*IP	Blank	Blank
Cart Contents	63041×1 70152×5	70152×5	70152×7	Empty	Empty
Cart Total	+5*IP	$-1*IP_{63041}$	+2*IP	0.00	0.00
Checkout	No	No	Yes	No	No

TEST NUMBER	16	17	18	19
Inputs, Actions				
Item ID	9999	Null	Fill cart	Fill cart 0.01
Quantity	3	5	to limit	past limit
Next Action	Continue	Continue	Checkout	Checkout
Expected Results				
Error Msg?	No	Yes	No	Yes
Item Price (IP)	Confirm	Blank	Confirm	Confirm
Item Total	3*IP	Blank	Confirm	Confirm
Cart Contents	3x09999	Empty	Confirm full	Confirm (near) full
Cart Total	3*IP	0.00	999.99	(<)= 999.99
Checkout?	No	No	No	Yes

TEST NUMBER	20	21	22
Inputs, Actions			
Item ID	34572	23897	89457
Quantity	0	-1	100
Next Action	Continue	Continue	Continue
Expected Results			
Error Msg?	Yes	Yes	Yes
Item Price (IP)	Blank	Blank	Blank
Item Total	Blank	Blank	Blank
Cart Contents	Empty	Empty	Blank
Cart Total	0.00	0.00	0.00
Checkout?	No	No	No

I've assumed that the system will accept the item ID either as an integer (without leading zeros) or as a five-character field with numeric characters only (with leading zeros). That's the permissive way to define the system, and I think systems should be permissive when possible.

I've instructed the tester to confirm the prices, probably using a paper catalog or price list and a calculator. When a reliable test oracle will be both readily available and changing over time, it's better not to introduce redundancy and ultimately discrepancies by hard-coding the expected result in the test case. Instead, you can make a note to check the expected result during test execution and possibly provide some information about where to find the test oracle.

In test 3, you might have noticed that I'm assuming you can order 100 (or more) of a single item simply by entering two orders. Should that be okay? Well, if the objective of the limit is to prevent people from accidentally ordering too many of a single item, forcing the user to enter two orders makes it obvious that the large order quantity is deliberate. If the system rejected this value with a message like, "Sorry, but you can only order a total quantity 99 of any given item," then most likely that would not be an error. However, you would need to add another test where you ordered quantity 99 of an item in a single order.

Also in test 3, the leading + in the cart total indicates that you should expect the cart total to include the previous cart total plus the addition item total for this item. In test 4, the leading = in the cart total indicates that you should expect the cart total to be unchanged from the previous cart total.

In test 5, I'm assuming that the item total for this item — the most expensive in the catalog — together with the 100 least-expensive items, will not exceed the $999.99 order total limit. If it does, then I might have to remove items from the cart or check out before running test 5.

In test 6 — and really, in all the tests — I'm assuming that the item ID I've entered corresponds to an actual item in the catalog. It's possible that the item IDs might be sparse, in the sense that most legal item ID numbers don't actually correspond to an item in the catalog. In that case, the test would have to pick the nearest possible item ID to achieve the same effect for many of the tests. You'd also want to check what happens when you enter an item ID that is legal but not in the catalog.

Notice that I've exercised boundary values on actions and outputs, not just inputs. For example, test 6 verifies checking out with a single item in the cart. Tests 7 and 9 verify trying to check out with no items in the cart. Test 7 should result in two error messages, one for a bad item ID and one for checking out with nothing in the cart. Test 9 should result in a single error message for checking out with nothing in the cart. Other tests verify checking out with multiple items in the cart.

In test 13, I've assumed that entering an item ID and a valid quantity for something already in the shopping cart adds to the total for that item. However, it might overwrite the total. Without a clear explanation of why the system should overwrite rather than add to the total, I'd report that as a bug. As a user, I'd expect it to add, not overwrite, so that judgment will be reflected in my test result interpretation.

There's no stated limit on how many *items* can be in the cart, but there is a stated limit on the *total cost* of the items. That's covered by tests 18 and 19. In test 18, the system should allow me to buy $999.99 worth of items. In test 19, the system should reject the last item I add — the one that puts my cart total as close as possible to $1,000.00 — but should allow me to purchase the other items I've already added to my cart.

To some extent, this example leaves to the tester's judgment or the requirements specification the questions of whether a European-style decimal point or currency symbol in the result would be correct. I usually prefer to have smart testers make this decision as they run the tests. That way, if the system is globalized for another locale later, I don't need to change the tests.

Nonfunctional Boundaries and Classes

Now, let's move on to nonfunctional areas. Referring to the Omninet Marketing Requirements Document and System Requirements Document, identify interesting nonfunctional boundaries for testing. Describe how you would test them on a blank page. I suggest 30 minutes as a time limit. When you're done, check out my solution in the following two tables. There, I list the elements of the Omninet Marketing Requirements Document (v0.3) and Omninet System Requirements Document (v0.2) that have nonfunctional boundary test implications, along with my approach for testing them.

Omninet Marketing Requirements Document (v0.3)

SECTION	DESCRIPTION	TEST APPROACH
2.	The first set of 1,000 Omninet kiosks shall be live, accepting payment and accessing the Internet…	Test 1,000 kiosks, all accessing the servers simultaneously for an extended period, probably using a simulator or automated tool. Increase the number of simulated kiosks until failure occurs to ensure graceful degradation under load.
3.1.2	The kiosk shall sell blocks of time in five (5) minute increments, up to one (1) hour.	This is a functional boundary, and I would cover it under functional testing. The sameapplies to other time and money accounting boundaries.
3.1.3	…each Omninet kiosk shall provide the user with a choice of the latest version of Netscape, Opera, or Internet Explorer (available on Windows kiosks only)…	Attempt to load an unsupported browser or a back-level version of a browser.
3.1.4	On kiosks operating with a PSTN connection, users shall have greater than 50 Kbps connection speed.	Test sustained throughput under kiosk and server load of at least 50 Kbps.
3.1.4	On kiosks operating with DSL or cable connections, users shall have greater than 128 Kbps connection speed.	Test sustained throughput under kiosk and server load of at least 128 Kbps.
3.2.1	If the update application on the application server tells the kiosk that it is overloaded, the kiosk shall disconnect, then retry at a later time. The delay for retry is a random period between ten (10) and sixty (60) minutes.	Force repeated disconnects during attempted update. Test to ensure proper retry delays. Test to see what happens if the update never succeeds.

Omninet System Requirements Document (v0.2)

ID	DESCRIPTION	TEST APPROACH
020-010-010 – 020-010-030	These subsections deal with delays for OS and browser patches and the need for no delay on security updates and patches.	Test to ensure that the different types of patches are distinguished from each other correctly.
030-030-010	The kiosk user interface shall not require the user to navigate through more than five unique pages before accessing the Web browser.	A straightforward test, but need to make sure that variations in browser and language are covered.
030-030-020	The call center desktop agent user interface shall not require the user to navigate through more than five unique pages before accessing any of the major call-center functions.	Same as 030-030-010.
040-010-010 –		
040-010-020	These subsections deal with timing and performance parameters for repeated actions.	Use an automated tool to force multiple (thousands of) cycles. Gather statistically valid information on conformance to these specifications.
040-020-010	The server farm shall support 1,000 kiosks, all of which may be simultaneously active.	See MRD section 2 test approach.
040-020-020	The server farm shall support 25 call center agent desktops, all of which may be simultaneously active.	As with 040-020-010, but test at the call center.
050-020-010	The server farm shall support up to 100 call center agents.	Hopefully, the test-to-failure run for 040-020-020 shows that failure occurs gracefully at more than 100 agents.
050-020-020	The server farm shall support up to 5,000 kiosks.	Hopefully, the test-to-failure run for 040-020-010 shows that failure occurs gracefully at more than 5,000 kiosks.

## CHAPTER 12

Use Cases, Live Data, and Decision Tables

In this chapter, I present some additional techniques for black-box testing. These techniques share in common a focus on testing the internal business logic of the system and how it handles realistic situations in which it must operate.

I'll start by discussing the test application of use cases. Use cases are a common object-oriented design technique that you can utilize for testing if you work on a project where they are available. In non-object-oriented projects, scenario tests are a similar approach.

Next, I'll discuss the use of live data and customer workflows for testing. Such test resources may be available for both IT and commercial software development and maintenance projects.

Finally, we'll get to the topic of decision tables. Decision tables are a useful way to describe the internal logic of a system. When provided to or created by a tester, they are a powerful testing resource too.

Use Cases and Scenario Tests

The essence of both use case-based tests and scenario tests is simple. You design various cases that reflect typical or challenging real-world uses of the system. For example, suppose you're testing a home equity loan application. You design tests around a hypothetical family, the Stevens. The Stevens are going to apply for a home equity loan using the application you're testing. You flesh out the scenario as follows:

- John and Jenny Stevens have three kids.
- They own a house worth $400,000. They owe $350,000 on the house on their first mortgage.
- They also own two cars worth $25,000 total. They have outstanding balances on their car loans totaling $17,000.
- John works as a college teacher. Jenny works as a stockbroker. They have incomes of $45,000 and $75,000, respectively.
- They have a good credit history, with only two derogatory entries. They have one late payment on their Visa card and one late car payment. These entries occurred 17 months and 35 months ago, respectively.
- The Stevens are applying for a $15,000 home equity loan.

The test case confirms that they are indeed given the loan for the request amount. The test case also confirms the term and interest rate.

Some object-oriented design methodologies make this easy for you. In these techniques, designers create use cases. Use cases can form the framework of scenarios like the preceding one. All you do is fill in the particulars, as shown. If you don't have use cases available, you can create scenarios like this too. You must first understand the intended uses of the system, which means understanding what the real users will do. Remember that different users might use the system differently.

You can and should combine the use case and scenario technique with equivalence classes to make sure that every equivalence class is covered. You can also use boundary value analysis to create challenging tests. Such tests should explore the boundaries where the behavior of the system should change.

This brings us back to the question posed in Chapter 10: Does testing at boundaries bring us beyond the realm of reasonable usage scenarios? For example, suppose you're testing an e-commerce system. If the system uses a 4-byte unsigned item counter variable, do you want to allow ordering 32,000 or more items? After all, the internal data representation of the software would support such an order.

Some of these questions are less obvious. Should a travel system allow departure dates after arrival dates for an air travel segment? Thanks to the international date line, the answer is, "It depends on the departure and arrival cities." A clever tester can sometimes design test scenarios where accepting a "ridiculous" input is required. You need to think very carefully about such uses to find such bugs.

Scenario testing is not just for testing functionality. Scenario tests can be used for other quality risks, including security, usability, and reliability.

For example, a number of years ago I managed a test group in charge of system testing a complex network operating system. This operating system,

AIX, was a Unix variant that ran on Intel PCs and mainframes. One of the tests we had to run was a reliability test. We used a scenario test that created the maximum possible load on each server in the maximum supported configuration, 31 servers acting as an AIX cluster. The server network configuration is shown in Figure 12-1.

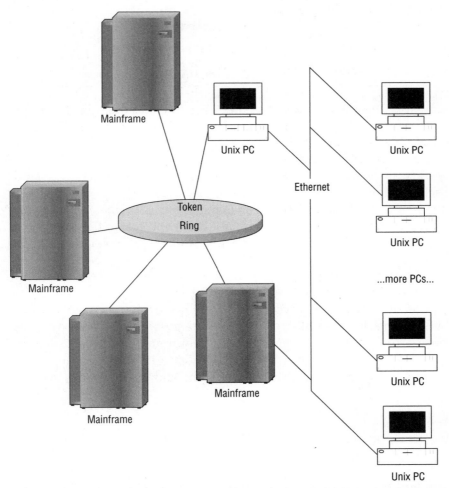

Figure 12-1: MaxConfig, a server network configuration for a scenario reliability test

The load was created through load generators that ran on each PC and mainframe. These load generators were simple C programs that used Unix system and library calls to carry out various activities:

- Creating, read, writing, and deleting files
- Sending and receiving interprocess communications

- Migrating running processes from one server to another
- Sharing files across the network

In this straightforward way, we created high and random load combinations that surpassed almost all foreseeable loads that real applications would create. This test was thus a worst-case scenario. The criteria were simple: If the servers stayed up to 48 hours, and no abnormal process termination, data loss, or communication failures occurred, then the test passed.

Nouns and Verbs, Adjectives and Adverbs

A refinement of the scenario-based technique is to try to think of the system behavior grammatically. In other words, if you can describe the intended behavior of the system in simple sentences, you can analyze the grammar of these sentences to derive test cases.

Many software systems exist to manipulate specific kinds of data. The kinds of data sets are the nouns. These data sets are the subjects — the actors — and the objects — the things acted upon. The manipulations are the verbs. In other words, these are actions the system will take on the objects at the direction of the actors. As in grammar, adjectives and adverbs affect the way the manipulation occurs.

So, you start by identifying these data items. You can then write the descriptions of the system actions in sentences. You can analyze these sentences grammatically and test accordingly. You can even trace your test coverage back to these sentences that describe the system. In effect, the short sentences become a form of use case or requirements specification for the system.

Let's consider an example. An ATM system should do things like the following:

- Accept deposits
- Process withdrawals
- Answer inquiries

You can take this further and describe the kinds of deposits, withdrawals, and inquiries. You can then look at adverbs and adjectives that modify the system's actions. Should the actions be performed quickly? How about securely?[1]

---

[1] This test design technique comes from Elisabeth Hendrickson. For more, see www.qualitytree.com.

Live Data and Customer Tests

So far, I've talked about what the user *should be able* to do with the system. Live data and customer tests consider what users *actually* do with the system. Such tests are like use cases or scenarios. However, these tests are not hypothetical. They are real tests. You use live data and actual customer experiences and workflows to construct the test cases.

For extremely complex scientific applications, such tests may be the only way to explore the system realistically. The number of specific use cases or scenarios for complex applications may be infinite or very close to infinite. For example, consider a seismic modeling system used for oil exploration. The potential number of configurations of the earth's crust is inconceivably enormous. Consider integrated circuit design software. How many different types of chip layouts are there?

In some cases, the tester might use live data from customers to create tests. The tester might also receive workflow descriptions from users for testing. When I was the test manager for a database query application, we had a process for adding a new set of tests to our automated test system every time a customer reported a bug. We used their workflows and data to create the tests.

In other cases, actual users perform the tests. Beta and pilot testing are examples. Here, the test team, marketing staff, or other stakeholders oversee a program where they provide early versions of the system to a subset of the customers under controlled conditions to see what happens when the system is used to solve real-world problems.

When planning to use customer data, customer workflows, and typical values for testing, be sure to remember one important caveat. Most natural processes and behaviors follow a statistical distribution, often the normal distribution. This means that most of the test data, workflows, and values are very much alike. Do not automatically assume you've covered a large number of unique and interesting test conditions simply because you've used a large volume of customer data or run a large number of realistic customer workflows. You'll need to augment your tests with special test data and unusual workflows to find some of the more interesting and exotic bugs. See Figure 12-2 for an illustration.

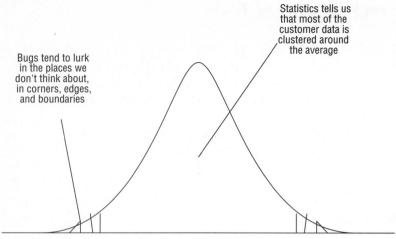

Figure 12-2: The limitations of customer data as test data

Decision Tables

Use cases, scenario tests, grammar-based tests, live data, and customer work-flow tests have something in common: They are typically focused on testing the internal workings of the system. These internal workings are sometimes called business rules.

The business rules can often be described or implemented through decision tables. For example, an e-commerce system has business rules that decide how to process an order. The decision looks at conditions like the size of the order, the inventory of the item order, the state or country to which the order will be shipped, and so forth.

Business rules can be described in flow charts or as decision tables. You can translate a flow chart representation into a decision table as a first step in creating tests. These tests follow directly from the decision tables. Let's take a look at an example.

The decision table in Table 12-1 shows some of the business logic for an ATM. This table specifies the correct handling of cash withdrawal transactions. Other decision tables could specify the correct handling of other types of transactions. These related decision tables might be very similar.

Table 12-1   ATM Decision Table

	BUSINESS RULES				
	1	2	3	4	5
Condition					
User Inserts Valid Card	N	Y	Y	Y	Y
User Enters Valid PIN	-	N	N	Y	Y
Three Invalid PINs Attempts	-	N	Y	N	N
Sufficient Balance for Request	-	-	-	N	Y
Action					
Reject Card	Y	N	N	N	N
Prompt to Reenter PIN	N	Y	N	N	N
Keep Card	N	N	Y	N	N
Prompt to Reenter Request	N	N	N	Y	N
Dispense Requested Cash	N	N	N	N	Y

The table is read columnwise. The leftmost column specifies first the conditions, then the actions. The conditions listed are those that influence the behavior of the system for the particular transaction under consideration. The actions listed are those actions the system might carry out depending on the conditions when handling this transaction. Each subsequent column to the right indicates, under the specified combination of conditions, which specified actions should and shouldn't take place.

The dashes (-) indicate conditions that aren't reached as part of this rule. For example, if someone tries to insert their driver's license or frequent flyer card into the ATM, the system should not try to validate the PIN or request and validate a withdrawal amount. Indeed, it would be nonsensical and impossible for the system to try to do so. Rather, under this condition, the ATM should simply reject the card. It should do nothing else, particularly not dispense any cash!

In this decision table, the rules are mutually exclusive. Only one rule can apply at any one moment of time. However, that is not true for all decision tables. In some situations, a decision table can describe a situation in which more than one rule could apply at one time. Also, in this decision table, the actions are mutually exclusive. That is not necessarily true for all decision tables, either.

In Chapter 10, I mentioned the use of layered system architecture. The business logic layer is usually under the user interface layer. The data-access layer is below the business logic layer.

If the user interface and data access were tested separately as part of integration testing, you can assume that the input-checking and data-integrity checking logic were already tested. So by the time you get to testing the business logic, you can assume that individual data items flowing to the business logic are already validated.

To use this table for testing, you need to have at least one test that covers each business rule. If there are multiple situations in which a condition might take on a particular value, then you might want to test some or all of those situations.

Okay, so that's the basic concept of decision tables and how they can be used for testing. However, you can and should take the concept much further than just the basics. To learn how to do so, proceed to the next chapter, which provides some exercises and further discussion on this useful technique.

Decision Table Exercise

Let's apply the decision table test technique to the Omninet project.

Decision Table Tests

Referring to the payment decision table in the Omninet System Requirements Document (Appendix B), develop tests for this function. I've provided an informal template in Table 13-1. I suggest 30 minutes as a time limit. When you're done, keep going in the chapter to see my solution.

Table 13-1 Decision Table Test Template

TESTER ACTION AND DATA	EXPECTED RESULT

Continued

Table 13-1   *(continued)*

TESTER ACTION AND DATA	EXPECTED RESULT

My Solution and Comments

In my solution to the quality risk analysis exercise, I identified "valid payment rejected/invalid payment accepted" as a very low technical risk but a high business risk. Based on that, I decided that this risk item should receive broad testing.

Did you remember to refer back to your quality risk analysis for guidance on how thoroughly you should test this function? If you're doing risk-based testing, that's important. You can easily misalign your tests with the level of risk during test design and development. In such cases, you'll overtest some low-risk items and undertest some high-risk items. In risk-based testing, your quality risk analysis is your road map.

Of course, your risk assessment can change over the course of the project. If, during test design, development, or execution, you obtain new information or insights that tell you that the risk assessment is wrong, you should revise the risk assessment rather than following a flawed road map.

Broad testing, for this decision table, means that every condition in the decision table is covered (see Table 13-2). Rules 5 and 6 involve a compound condition, "Valid PIN (for debit) or no PIN required (for credit)." So, I need one test each for rules 1 through 4, while rules 5 and 6 need two tests each. My solution is shown in Table 13-3.

Table 13-2   Omninet Payment Processing

| | Business Rules | | | | | |
Condition	1	2	3	4	5	6
Valid money	No	Yes	-	-	-	-
Valid card	-	-	No	Yes	Yes	Yes
Valid PIN (for debit) or no PIN required (for credit)	-	-	-	No	Yes	Yes
Amount approved	-	-	-	-	No	Yes
Action						
Reject cash	Yes	No	No	No	No	No
Reject card	No	No	Yes	Yes	No	No
Prompt for lower amount	No	No	No	No	Yes	No
Sell time block	No	Yes	No	No	No	Yes

Table 13-3   Omninet Payment Processing Tests

#	TESTER ACTION AND DATA	EXPECTED RESULT
1	Insert invalid money (e.g., cut out a piece of paper in the size and shape of a $20 bill, color it green, and feed it into the bill slot).	Fake money is rejected. The kiosk does not give the user any browsing time.
2	Insert valid money (e.g., $20 bill).	Money is accepted. The kiosk gives the user the appropriate block of time. (Refer to current rate sheet to determine how many minutes this is.)

Continued

Table 13-3 *(continued)*

#	TESTER ACTION AND DATA	EXPECTED RESULT
3	Insert an invalid card (e.g., a frequent flyer card or driver's license).	Card is rejected. The kiosk informs the user that the card is not a valid debit or credit card. The kiosk does not give the user any browsing time.
4	(1) Insert a valid debit card. (2) Enter an invalid PIN. (3) Enter a valid amount (i.e., a legal time block size).	Card is rejected. The kiosk informs the user that the network did not validate the card. The kiosk does not give the user any browsing time.
5	(1) Insert a valid debit card. (2) Enter a valid PIN. (3) Enter an amount that is not a legal time block size.	Card is accepted. The kiosk informs the user that the requested time block is not allowed. The kiosk prompts for a legal time block amount. The kiosk does not give the user any browsing time until a legal time block is entered.
6	(1) Insert a valid credit card. (2) Enter a legal time block size amount that exceeds the credit limit.	Card is accepted. The kiosk informs the user that the requested amount exceeds the available balance. The kiosk prompts for a lower amount. The kiosk does not give the user any browsing time until a lower value is entered.
7	(1) Insert a valid debit card. (2) Enter a valid PIN. (3) Enter an amount that is both a legal block size amount and within the available account balance.	Card is accepted. The kiosk gives the user the appropriate block of time. (Refer to current rate sheet to determine how many minutes this is.)
8	(1) Insert a valid credit card. (2) Enter an amount that is both a legal block size amount and within the available account balance.	Card is accepted. The kiosk gives the user the appropriate block of time. (Refer to current rate sheet to determine how many minutes this is.)

In the course of designing this test, I found a potential bug in the decision table. The condition "Amount approved" can actually be untrue for two reasons. First, the amount could exceed the amount available in the account, which is what the table foresees.

However, what's apparently missing is the possibility that the user might enter an amount that does not correspond to a time block. For example, if time is sold in increments of 10 minutes at 1 dollar, then what should the kiosk do if the user enters an amount like $1.75?

So the action "Prompt for lower amount" is not sufficient. The action really should be "Prompt for legal amount."

From a test point of view, I would want to test both ways the condition might not be met in rule 5. However, since there's no reason to think that the use of a debit or credit card would influence the kiosk logic in terms of legal time blocks, there's no need to increase the number of tests to try all permutations.

From a system design point of view, we could prevent this problem by using a pull-down list to prompt the user for an amount. The list would contain only valid amounts.

Another test issue is that we'll need some props for this test. We need at least one valid debit card and one valid credit card. These cards must be tied to accounts that have appropriate balances. Getting these kinds of test props is often difficult, so you should start work on obtaining them as soon as you know you'll need them.

Decision Tables and Boundary Values

In this next exercise, you'll combine decision table testing with boundary value analysis. I suggest the use of scenarios as a way to define your test cases.

An increasing number of police departments in the United States issue traffic cops handheld information appliances. These take violator and vehicle information during traffic stops and sometimes even take credit cards to allow ticketed motorists to pay for moving violations. Suppose you're testing such a system. You'll find a decision table for the system in Table 13-4. The conditions that determine the actions the system is to take are shown in this table.

In this exercise, I suggest that you use boundary value analysis to create test scenarios from this decision table. I've provided a template in Table 13-5. I suggest 30 minutes as a time limit. When you're done, keep reading to see my solution.

Table 13-4 Traffic Cop Computer Decision Table

				Business Rules				
Condition	1	2	3	4	5	6	7	8
License OK	No	-	-	-	-	-	-	-
Warrant	-	Yes	-	-	-	-	-	-
Registration OK	-	-	No	-	-	-	-	-
Vehicle OK	-	-	-	No	-	-	-	-
Excess Speed	-	-	-	-	1-10	11-20	21-25	>25
Action								
Arrest	Yes	Yes	-	-	-	-	-	Yes
Fix-It Ticket	-	-	Yes	Yes	-	-	-	-
Warning	-	-	-	-	Yes	-	-	-
Fine	+250	+250	+25	+25	+0	+75	+150	+250

Table 13-5 Scenario Template

#	SCENARIO	EXPECTED RESULT

#	SCENARIO	EXPECTED RESULT

My Solution and Comments

In this decision table, unlike with the previous exercise, the business rules are not all mutually exclusive. Clearly, a motorist can be both speeding and driving with an invalid license.

Therefore, the conditions associated with rules 1 through 4 are independent. The dashes (-) mean that it doesn't matter whether a particular condition is true or false. If a motorist is driving with an invalid license, that person will be arrested and fined at least $250. Other conditions that apply could lead to additional citations and fines.

So I combined rules in a scenario. When I did so I ensured that I didn't combine two rules that have the same result. For example, if I combined rules 1 and 2, the system might calculate the correct fine, $500, and the system might say to arrest the motorist. But how do I know which of the two rules triggers the arrest action? What if there's a bug in the implementation of one of the rules where the fine calculation is correct but the arrest action is not handled properly. I avoided combining rules where the correct handling by the system of one rule masks a bug in the system's ability to handle another rule.

To start the test design, I first performed an equivalence classes and their boundary value analysis on the conditions. The first four business rules are driven by Boolean conditions like Warrant or License OK. So the equivalence classes and their boundary values are True and False. The last four business rules are driven by the Excess Speed condition. That's an integer field. There are 7 equivalence classes. There are 11 boundary values. The analysis in Figure 13-1 turns up gaps you need to fill in to the decision table during test design.

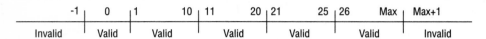

Figure 13-1: Excess speed equivalence partitions and boundary values

While the table doesn't say so, there must be such a thing as an Excess Speed value that is invalid because it is too low and another that is invalid because it is too high. You can assume that −1 is the upper boundary of the invalid too low class. Zero must be a valid Excess Speed entry. For example, suppose the motorist is pulled over for a faulty brake light? In that case, the cop will need to enter 0 in the Excess Speed field while entering the other information for the fix-it ticket.

The boundary between the maximum valid Excess Speed equivalence class and the invalid too high equivalence class is undefined. I've used the notation Max to remind myself that I need to clarify this with the designers. This ambiguity could indicate a lurking bug. Suppose the GUI designer allows only two-digit Excess Speed values. What if a cop pulls over a motorcyclist going 150 miles per hour in a 30 mile-per-hour zone?

As I mentioned in Chapter 12, this testing of the invalid equivalence classes might not be necessary. If I can assume that the user interface and data access layers of the system were previously tested, then I can skip those tests. In this case, though, I've decided to include the two scenarios that attempt to stuff an invalid number into the Excess Speed field. This creates an additional system action, Reject, which should occur when the system is confronted with an invalid data set.

I needed to ensure complete coverage of these equivalence classes and boundary values in this decision table. So I modified the decision table to show the equivalence classes and their boundary values. This coverage analysis is shown in Table 13-6. Note that the *V* in the Excess Speed row indicates that I must select a *valid* excess speed value when generating this scenario, but other than that I am free to select any excess speed value.

APPLICABLE BUSINESS RULE (~ INDICATES NEAR BUT OUTSIDE THAT RULE)																			
Condition	1	~1	2	~2	3	~3	4	~4	~5	5	5	6	6	7	7	8	8	8	~8
License OK	No	Yes	-	-	-	-	-	-	-	-	-	-	-	-	-	-	-	-	-
Warrant	-	-	Yes	No	-	-	-	-	-	-	-	-	-	-	-	-	-	-	-
Registration OK	-	-	-	-	No	Yes	-	-	-	-	-	-	-	-	-	-	-	-	-
Vehicle OK	-	-	-	-	-	-	No	Yes	-	-	-	-	-	-	-	-	-	-	-
Excess Speed	V	V	V	V	V	V	V	V	-1	0	1	10	11	20	21	25	26	Max	Max+1
Action																			
Arrest	Yes	-	Yes	-	-	-	-	-	No	-	-	-	-	-	-	-	Yes	Yes	Yes
Fix-It Ticket	-	-	-	-	Yes	-	Yes	-	No	-	-	-	-	-	-	-	-	-	-
Warning	-	-	-	-	-	-	-	-	No	Yes	Yes	-	-	-	-	-	-	-	-
Fine	+250	+0	+250	+0	+25	+0	+25	+0	+0	+0	+0	+75	+75	+150	+150	+250	+250	+250	-
Reject	No	No	No	No	No	No	Yes	No	No	No	No	No	No	No	No	No	No	No	Yes
	1	4	2	4	2,6	4	1,8	4	3	2	1	4	5	6	7	8	9	10	11

Primary Covering Scenario(s) (Other Scenarios May Also Cover)

Table 13-6 Extended Traffic Cop Test and Coverage Table

This is not a decision table, but rather a table that shows the specified actions under chosen test conditions. It shows the applicable business rule for each column. It also shows traceability from each condition to the scenario(s) that cover it.

Now, armed with this revised table, I constructed the test scenarios, given three additional rules:

1. Combine as few rules as possible because the main focus of the test is to verify each business rule in the decision table.

2. Don't combine invalid conditions with any other condition because the rejection of the invalid conditions will prevent testing of the other conditions.

3. Don't combine two rules that have the same action because the failure to trigger the proper action for one rule might be masked by correct behavior of the other rule.

The test scenarios are shown in Table 13-7.

Table 13-7 Traffic Cop Tests

#	SCENARIO	EXPECTED RESULT
1	Suzy Scofflaw was driving at 1 mile per hour over the limit with an invalid driver's license when Officer Pain stopped her after noticing her car's exhaust pipe dragging on the road, shooting sparks.	The system accepts the input. Suzy is arrested, issued a fix-it ticket, warned about violating the speed limited, and fined $275.
2	Freddy Felon was driving exactly at the posted speed — always suspicious — when Officer Friendly pulled him over for expired vehicle registration. Freddy turned out to have an outstanding warrant for bank robbery in another state.	The system accepts the input. Freddy is arrested, issued a fix-it ticket, and fined $275.
3	Sammy Slowpoke was driving in the left lane of a public highway, signaling a lane change, going 1 mile an hour under the speed limit, and being passed by angry motorists on the right when Officer Righteous pulled him over for impeding the flow of traffic.	The system rejects Officer Righteous' entry of -1 as the excess speed. No ticket is issued. Sammy is not arrested or fined. [TBD: How does Officer Righteous cite Sammy for impeding the flow of traffic?]
4	Hank Hurriup was driving at 10 miles per hour over the limit. Officer Handicuff pulled him over, but found Hank's vehicle, license, registration, and warrant status clean.	The system accepts the information on Hank. No ticket is issued. Hank is not arrested or fined. Officer Handicuff gives Hank a verbal warning.

#	SCENARIO	EXPECTED RESULT
5	David Bassoon was late driving his kids to day care, going 11 miles per hour over the limit. Officer Hornblower pulled him over. David's vehicle, license, registration, and warrant status were clean.	The system accepts the information on David. He receives a speeding ticket and a $75 fine but is not arrested.
6	Rush Rampart was driving his brand-new Porsche 911 at 20 miles per hour over the limit. Officer Cadena discovered that Rush had forgotten to file the registration paperwork, but his vehicle, license, and warrant status were clean.	The system accepts the information on Rush. He receives a speeding and fix-it ticket and a $100 fine but is not arrested.
7	Governor Grandstand was driving his government-issued sedan, featuring a burnt-out headlight, at 21 miles per hour over the limit at 2:00 A.M. Officer Nowata pulled him over. The governor's license, registration, and warrant status were clean.	The system accepts the governor's information. He receives a speeding and fix-it ticket and a $175 fine but is not arrested.
8	Ricky Reckless was driving his Cadillac SUV down the street at 25 miles per hour over the limit. Officer Café pulled him over. Ricky's vehicle, license, registration, and warrant status were clean.	The system accepts Ricky's information. He receives a speeding ticket and a $150 fine but is not arrested.
9	Javier Arriba was driving at 26 miles per hour over the limit. Officer Mas-Despacio pulled him over and checked his vehicle, registration, license, and warrants. Nothing beyond reckless driving.	The system accepts Javier's information. Javier receives an arrest citation, a $250 fine, and a free night's room and board in the county jail.
10	Jacques Canard was driving so fast over the speed limit that he is maxing out the excess speed field. [TBD: What is the maximum entry?] Officer Verdadoso pulled him over and checked his vehicle, registration, license, and warrants. Nothing beyond reckless driving.	The system accepts Jacques's information. Jacques gets an arrest citation, a $250 fine, and a night in jail.
11	Lois Lane was driving exactly at the speed limit. Officer Kent pulled her over and checked her vehicle, registration, license, and warrants but found nothing.	The system rejects Officer Kent's entry of Max+1 as the excess speed. No ticket is issued. Lois is not arrested or fined. [TBD: What should the system do when an officer aborts the writing of a ticket?]

In the course of developing these tests, I found something that is probably missing from the table. I wanted to test what happens when a cop enters an invalid excess speed entry. The system should reject that excess speed.

Of course, scenario 3 *does* indicate that Sammy was violating the law: Driving in the passing lane at a speed slower than that of prevailing traffic is an offense, impeding the flow of traffic. That offense is missing from the decision table.

Other offenses might be missing as well. As with the ATM exercise, one option is to separate different types of violations into their own decision tables and apply each separately.

I've deliberately created the tests so that funny, sometimes dramatic things happen in these scenarios. Such scenarios are examples of what Hans Buwalda calls *soap opera tests*. Designing scenarios that are humorous, dramatic, and extreme makes testing interesting.[1]

In this exercise, I've not tested the possible interactions of factors. When you want to check the interaction of factors, the technique to pick is called domain analysis. Do combinations of rules result in interesting interactions? Could we apply boundary value analysis to the outputs and results as well as the conditions? What is the maximum fine someone can receive? Under what scenario does it occur? What is the minimum fine? Under what scenario does it occur? I'll cover domain testing in Chapter 16.

Building a Decision Table for Testing

In this final decision table exercise, you'll first create a decision table from a flowchart. After doing so, you'll create tests from the decision table.

In this exercise, you are testing a first-person action video game called Grays and Blues. This game is set during the American Civil War, which ran from 1861 to 1865. Since this was before the advent of smokeless gunpowder and modern cartridge-based firearms, the war was fought primarily with three types of small arms:

- The officer's sword. A sword does not require any ammunition, of course. Hung at the side in a scabbard, it is always ready to use and treated as "loaded."

- The cap-and-ball revolver. Most of the Civil War models held up to six shots. The game assumes that each chamber can be loaded in 10 seconds, though this certainly takes a very proficient — or motivated — soldier!

- The musket. The game assumes that the musket holds one shot and can be loaded in 30 seconds.

A Grays and Blues player may have none, one, two, or all three of these weapons in her possession at any given time. However, a player can only have one weapon in hand at any given time. The player uses the S, R, and M keys to

---

[1] You can find some of Buwalda's work on soap opera testing at www.stickyminds.com.

request a selected weapon. This is useful when a player wants to switch from a musket to a pistol for close action, for example. Figure 13-2 shows the decision-making logic for weapon selection. While this flow chart appears reasonable at first glance, you'll find bugs in it through test design.

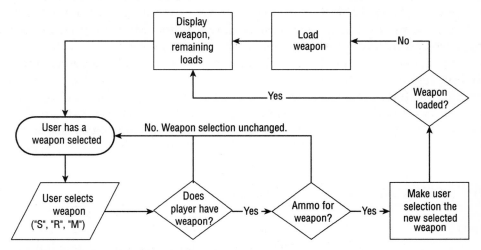

Figure 13-2: Weapon selection flowchart

Here are some other rules that influence weapon selection.

1. A player starts the game with only the musket but can collect other weapons by capturing them, by battlefield scavenging, or by promotion to the officer's ranks.

2. A player starts the game with the musket loaded and with 20 spare loads in the kit bag. (A load is powder, a wad, and a ball.) The kit bag can hold from 0 to 100 spare loads. As with weapons, players can collect loads through capture or scavenge and also by visiting the supply wagon between battles.

3. A player can use the loads interchangeably between musket and revolver. However, once a player has placed a load in a weapon, the player cannot remove that load to use it in another weapon.

Antique firearms and Civil War buffs will no doubt note that not all these rules are realistic, but they keep the game simpler.

The goal of the exercise is to test weapon selection using decision tables, equivalence class partitioning, and boundary value analysis. The exercise consists of three parts:

1. Assisted by the rules given earlier, translate the flowchart into a decision table.

2. Perform equivalence class partitioning and boundary value analysis.

3. Use the classes, boundary values, and the decision table to create tests.

I've not provided a template, but you can use a blank page of paper.

I suggest 120 minutes as a time limit for this exercise. If it takes you longer than that, you're probably — pardon the phrase — shooting wide of the mark.

When you're done, keep reading to see my solution. My solution is not the only correct solution, just an example of one correct solution.

Some people deprecate this exercise, saying, "Hey, I don't test games; I test real business systems." Think twice before you skip it. While I've used a video game to illustrate the technique, you can use this approach for real business systems too. I once created decision-table-based tests from a flowchart that described the rules for deciding whether an applicant was eligible for a car loan. You can't get more "real business system" than that.

My Solution and Comments

First, I created the decision table, shown in Table 13-8. I translated the flow-chart to the decision table mechanically. I turned the user input parallelogram and the decision diamonds into conditions. I turned the action rectangles into actions. Since the flowchart is sequential, the business rules in this decision table are mutually exclusive.

Table 13-8 Weapon Selection Decision Table

	Business Rules				
Condition	1	2	3	4	5
User Requested Weapon	S or R or M	S	R or M	R or M	R or M
Has Weapon?	No	Yes	Yes	Yes	Yes
Has Ammo?	-	-	No	Yes	Yes
Weapon Loaded?	-	-	-	No	Yes
Action					
Make Selected Weapon	Unchanged	S	Unchanged	As Selected	As Selected
Load Weapon	No	No	No	Yes	No
Display Weapon, Loads	No	Yes	No	Yes	Yes

I could use this decision table as a set of tests by simply setting arbitrary values for the Has Ammo and Weapon Loaded conditions to achieve decision coverage in rules 1, 3, 4, and 5. That would give me the table shown in Table 13-9. By covering each column in this test table, I could call the testing complete.

Table 13-9   Weapon Selection Test Table

APPLICABLE BUSINESS RULE									
Condition	1	1	1	2	3	3	4	4	5	5
User Requested Weapon	S	R	M	S	R	M	R	M	R	M
Has Weapon?	N	N	N	Y	Y	Y	Y	Y	Y	Y
Has Ammo?	-	-	-	-	N	N	Y	Y	Y	Y
Weapon Loaded?	-	-	-	-	-	-	N	N	Y	Y
Action										
Make Selected Weapon	U	U	U	S	U	U	R	M	R	M
Load Weapon	N	N	N	N	N	N	Y	Y	N	N
Display Weapon, Loads	N	N	N	Y	N	N	Y	Y	Y	Y
	1	2	3	4	5	6	7	8	9	10

Test Steps

However, I also want to consider the equivalence classes and boundary values that might affect these tests. The equivalence classes and boundary values that affect the conditions Has Weapon and Has Ammo are shown in Figure 13-3. The equivalence classes that affect the Load Weapon action are shown in Figure 13-4. So, to create tests using these equivalence classes and boundary values, I made sure that each valid equivalence class and its boundary values, if any, were represented in at least one column in Table 13-10.

Equivalence Classes and Boundary Values for Loads in Kit Bag

Equivalence Classes and Boundary Values for Revolver

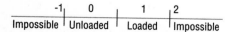

Equivalence Classes and Boundary Values for Musket

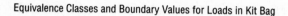

Figure 13-3: Equivalence classes and boundary values for weapon selection

Equivalence Classes for Revolver Load Delays

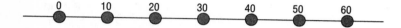

Equivalence Classes for Musket Load Delays

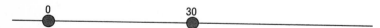

Figure 13-4: Equivalence classes for load delays

Table 13-10   Extended Weapon Selection Test Table

APPLICABLE BUSINESS RULE										
Condition	1	1	1	2	3	3	4	4	4	4
User Requested Weapon	S	R	M	S	R	M	R	M	R	R
Has Weapon?	N	N	N	Y	Y	Y	Y	Y	Y	Y
Loads Available	20	20	20	20	0	0	20	100	99	21
Loads in Weapon	-	-	-	-	-	-	0	0	1	5
Action										
Make Selected Weapon	U	U	U	S	U	U	R	M	R	R
Load Delay	0	0	0	0	0	0	60	30	50	10
Display Weapon	N	N	N	Y	N	N	Y	Y	Y	Y
Display Loads	N	N	N	20	N	N	14	99	94	20
	1	2	3	4	5	6	7	8	9	10

Test Steps

APPLICABLE BUSINESS RULE							
Condition	4	4	4	4	4	5	5
User Requested Weapon	R	R	R	R	R	R	M
Has Weapon?	Y	Y	Y	Y	Y	Y	Y
Loads Available	1	1	5	6	19	3	50
Loads in Weapon	4	5	2	4	3	6	1
Action							
Make Selected Weapon	R	R	R	R	R	R	M
Load Delay	10	10	40	20	30	0	0
Display Weapon	Y	Y	Y	Y	Y	Y	Y
Display Loads	0	0	1	4	16	3	50
	11	12	13	14	15	16	17

Test Step

I omitted any setup steps required to get the system ready for each test step. For example, between test step 7 and 8, the player must visit the supply wagon to obtain more ammunition.

As I designed tests from this figure, I came across three problems with the flowchart.

First, what if the player has no loads available in the kit but the selected weapon is already loaded? Shouldn't the player be allowed to select it? The flowchart says that the player cannot.

Second, what if the weapon is partially loaded? Shouldn't the player be allowed to use it immediately rather than having to spend time loading it? The flowchart is ambiguous on this question, since the decision block with the "Weapon loaded?" label doesn't allow for a partially loaded outcome. Test step 11 shows the expected results in this condition, assuming that players are indeed forced to load the weapon if it is partially loaded.

Finally, what if the player wants to load fewer chambers in the revolver than are currently empty? If you have say, 15 seconds before an enemy closes in on you, you might want to load one chamber in your empty revolver and fire. In the flowchart, it's unclear that such an action is allowed, or even how you tell the game that you wanted to do so.

This exercise brings up four important points.

First, as I've mentioned before, the very act of test design often reveals potentially serious bugs. We've seen that again in this case.

Second, a simple diagram can hide a complex testing situation. The flowchart is simple. However, the test analysis revealed a complex set of tests, as well as problems hiding in the flowchart. This is a fairly typical experience. When I analyzed the simple one-page flowchart for the auto loan processing application I mentioned at the outset of this exercise, it turned into the large and complex spreadsheet you will find on our website.

Third, I like exploratory testing. I consider it a testing best practice that no project should do without. However, can you imagine an exploratory tester, working in a time-boxed session of one or two hours, doing this kind of analysis? What do you think the odds are of any but the most skilled exploratory tester finding the subtle bugs in the weapon selection logic? Clearly, exploratory testing would not reveal bugs during system design since exploratory testing does not begin until a running system arrives, being a purely dynamic form of testing.

Finally, you might be thinking that the tests shown earlier won't cover all the interesting test situations. If so, you're right. In Chapter 14, I cover state transition diagrams and their uses for testing. You might be interested in testing the behavior of the game when the player is in the states related to loading a weapon. In Chapter 16, I cover domain analysis and its use for testing. You might be interested in how factors like the currently selected weapon and the other weapons in possession interact to affect the weapon selection logic.

The point is that any test design technique can reveal only the bugs it helps you look for. Decision tables will help you find bugs related to the incorrect implementation of simple rules in the program. Enough of these kinds of bugs occur that this is often a useful technique.

State Transition Diagrams

In this chapter, I present a powerful technique for black-box testing. In some systems, the correct behavior of the system depends not only on what's happening right now, but also on what events have occurred so far. A system that has some awareness of what has happened in the past has state-dependent behavior. State transition diagrams and state tables are powerful tools for analyzing and testing such systems. In this chapter, you'll see how.

Describing Systems with States Using State Transition Diagrams

The process of applying state-based testing concepts to a system can be easily described.

1. Pick a perspective from which to view the world. This is often, but not always, the viewpoint of the system, a direct or indirect user of the system, or some real-world object that the system is aware of.

2. Understand the various states that the system, user, or object can be in, including the initial and final states.

3. Identify transitions, events, conditions, and actions that can — and can't — apply in each state.

4. Use a graph or table to model the system. This graph or table also serves as an oracle to predict correct system behavior along with a requirements specification and common sense.

5. For each event and condition — that is, each transition — verify that the correct action and next state occurs.

While this is easily stated, the actual application of this process is tricky indeed. Let's take a look at an example.

Figure 14-1 shows a state-transition diagram for a point-of-sales system. The diagram shows the point-of-sales system from the cashier's point of view.

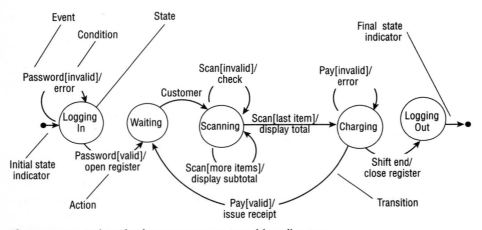

Figure 14-1: Point-of-sales system state transition diagram

The various elements of the state-transition diagram are labeled.

State: Representation of the situation the cashier is in. The state captures the essence of what is going on and what should happen next. States often involve waiting for an event to occur or complete.

Initial state indicator: State the cashier is in when he is first interacting with the point-of-sale system.

Event: Occurrence that can trigger a change in state. It can be something the cashier does, something the customer does, something the system does, or even something external to all the actors.

Condition: Criterion or criteria that divide an event into different possible resulting states.

Transition: Event-triggered — and possibly condition-influenced — change into a different state or perhaps back into the same state.

Action: Output, behavior, or other result associated with a transition.

Final state indicator: State the cashier is in when he is done interacting with the point-of-sale system (at least for that shift).

While this description is specific to the point-of-sales system, state transition diagrams usually contain the same seven major elements.

Spend a minute thinking about how the state transition diagram would look from the customer's point of view. How about from the system's?

This state transition diagram contains a bug. Do you see it? You will if you try to design a set of tests from it.

To design a set of functional tests from a state transition diagram, the rules are simple:

- Visit every state.
- Cover every transition.
- Ensure that no states are unreachable or unleavable.

As you do this, make sure that you refer to the requirements specification and your built-in tester's skepticism. Now do you see the bug?[1]

So far I've talked about using state diagrams for functional testing, but you can also use a state diagram to create reliability and load tests. In such a case, the load generator will frequently create a sequence of events that causes the system to traverse the state transition diagram randomly, creating interesting test conditions along the way. If the system crashes, hangs, or stops responding to input, the test has failed. After some period of time, the test is finished if no such failure has occurred.

State Tables

A problem with using state transition diagrams is that they don't show all possible combinations of states and events. Consider an e-commerce system. Unless the programmer takes steps to avoid it, the user can trigger both legal and illegal events by clicking buttons on the screen. This is why many e-commerce systems give customers strong cautions about not clicking the Check Out button more than once since that can trigger multiple charges to the customers' credit cards. Likewise, consider an event-driven or real-time system. Just about any event or interrupt can occur at any time.

State transition diagrams will usually show only transitions for events that are legal in a given state. State transition tables allow you as a tester to overcome this limitation by combining every known state with every event/condition

---

[1] The main bug is that the system seems to force the shift end to occur only in the midst of charging the customer, which is nonsensical. There is also a missing exception condition, which is the handling of a situation in which a customer abandons a purchase.

combination that can occur. You can then specify the correct action or next state. If you find a combination of state, event, and condition for which the attendant action and subsequent state are not specified, congratulations. You've found a potential bug.

Table 14-1 shows a portion of the state transition table for the point-of-sales system. A state-transition table can also represent complex state-transitions that won't fit on a graph. However, the complexity might indicate bad design, or that you don't really understand the set of states and transitions.

Table 14-1   A Portion of the State Table for the Point-of-Sales System

CURRENT STATE	EVENT[CONDITION]	ACTION	NEW STATE
Logging In	Password[invalid]	Error	Logging In
Logging In	Password[valid]	Open register	Waiting
Logging In	Customer	[Undefined]	[Undefined]
Logging In	Scan[any]	[Undefined]	[Undefined]
Logging In	Pay[any]	[Undefined]	[Undefined]
Logging In	Shift end	[Undefined]	[Undefined]

Printer Server State Transition Diagram

Let's look at another example. The print server shown in Figure 14-2 can be in one of the following states:

- Awaiting job
- Queuing job
- Printing job
- Awaiting user intervention
- Awaiting operator intervention

The print server responds to events (user or printer inputs) based on the state it's in.

In this diagram, I've used an alternate notation for the initial state: the double-walled state bubble. You'll sometimes see this notation used because it's common in some computer science texts for finite state machines. In this case, there is no final state because the print server, once booted, is intended to run indefinitely. Of course, the reality is that exception events like system crashes and shutdowns can take a print server offline. It's often the case that state transition diagrams omit such details to focus the testing where it's needed.

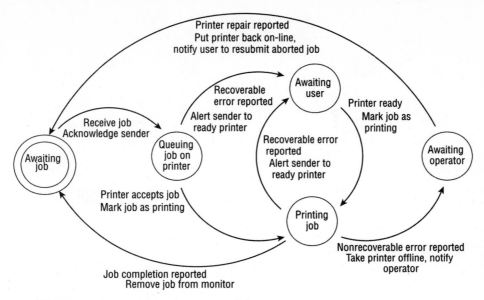

Figure 14-2: Print server state transition diagram

So, as with Chapter 12, which introduced decision tables, in this chapter I have introduced you to a powerful technique for test design. In the next chapter, as with decision tables, I'll give you a chance to apply this technique to an exercise and use that exercise to discuss further important matters related to the technique.

## CHAPTER 15

State Transition Diagram Exercise

In this chapter, you'll work through a series of exercises related to state testing. In this first exercise, you'll create a state transition diagram for the Omninet kiosks, then build test cases to cover that diagram.

Kiosk States

The public Internet access kiosks can be in various states based on receipt of payment and active sessions. As you do the exercise, refer to the Marketing Requirements Document and the System Requirements Document for Omninet.

The exercise is three parts:

1. Draw a state diagram for the kiosk.
2. Create a state table to identify additional state/event combinations.
3. Create test cases based on that diagram.

I suggest 60 minutes as a time limit. When you're done, keep reading to see my solution.

My Solution and Comments

First, I drew the state transition diagram, as shown in Figure 15-1.[1] Notice that the model views the world from the kiosk's point of view. The transitions in this diagram are defined in the Marketing Requirements Document and System Requirements Document.

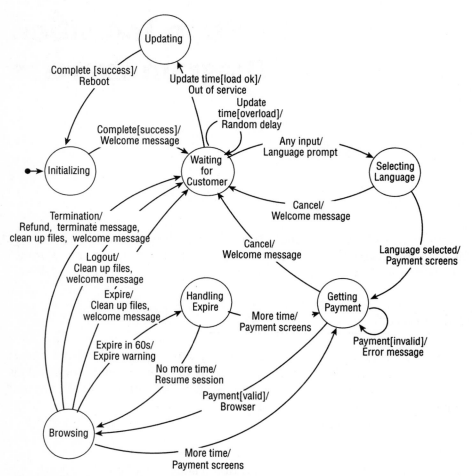

Figure 15-1: Kiosk state transition diagram

---

[1] Some people draw this diagram with a Checking Content state. The Checking Content state is entered via a Submit URL event during browsing. The Checking Content state is then exited back to Browsing state with the events Accept URL and Reject URL. Alternatively, some people show two looping event/action pairs where URL[good] and URL[bad] are the event/condition pairs that determine which loop to take. In addition, others like to allow for a Time Expire event from the Handling Expire and Checking Content state.

In the course of drawing the diagram, I discovered the following issues in the Marketing Requirements Document and the System Requirements Document:

- What happens if the system encounters a serious problem while running? Should it try to initialize itself? Should the current customer — if any — receive a refund?

- What happens if the kiosk doesn't initialize properly? There was a problem with a Mars spacecraft where the failure to initialize after a serious problem (out of file space) lead to an endless sequence of reboots.

- What happens if an update fails?

- I've assumed that the kiosk can begin fetching updates only when it is idle. However, that's not clear in the requirements. This should be clarified.

I assumed that the hourly status report to the server should happen in the background. I also assumed that security event logging would occur in the background. Those would involve different state transition diagrams. The diagram in the figure shown addresses only foreground events and activities. I chose to represent the payment activities as a single state. I could also have broken this out into a sequence of states. When using state-based testing techniques, you sometimes have to choose where to focus the testing and where to simplify.

Next, I created the state table shown in Table 15-1 to identify additional state/event combinations.

There are only 17 state transitions defined in the diagram. There are 124 rows in the table, so we have 107 situations that are undefined in the diagram. Most of these I've marked as with a dash (-).

Before trying to define tests for these, I would attempt to get clarification on correct kiosk behavior in these circumstances. If I were unable to get such clarification, I would then take my best guess.

If someone were to tell me, "Hey, none of those state/event combinations can happen," I would test many of those combinations anyway. The "impossible" event, the "no real user would ever do that" input, the situation that could never arise: These are usually fertile ground for bugs.

Experience tells us to be especially skeptical and alert — in a quiet, professional way — when the programmer who wrote the code in question tells you something "can't happen." He is telling you about an assumed precondition in his code. Can you violate that precondition? You should try.[2]

Some state/event combinations really can't (or probably can't) happen. I've marked the ones that can't happen as N/A in the table. I've marked the "probably can't happen" as N/A? in the table. Screen prototypes would help answer some of these questions.

---

[2] One reviewer, Judy McKay, mentioned when reviewing this chapter that she once received an error message while testing that read, "This can't happen." At least the programmer had been wise enough to code a check for the allegedly impossible situation!

Table 15-1   Kiosk State Transition Table

INITIAL STATE	EVENT[CONDITION]	ACTION	NEXT STATE
Initializing	Complete[success]	Welcome message	Waiting for Customer
	Update time [load ok]	-	-
	Update time [overload]	-	-
	Any input	-	-
	Cancel	N/A	N/A
	Language selected	N/A	N/A
	Payment[valid]	N/A	N/A
	Payment[invalid]	N/A	N/A
	More time	N/A	N/A
	No more time	N/A	N/A
	Expire in 60s	-	-
	Expire	-	-
	Logout	N/A	N/A
	Terminate	N/A	N/A
Waiting for customer	Complete[success]	-	-
	Update time [load ok]	Out of service	Updating
	Update time [overload]	Random delay	Waiting for customer
	Any input	Language prompt	Selecting language
	Cancel	N/A	N/A
	Language selected	N/A	N/A
	Payment[valid]	N/A	N/A
	Payment[invalid]	N/A	N/A
	More time	N/A	N/A
	No more time	N/A	N/A
	Expire in 60s	-	-
	Expire	-	-
	Logout	N/A	N/A
	Terminate	-	-

INITIAL STATE	EVENT[CONDITION]	ACTION	NEXT STATE
Updating	Complete[success]	Reboot	Initializing
	Update time [load ok]	-	-
	Update time [overload]	-	-
	Any input	N/A?	N/A?
	Cancel	N/A?	N/A?
	Language selected	N/A?	N/A?
	Payment[valid]	N/A?	N/A?
	Payment[invalid]	N/A?	N/A?
	More time	N/A?	N/A?
	No more time	N/A?	N/A?
	Expire in 60s	-	-
	Expire	-	-
	Logout	N/A?	N/A?
	Terminate	-	-
Selecting language	Complete[success]	-	-
	Update time [load ok]	-	-
	Update time [overload]	-	-
	Any input	-	-
	Cancel	Welcome message	Waiting for customer
	Language selected	Payment screens	Getting payment
	Payment[valid]	N/A?	N/A?
	Payment[invalid]	N/A?	N/A?
	More time	N/A?	N/A?
	No more time	N/A?	N/A?
	Expire in 60s	-	-
	Expire	-	-
	Logout	N/A?	N/A?
	Terminate	-	-

Continued

Table 15-1 *(continued)*

INITIAL STATE	EVENT[CONDITION]	ACTION	NEXT STATE
Getting payment	Complete[success]	-	-
	Update time [load ok]	-	-
	Update time [overload]	-	-
	Any input	N/A?	N/A?
	Cancel	Welcome message	Waiting for customer
	Language selected	-	-
	Payment[valid]	Browser	Browsing
	Payment[invalid]	Error message	Getting payment
	More time	N/A?	N/A?
	No more time	N/A?	N/A?
	Expire in 60s	-	-
	Expire	-	-
	Logout	N/A?	N/A?
	Terminate	-	-
Browsing	Complete[success]	-	-
	Update time [load ok]	-	-
	Update time [overload]	-	-
	Any input	Note: Most inputs go to browser.	
	Cancel	N/A?	N/A?
	Language selected	N/A?	N/A?
	Payment[valid]	N/A?	N/A?
	Payment[invalid]	N/A?	N/A?
	More time	Payment screens	Getting payment
	No more time	N/A?	N/A?
	Expire in 60s	Expire warning	Handling expire
	Expire	Clean up files Welcome message	Waiting for customer
	Logout	Clean up files Welcome message	Waiting for customer

INITIAL STATE	EVENT[CONDITION]	ACTION	NEXT STATE
	Terminate	Refund Terminate message Clean up files Welcome message	Waiting for customer
Handling expire	Complete[success]	-	-
	Update time [load ok]	-	-
	Update time [overload]	-	-
	Any input	N/A?	N/A?
	Cancel	N/A?	N/A?
	Language selected	N/A?	N/A?
	Payment[valid]	N/A?	N/A?
	Payment[invalid]	N/A?	N/A?
	More time	Payment screens	Getting payment
	No more time	Resume session	Browsing
	Expire in 60s	-	-
	Expire	-	-
	Logout	-	-
	Terminate	-	-

Fair questions you might ask are: Must I always create a state table for testing? Can I simply cover the state transition diagram? The answers are no and sometimes because (of course) the right extent of testing depends on the risks involved.

This state transition diagram covers many of the risks identified in the quality risk analysis. (For the most part, it covers these risks indirectly.) Some of those risks require extensive testing. Therefore, it makes sense to try every possible combination of states and events for this diagram. In a situation where the state-based tests relate only to medium- and low-risk items, then simply covering the diagram may be sufficient.

The basic difference between covering the diagram and covering the table is that the table takes into account the "can't happen" and "shouldn't happen" situations. Where extensive testing or considerable error handling and robustness tests are required, then you should plan to cover the table.

Finally, I created test scenarios to cover the state transition diagram, shown in Table 15-2. Once I received information on how the undefined situations in the table were to be handled, I'd include those as additional scenarios.

Table 15-2   Kiosk State Tests

#	SCENARIO	EXPECTED RESULT
1	Kiosk starts off.	
	1. Boot the system.	1. Check Welcome screen.
	2. Touch keyboard.	2. Check Language prompt.
	3. Select language.	3. Check Payment screens.
	4. Make a valid payment.	4. Check Browser. (Note: Should be the browser selected by the user.)
	5. Allow timer to 60 seconds of expiration.	5. Check Expire warning.
	6. Select no more time.	6. Check return to Browser, with session uninterrupted.
	7. Allow time to expire.	7. Check Welcome screen. Verify clean up of files.
2	Kiosk starts at Welcome screen.	
	1. Touch keyboard.	1. Check Language prompt.
	2. Cancel transaction.	2. Check Welcome screen.
3	Kiosk starts at Welcome screen.	
	1. Repeat scenario 2 but do not cancel. Instead, select language.	1. Check Payment screens.
	2. Cancel transaction.	2. Check Welcome screen.
4	Kiosk starts at Welcome screen.	
	1. Repeat scenario 3, but do not cancel. Instead, enter an invalid payment.	1. Check Error message.
	2. Make a valid payment.	2. Check Browser. (Note: Should be the browser selected by the user.)
	3. Before the 60-second warning appears, buy more time.	3. Check Payment screens.
	4. Enter a valid payment.	4. Check return to the Browser, with session uninterrupted.
	5. Before the 60 second warning appears, log out.	5. Check Welcome screen. Verify clean up of files.
5	Kiosk starts at Welcome screen.	
	1. Repeat 4, but allow the 60-second warning to appear and buy more time.	1. Check Browser. (Note: Should be the browser selected by the user.) Check payment screens.

#	SCENARIO	EXPECTED RESULT
	2. Before the 60-second warning appears, have a call center agent terminate the session.	2. Check refund and termination message. Check Welcome screen. Verify cleanup of files.
6	Kiosk starts at Welcome screen. Set local time to slightly before 2:00 a.m.. Do not load update server.	
	1. Allow time to reach 2:00 a.m..	1. Check update start. Verify Out of Service message.
	2. Allow update to successfully complete.	2. Verify reboot.
	3. Allow initialization to successfully complete.	3. Check Welcome message.
7	Repeat setup for scenario 6, but heavily load the update server.	
	1. Repeat scenario 6.	1. Check random delay.
	2. Remove heavy load from update server. Let the delay expire and the update to start.	2. Verify Out of Service message.
	3. Allow update to successfully complete.	3. Verify reboot.
	4. Allow initialization to successfully complete.	4. Check Welcome message.

You might, as an additional set of tests, exercise loops in the state diagram. For example, you could continue to maintain the load on the server in scenario 7 for a few hours, verifying multiple random delays.

If you can automate the tests — which might in this case prove somewhat challenging — you could have an automated tool continuously traverse the states, creating both defined and undefined state/event combinations, to see how the system behaves. You can discover memory exhaustion problems, intermittent lock-ups and crashes, and other such bugs with such tests.

ATM State Models

In this next exercise, you'll create a state transition diagram for an ATM. Suppose you're testing a withdrawal-only ATM machine. The ATM accepts cards from any bank in its network. The ATM will validate the customer's PIN, then allow a withdrawal. It dispenses the cash and returns the customer's card all at once at the end of the transaction. The customer can cancel instead of entering the PIN or a withdrawal request. If so, the ATM returns the customer's card. The ATM will also return the customer's card after three invalid PIN attempts.

For the exercise, draw a state diagram for this ATM, then translate the state diagram into test cases. I suggest 30 minutes as a time limit. When you're done, keep reading to see my solution.

My Solution and Comments

First, I drew the state transition diagram, shown in Figure 15-2.

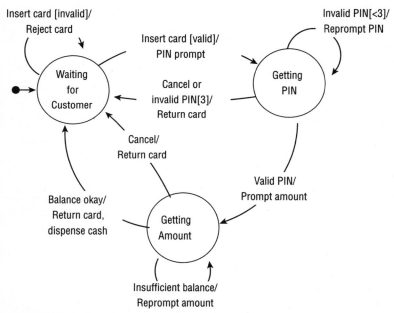

Figure 15-2: ATM state transition diagram

This is a simplified state diagram, of course. It does not include states involved in initializing and handling errors. However, for testing low-risk situations — for example, regression testing the ATM after a minor change to the back end — then it might suffice.

Next, I created the test cases as shown in Table 15-3. You will need a prop for this test. You need a valid account with some money in it, but not too much. The account should have an available balance small enough that it is possible to make a withdrawal request that exceeds the available balance.

Table 15-3 ATM Test Cases

#	TEST STEP/SUBSTEP	EXPECTED RESULT
	In all cases, the ATM starts in the waiting for customer state.	
1	1. Insert invalid card.	1. ATM rejects card.
	2. Insert valid card.	2. ATM prompts for PIN.
	3. Enter invalid PIN twice.	3. ATM reprompts for PIN.
	4. Enter invalid PIN a third time.	4. ATM returns card, goes back to the waiting for customer state.
2	1. Insert valid card.	1. ATM prompts for PIN.
	2. Press cancel.	2. ATM returns card, goes back to the waiting for customer state.
3	1. Insert valid card.	1. ATM prompts for PIN.
	2. Enter valid PIN.	2. ATM prompts for amount.
	3. Enter an amount that exceeds the available balance.	3. ATM reprompts for a lower amount.
	4. Press cancel.	4. ATM returns card, goes back to the waiting for customer state.
4	1. Repeat the first two substeps of test case 3.	1. Verify correct behavior of as specified in 3.1 and 3.2.
	2. Enter a valid amount.	2. ATM returns card, dispenses cash, goes back to the waiting for customer state.

Grays and Blues and State Transition Diagrams

In this final state exercise, you'll test how the behavior of the Grays and Blues game varies depending on the state the player is in with respect to loading a weapon. You'll apply state transition diagram analysis to reveal even more potential hiding places for bugs.

In one exercise in Chapter 13, you were testing a first-person action video game called Grays and Blues. Let's rejoin the exercise in progress. If you didn't do that exercise, don't worry, I'll recap the essential parts for this exercise.

The Grays and Blues game is set during the American Civil War, which ran from 1861 to 1865. Since this time period was prior to the advent of smokeless gunpowder and modern cartridge-based firearms, the war was fought primarily with three types of small arms:

- The officer's sword. A sword does not require any ammunition, of course. Hung at the side in a scabbard, it is always ready to use and the game treats it as "loaded."

- The cap-and-ball revolver. Most of the Civil War models held up to six shots. The game assumes that each chamber can be loaded in 10 seconds, though this certainly takes a very proficient — or motivated — soldier!

- The musket. The game assumes that the musket holds one shot and can be loaded in 30 seconds.

A Grays and Blues player may have none, one, two, or all three of these weapons in her possession at any given time. However, a player can have only one weapon in hand at any given time. The player uses the S, R, and M keys to select which weapon to have in hand. This is useful when a player wants to switch from a musket to a pistol for close action, for example.

Figure 15-3 shows the decision-making logic for weapon selection. All of the decisions and actions are immediate except the loading. Loading entails the delays specified in the list of arms.

The goal of the exercise is to create a state transition diagram from the flowchart, then identify bugs in the system design by analyzing the state transition diagram. I suggest 30 minutes as a time limit for this exercise. If it takes you longer than that, you're probably headed in the wrong direction. When you're done, keep reading to see my solution. My solution is not the only correct solution, just an example of one correct solution.

My Solution and Comments

Based on the flowchart, I created the state diagram in Figure 15-4 that describes the loading. And it shows the bug clearly, if you read it properly.

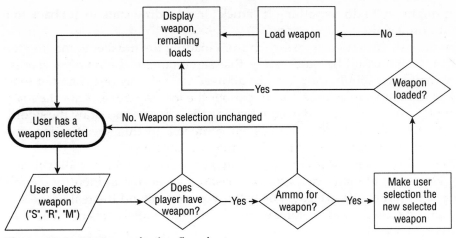

Figure 15-3: Weapon selection flowchart

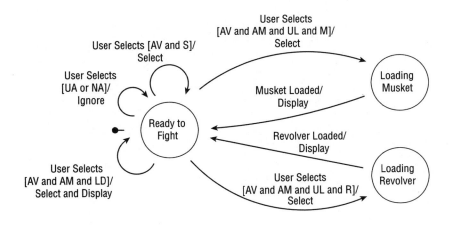

Legend
UA   Weapon unavailable
AV   Weapon available
NA   No ammunition available (does not apply to sword)
AM   Ammunition available (does not apply to sword)
UL   Weapon unloaded
LD   Weapon loaded
S   Sword selected
M   Musket selected
R   Revolver selected

Figure 15-4: Weapon selection state diagram

A delay is a potential problem for a player. While the player is wielding a weapon, the player is ready to fight. However, while the player is loading a weapon, the player is not ready to fight. So, it's reasonable to expect that the player might try to do something if "stuck" in a loading state to get back to a ready-to-fight state.

However, there is no way to switch from loading the musket to loading the revolver, which could be quicker. On that same note, if the revolver has six empty chambers, should the player be allowed to load only one chamber to be ready to fight as soon as possible? In neither the loading musket nor the loading revolver state can the player stop loading the weapon and draw the sword.

Even — or especially — if the system conforms to this specification precisely, the game will possess these three major problems.

This is a key lesson for testers. Conformance to requirements is all well and good. However, in many cases the tester should feel free to identify conformance to requirements *as a bug*. The better you understand the real usage scenarios and the users' and customers' needs, the more likely it is that you'll be able to find such bugs.

Domain Testing

In this chapter, I'll present an advanced technique for black-box testing. Domain analysis is an analytical way to deal with the interaction of factors or variables within the business logic layer of a program. It is appropriate when you have some number of factors to deal with. These factors might be input fields, output fields, database fields, events, or conditions. They should interact to create two or more situations in which the system will process data differently. Those situations are the domains. In each domain, the value of one or more factors influences the values of other factors, the system's outputs, or the processing performed.

Combinatorial Explosions

In some cases, the number of possible test cases becomes very large due to the number of variables or factors and the potentially interesting test values or options for each variable or factor. For example, suppose you have 10 integer input fields that accept a number from 0 to 99. There are 10 billion billion valid input combinations. Equivalence class partitioning and boundary value analysis on each field will reduce but not resolve the problem. You have four boundary values for each field. The illegal values are easy, because you have only 20 tests for those. However, to test each legal combination of fields, you have 1,024 test cases.

But do you need to do so? And would testing combinations of boundary values necessarily make for good tests? Are there smarter options for dealing with such combinatorial explosions?

There are two general cases:

- The factors should interact. One or more factors should partition the system's behavior into two or more domains, situations in which the system processes data differently. In addition, one or more factors interact in the system data processing. The value of one or more factors influences the values of other factors, the system's outputs, or the processing performed. For example, on typical multiscreen forms or business logic, you have different fields and operations, you can fill the fields in various orders, and so forth. The value of one field can determine the way subsequent fields are handled.

- The factors should not interact. The system should process data in substantially the same way no matter what value the factors take on. For example, to test application compatibility, you have to consider platforms, operating systems, printers, cohabitating applications, networks, and modems. The application should work the same in all supported configurations.

In Chapter 18, which covers orthogonal arrays and all pairs testing, I'll examine a test technique that works when the factors should not interact. In this chapter, we'll look at domain analysis, a technique that works when they should interact.

A Domain Example Using Frequent-Flyer Programs

One of the occupational hazards of being an international consultant is spending too much time on airplanes. To attempt to gather some benefit from that wasted time and (especially lately) aggravation, I collect frequent-flyer points, usually enough to fly my family around during vacations at the airlines' expense.

Airlines don't give my family free tickets because they like me. Airlines give frequent-flyer points to ensure customer loyalty. So the more loyal I am, the more richly they reward me. Each airline assigns me a status level based on the distance I traveled in their planes in the last year. Table 16-1 shows the way some airlines calculate bonus points based on the domains formed by the status levels.

Table 16-1   Status Levels Forming Domains of Point Calculations

STATUS LEVEL	NONE	SILVER	GOLD	PLATINUM
Trip Bonus	0%	25%	50%	100%
Distance Traveled	d	d	d	d
Points Awarded	d	1.25*d	1.5*d	2*d

The points awarded for any trip is a function of the traveler's status level and the distance traveled:

```
points = (1+bonus)*distance
```

The distance traveled in the last year determines the status level, which creates four domains of processing. The distance and trip bonus variables interact, and the result is the points variable.

Certainly, from the point of view of input and output verification, you might want to try maximum and minimum distances and points. Boundary values are useful for that. As I mentioned in Chapters 10 and 12, systems are often built in layers. At the user interface and the data access layers, checking fields and variables at the boundaries is smart. However, notice that testing a distance of zero with each status level is not only nonsensical, it is also unlikely to tell us whether the formula that calculates the points is incorrect.

So, suppose we are concerned that the system will miscalculate the points awarded? We need to test at least one trip for each traveler status. In Figure 16-1, you see four points that covers the four domains (i.e., the four calculations). Like the decision table technique, domain analysis focuses on central layers of the system architecture that implement the processing, not the user or data interface layers. Good system design principles says that, as much as possible, accepting valid inputs, displaying valid outputs, rejecting invalid inputs, and marking invalid outputs should reside in the user or data interface(s). You can test those interfaces using boundary values or equivalence partitioning.

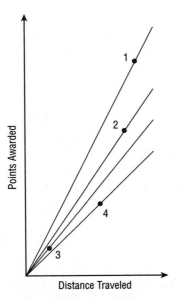

Figure 16-1: Graphical view of the bonus-points domains

Possible Domain Test Values

Much of the original work in the area of domain testing was done by Boris Beizer and lately has been carried on by Robert Binder and Lee Copeland.[1] They have written that in order to test a domain, there are four types of interesting test values, as shown in Table 16-2. This table also includes an analysis of the four points shown in Figure 16-1.

Table 16-2 Domain Test Values

NAME	DESCRIPTION	FREQUENT-FLYER EXAMPLE
On	A value on a domain boundary that may be inside or outside of the domain	1 (on platinum), 2 (on gold), 3 (on silver), 4 (on none)
Off	A value just off a domain boundary by the smallest recognizable amount and outside of the domain	1 (off gold), 2 (off platinum), 2 (off silver), 3 (off gold), 3 (off none), 4 (off silver)
In	A value inside the domain, not on or off	No such value possible
Out	A value outside the domain, not on or off	No such value possible

In case you're wondering about the *in* and *out* values for this example, because the domains are actually lines, you can only be on or off. Being off one line means you are on another because those are the only possible values. So, if you look at point 1, you see it is on the platinum line and off the nearest next line, which is gold.[2]

Because this is the point where a lot of people get lost when they learn domain analysis, let's back up for a minute to the single-factor situation. In Chapter 10, I gave a very simple example: a "quantity ordered" field in an e-commerce application. The application accepts quantities that are greater than zero and less than 100. Boundary values and equivalence partitioning say you need to test at least 0, 1, 99, and 100, with the added possibility of an interior value in each class like –7, 15, and 126.

---

[1] See, for example, Beizer's book *Software Testing Techniques*, Binder's book *Testing Object-Oriented Systems*, and Copeland's book *A Practitioner's Guide to Software Test Design*.

[2] I thank Judy McKay for this neat way of explaining this fact.

Let's apply domain analysis. First, I identify three domains, which are simply the three equivalence classes:

- Invalid too low
- Valid
- Invalid too high

Now, in Table 16-3, I identify the four different types of domain test values, reusing them where I can to keep the testing efficient.

Table 16-2 Domain Test Values for Quantity Ordered

DOMAIN	ON	OFF	IN	OUT
Invalid too low	0	1	-7	15
Valid (lower boundary)	0	-1	15	-7
Valid (upper boundary)	100	101	15	126
Invalid too high	100	99	126	15

Notice that the domain analysis is applied boundary by boundary so that the valid domain has two analyses: one at the boundary with the invalid too high domain and one at the boundary with the invalid too low domain. Also, notice that you can use the same set of tests you used with boundary values and equivalence partitioning, with the addition of the –1 and 101 values.[3] Finally, notice that, had you defined the quantity ordered field as accepting values that are greater than or equal to 1 and less than or equal to 99, you would still test with the same boundary value and equivalence partitioning data, but in this case you would add 2 and 98 rather than –1 and 101.

This close relationship between the boundary value and equivalence partitioning technique and domain testing leads to domain analysis being referred to as multivariable or multifactor equivalence partitioning by some.

An Aerospace Example

With the concept of on, off, in, and out points firmly in hand, let's go back to the multifactor situation. Figure 16-2 shows an aerospace example. For a missile defense system, one needs to be able to calculate the current — and projected — vertical and horizontal positions of a large falling object, in this

---

[3] In fact, some variants of boundary value and equivalence partitioning test design would include these two values as well.

case an incoming ballistic missile. A measurement is taken with a laser or radar, but time elapses during the measurement period. When the radar or laser gets back to the measuring station, the object is no longer where it was when it was measured. It has moved.

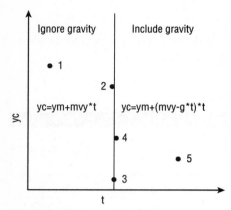

Figure 16-2: An aerospace domain

The situation with horizontal position and velocity is straightforward, as no forces are acting on the missile in this dimension. However, vertically, gravity is accelerating the missile downward. To simplify the calculation, we ignore the effect of gravity if a small enough period of time has elapsed, but we will include the effect of gravity if the time elapsed is 1 millisecond or more. Now we have two domains, as shown in Figure 16-2.

To define the five points shown in the figure, I performed the domain analysis shown in Table 16-3. I assumed that the smallest measurable difference in time is one microsecond. Notice that my choices of the *ym* and *mvy* values are arbitrary. What I'm trying to test here is that the boundaries between the two domains are defined properly and that the calculation is done correctly in each domain. Again, notice the similarity between the objectives of domain analysis testing and boundary value and equivalence class testing.

Table 16-3   Domain Test Values for Aerospace Example

DOMAIN	ON	OFF	IN	OUT
Ignore gravity	1.000 (point 3)	1.001 (point 4)	0.372 (point 1)	1.752 (point 5)
Include gravity	1.000 (point 3)	0.999 (point 2)	1.752 (point 5)	0.372 (point 1)

When Domain Rules Change

In the two examples so far, the rules for the domain and the calculations within each domain remain constant. However, it's possible for the rules to change within a domain, creating the need for additional tests.

Suppose we look at the total number of points awarded to a frequent flyer for a whole year. A traveler's status is based on the total distance traveled in the current year or the total distance traveled in the past year. At 25,000, the status increases to silver. At 50,000, the status increases to gold. At 100,000, the status increases to platinum. Any distance traveled after the status changes accrues bonus points based on the new status, both in the current year and the next year. Basically, these rules split three of the four domains into two or more subdomains.

Domain testing theory says that we should add some additional domain tests in this situation, specifically to cover values in each subdomain or rule segment. This adds one new test for travelers starting with gold status (if they move up to platinum), two new tests for travelers starting with silver status (if they move up to gold or platinum), and three for travelers starting with no status (if they move up to silver, gold, or platinum). These values are shown in Figure 16-3. Notice that, if you test this by adding points for completed flights one flight at a time, a traveler who, for example, started the year with silver status and ended with platinum would, at some point in the year, have silver status, gold status, and platinum status.

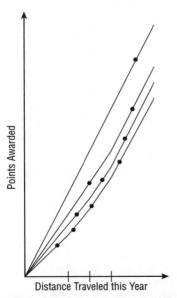

Figure 16-3: Yearly frequent-flyer point calculations

Notice that what I am testing with these values is only the calculation itself. If I wanted to add a test that checked whether the boundaries where a traveler's status changes were defined correctly, I'd have to add tests at these boundaries. To do so, I could apply the concept of domain analysis to each of the four lines. Notice that if I did so, domain analysis for each line would be the same as boundary value and equivalence partitioning.[4]

Domain Analysis Summary

Let's summarize what we've covered so far in the area of domain analysis before we take it to the next level of complexity.

In some cases, factors or variables should interact. More precisely, the system's behavior is only correct when the factors or variables interact properly. In the first frequent-flyer example, the status level determined the formula that calculated the number of points awarded from the distance traveled. Each status level formed a domain of processing.

In the aerospace example, the system should use one of two formulas to calculate the current vertical position, depending on the measured position, the measured vertical velocity, time, and in one domain, the acceleration of gravity. The time elapsed since the measurement formed the two domains of processing.

In the second frequent-flyer example, the initial status level (based on the last year) and the total distance traveled for the current year determined both the points awarded and the transition into the new status level. In that example, I analyzed the domains to test the correct points awarded. However, note that by adding more test points, I could have tested whether the promotion to the correct new status level was occurring at the correct points. Specifically, I would have needed *on* and *off* points for the boundaries at 25,000, 50,000, and 100,000, on each of the four lines corresponding to the initial status levels. We'll take a look at ways to cover multiple domains in a single test shortly.

In the aerospace example, the interaction took the form of formulas that influence how inputs interacted to create an output. In the frequent-flyer example, the inputs interacted with data about the traveler, likely from a database. One or more of the factors or variables combined to create domains of operation or processing that should be the same. Domains can be based on

---

[4] In *Software Testing Techniques*, Boris Beizer introduces some new terms for this situation. He calls domain tests that cover each rule segment *strong*. He refers to domain tests that do not cover each rule segment as *weak*. He then uses the phrase "strong 1x1 testing" to refer to domain tests that include at least one *on* and on *off* point for each subdomain. He calls domain tests that test each domain but not each subdomain "weak 1x1 testing."

inputs, outputs, or internal data sets. Domains can involve real numbers, integers, dates, sets, or other intrinsic or programmer-defined data types.

Here are some rules of thumb for constructing domain tests:

- You should cover at least the *on* and *off* values for each domain.

- If an *on* value for one domain is an *off* value for another, you needn't create additional values.

- In the case where the variable that determines the domain is an integer or real variable, as in the aerospace example, you should also cover *in* and *out* values.

- If an *in* value for one domain is an *out* value for another, you needn't create additional values.

- If the rules for a domain's boundary change or the processing changes in the domain, consider additional *on*, *off*, *in*, and *out* values to achieve *strong* domain coverage.

Finally, remember that typically you are not verifying basic data sanity checking, but rather that the internal core logic of the system is correct.

Complex Domain Testing Example

For real systems, we not only have multiple factors and variables interacting, we also have multiple interactions going on across multiple domains. Let's look at an example, using the moving violator decision table, shown in Table 16-5.

First, note that if you attempt to test all combinations of boundary values and equivalence classes, you have 208 tests.

There are four true/false equivalence classes:

- License OK

- Warrant

- Registration OK

- Vehicle OK

I can identify 8 equivalence classes related to excess speed, with 13 boundary values:

- Invalid too low (-1 and below)

- No excess speed (0)

- Insufficient excess speed (1–10)
- Ticketable excess speed (11–20)
- Severe ticket excess speed (21-25)
- Two-digit arrest excess speed (26–99)
- Three digit arrest excess speed (100–max)
- Invalid too high (max+1 and above)

So, there are

```
2x2x2x2x13=208
```

tests that you could run to cover all the combinations. Another way to look at the combinatorial explosion is in terms of all the possible fine calculations, shown in Figure 16-4.

Moving Violator Fine Calculations

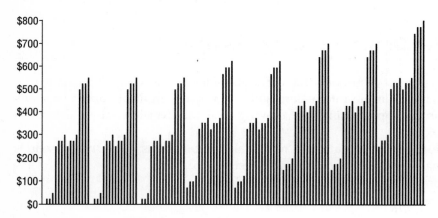

Figure 16-4: Moving violator fine calculations

However, what would be more efficient — and probably more effective — is to analyze the domains defined in the decision table and build tests that way. That way, I can test one violator in each domain and one just outside each domain.

Table 16-4   Moving Violator Decision Table

	Business Rules							
Condition	1	2	3	4	5	6	7	8
License OK	No	-	-	-	-	-	-	-
Warrant	-	Yes	-	-	-	-	-	-
Registration OK	-	-	No	-	-	-	-	-
Vehicle OK	-	-	-	No	-	-	-	-
Excess Speed	-	-	-	-	1-10	11-20	21-25	>=26
Action								
Arrest	Yes	Yes	-	-	-	-	-	Yes
Fix-It Ticket	-	-	Yes	Yes	-	-	-	-
Warning	-	-	-	-	Yes	-	-	-
Fine	+250	+250	+25	+25	+0	+75	+150	+250

Suppose you can assume that each individual business rule in the table was tested appropriately, as discussed in Chapter 13. Now you want to test bugs that arise from improper interaction of three sets of data.

The first is the excess speed. Suppose that you decide to use just seven classes:

- Invalid too low (-1 and below)
- No excess speed (0)
- Insufficient excess speed (1–10)
- Ticketable excess speed (11–20)
- Severe ticket excess speed (21–25)
- Arrest excess speed (26–max)
- Invalid too high (max+1 and above)

The second is that excess speed combines properly with the various Boolean conditions to result in the proper ticket. There are five classes:

- None
- Warn
- Fix-it
- Speeding
- Arrest

Finally, you want to make sure that the speed, the ticket issued, and the other conditions all interact properly in terms of the motorist's arrest class:

- Don't arrest
- Do arrest

You're going to assume that, if these interactions work properly, the rest of the possible inputs or outputs at boundaries should work properly. This is generally a safe assumption because the programmer would have to go out of his way to create bugs by adding logic and branching to create next classes in the processing.

A General Rule for Complex Domains

How do you tackle this problem? It's clearly more complex than the three examples. The additional complexity arises from trying to handle multiple factors, conditions, or variables at once along with the fact that the potential interactions are complex.

Here's a process that will help guide you.

1. Pick the "biggest" variable or factor, the one with the most equivalence classes. Perform the domain analyses on the processing you're testing. Define the condition(s) needed to cover the *on* and *off* (and possibly the *in* and *out*) values. You can use a variation on the decision table itself to keep track of where you are.

2. Pick the "next-biggest" variable or factor. Perform the domain analysis on the processing you're testing for this variable. Figure out which *on* and *off* (and possibly *in* and *out*) values are already covered, if any. Populate conditions (within existing tests, if possible) to cover those values. Add any additional tests needed.

3. Repeat step 2 until all the variables or factors are handled.

This process is simple to state but hard to carry out. However, the time spent in analysis and test design here will save you time later when there are fewer tests to run.

Table 16-6 shows the domain tests I built using the preceding process and the domains mentioned earlier. Spend a few moments studying it. Keep in mind that I built the table by starting in the Domain Analysis section at the bottom, selecting the *on* and *off* point for the speed factor. That determined the excess speed row in the Test Condition section.

I then did the domain analysis for the ticket type. Which column the various *on* and *off* points for that factor ended up in depended in part on the excess speeds I had already chosen. Once I had covered those points, I could then select the rest of the factors in the Test Condition section.

Table 16-5 Domain Tests for the Moving Violator Decision Table

Test Case

	1	2	3	4	5	6	7	8	9	10	11
Test Condition											
License OK	Yes	Yes	Yes	No	Yes	Yes	Yes	Yes	No	Yes	No
Warrant	No	No	No	No	No	No	Yes	No	Yes	No	Yes
Registration OK	Yes	No	Yes	Yes	Yes	No	Yes	No	No	Yes	No
Vehicle OK	Yes	Yes	Yes	Yes	Yes	No	Yes	No	No	Yes	No
Excess Speed	-1	0	1	10	11	20	21	25	26	Max	Max+1
Expected Result											
Fine	0	25	0	250	75	125	400	200	800	250	0
Ticket	N	F	W	W+A	S	S+F	S+A	S+F	S+F+A	S	N
Arrest	No	No	No	Yes	No	No	Yes	No	Yes	Yes	No
Reject Data	Yes	No	No	No	No	No	No	No	No	No	Yes
Domain Analysis											
Speed ON	1	0	1-10	1-10	11-20	11-20	21-25	21-25	>=26	>=26	1
OFF	0	1, 1-10	0	11-20	1-10	21-25	11-20	>=26	21-25	1	>=26
Ticket ON	N	F	W	WA	S	SF	SA	SF	SFA	S	N
OFF	WFSA	NWSA	NSFA	NSF	NWFA	NWA	NWF	NWA	NW	NWFA	WSFA
Arrest ON	Don't	Don't	Don't	Do	Don't	Don't	Do	Don't	Do	Do	Don't
OFF	Do	Do	Do	Don't	Do	Do	Don't	Do	Don't	Don't	Do

Finally, referring to the original decision table, I populated the Expected Result section.

As shown in the table, that reduced the 208 tests down to 11. However, you might say, "Okay, Rex, but the original calculation covered all the possible fines. You haven't."

That's a good point, to which I'd respond, "Do you really have to cover all possible fines if what you want to know is that the fine is calculated correctly?"

It's likely that the fine is calculated by adding the possible fines the violator could receive. In other words,

```
fine=license fine+warrant fine+registration fine+vehicle fine+speeding fine
```

Each of the possible fines could be calculated by looking up the fine in a table or database based on the condition that applies. So if I can assure that each of the five terms in the fine calculation takes every possible value at least once, as well as making sure that the maximum and minimum fines are calculated correctly, I should be safe.

You might object to my guessing about implementation details. However, I believe that as testers, we must do so. If we don't, the set of all possible bugs is so large that it threatens to overwhelm us.

We almost always make some implementation assumptions, consciously or unconsciously. As I mentioned in the chapter on equivalence classes and boundary values (Chapter 10), boundary value analysis is effective against bugs where we suspect the use of the wrong comparison operator or a close but wrong constant value. In other words, if the programmer writes

```
if ((c > '0') && (c < '9')) {
    // handle the digits
    ...
}
```

when she should have written

```
if ((c >= '0') && (c <= '9')) {
    // handle the digits
    ...
}
```

boundary value analysis can catch that bug.

However, if the programmer instead wrote

```
switch (c) {
    case `0': case `1': case `1': case `3': case `4':
    case `5': case `6': case `7': case `8': case `9':
        // handle the digits
        ...
        break;
```

the boundary value analysis will not catch the bug in this code fragment.

Some kinds of bugs are not amenable to discovery by testing. For example, suppose that the programmer of the moving violator fine logic, instead of looking up fine values in a table or database, hard-coded those values? A test that compares expected and actual results is unlikely to find that bug because the results will probably be correct at first. It's only once the fine values change — when the law changes, for example — that the results will be wrong.

Notice that code reviews would be effective against both the digit-handling bug and the hard-coded-values bug. As the saying goes, "You can't test quality into the system," and this is another manifestation of that aphorism.

One consideration that applies here is known as the "competent programmer assumption." Testing based on good guesses about implementation will work when you can assume the programmers are competent but fallible. You look for the mistakes they are likely to make.

If you can't assume that the programmers are competent, the set of likely bugs explodes. The number of bugs you will find explodes. Indeed, the situation is likely to be so hopeless, your head might explode! In the case of incompetent programming, test design techniques and niceties like what assumptions you are making about the quality of the code probably go out the window. You'll find bugs everywhere you look.

Domain Testing Exercise

Let's apply the domain testing test technique to the Omninet project.

The Omninet marketing team requests a change to the Marketing Requirements Document, section 3.1.2, to add the following paragraph:

> *A frequent surfer is someone who has used an Omninet kiosk in the last four weeks. A frequent surfer who purchases one or more blocks of time (at five minutes per block) receives a bonus block of time (also five minutes) for each block purchased. The total time given (paid plus bonus blocks) for any single payment transaction shall not exceed one hour.*

The exercise is to draw a graph showing the blocks of time purchased, the total (paid and bonus) blocks received by the customer, and the domain test values you would want to cover. Next, create a set of tests to cover the domain test values and ensure proper payment processing and time sold to frequent surfers and regular surfers. Finally, jot down any other test considerations this change creates, if any.

I haven't provided a template for this exercise because it would constrain your choices in how to analyze the domains. I suggest 60 minutes as a time limit. When you're done, keep reading to see my solution.

My Solution and Comments

If what you want to test is only the delivery of the proper number of time blocks to the two kinds of surfers, you might have drawn one graph, as shown in Figure 17-1. The figure shows the test points I would cover. Notice that I did subdomain analysis on each of the two domains to check the invalid subdomains above and below each valid surfer domain. If you assume that there is no way for an invalid input to sneak past the user interface, you could have omitted that.

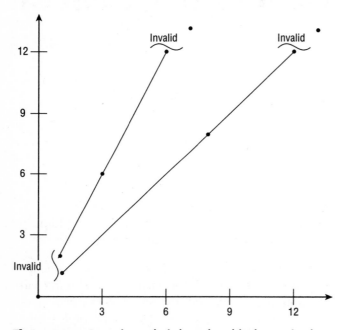

Figure 17-1: Domain analysis based on blocks received

Now, I created a set of tests to ensure proper payment processing and time sold to frequent surfers and regular surfers. Table 17-1 shows the domain analysis, the test conditions, and the expected results. Notice that I have omitted the out points because I'm not going to try to create test points in the interiors of the invalid regions.

Table 17-1   Domain Tests for the Frequent Surfer without Time Analysis

DOMAIN ANALYSIS		1	2	3	4	5	6	7	8	9	10
Frequent Surfer	On	I	1–6		1–6	I					
	In			1–6							
	Off	1–6	I		I	1–6					
Basic Surfer	On						I	1–12		1–12	I
	In								1–12		
	Off						1–12	I		I	1–12
Condition											
Block Purchased		0	1	3	6	7	0	1	8	12	13
Frequent Surfer		Y	Y	Y	Y	Y	N	N	N	N	N
Expected Result											
Blocks Received		0	2	6	12	0	0	1	8	12	0
Reject		Y	N	N	N	Y	Y	N	N	N	Y

Suppose that you want to make sure to test the operation that creates the domain, the time interval since the last surf. In that case, your graph might look more like the one shown in Figure 17-2.

Your set of tests might look like Table 17-2.[1] You might also want to add a test at 27 days, but I felt that the condition was adequately covered by the test at 28 days.

[1] I'd like to acknowledge Sophie Dusire of Eurocontrol for her contribution to this solution.

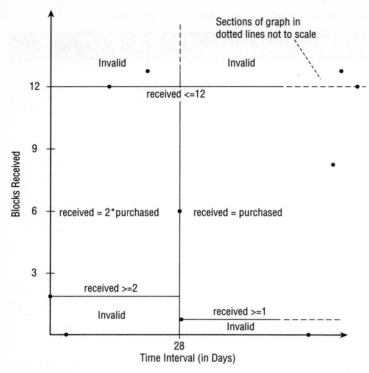

Figure 17-2: Domain analysis based on blocks received and time elapsed

I've identified a few obvious additional test considerations for this change.

- How does the kiosk recognize a frequent surfer? A logical way to recognize frequent surfers is by their credit card number, but what if the same person uses a different or new credit card? What about cash customers?

- Can the tester assume that the kiosk be connected and able to query the database of users at the time the decision about the legal number of blocks is made?

- How is the number of days since last surfing determined? Is that 28 calendar days or exactly 672 hours of elapsed time? Are time zones and the international date line going to be taken into account? The easiest and most robust approach is calendar days based on the kiosks' local clocks, so that's what I've assumed in my tests.

Perhaps you thought of others?

Table 17-2 Domain Tests for the Frequent Surfer with Time Analysis

DOMAIN ANALYSIS		1	2	3	4	5	6	7	8	9	10
Time Interval (days)	On		0–28	0–28				>29			
	In	0–28			0–28	0–28	>29		>29	>29	>29
	Off			>29				0–28			
Frequent Surfer	On	I	1–6		1–6	I					
	In			1–6							
	Off	1–6	I		I	1–6					
Basic Surfer	On						I	1–12		1–12	I
	In								1–12		
	Off						1–12	I		I	1–12
Condition											
Time Interval		4	0	28	12	23	76	29	457	∞[2]	365
Block Purchased		0	1	3	6	7	0	1	8	12	13
Frequent Surfer		Y	Y	Y	Y	Y	N	N	N	N	N
Expected Result											
Blocks Received		0	2	6	12	0	0	1	8	12	0
Reject		Y	N	N	N	Y	Y	N	N	N	Y

[2] The time interval is infinite if it's the user's first use of the kiosk.

## CHAPTER 18

Orthogonal Arrays
and All Pairs

In this chapter, I'll present two more advanced techniques for black-box testing. Both deal with the same test problem, that of combinations where factors should not interact but might. However, each technique solves the problem in a slightly different way.

Combinatorial Explosions

If you didn't go through the chapter on domain testing (Chapter 16), let me revisit the problem. Sometimes, the number of possible test cases becomes very large due to the number of variables or factors and the potentially interesting test values or options for each variable or factor.

For example, suppose you have 10 integer input fields that accept a number from 0 to 99. There are 10 billion billion valid input combinations.

Equivalence class partitioning and boundary value analysis will reduce but not resolve the problem. You have four boundary values for each field. The illegal values are easy, because you only have 20 tests for those. However, to test each legal combination of fields, you have 1,024 test cases.

But do you need to do so? And would testing combinations of boundary values necessarily make for good tests? Are there smarter options for dealing with such combinatorial explosions?

There are two general cases:

- The factors should interact. One or more factors should partition the system's behavior into two or more domains, situations in which the system processes data equivalently. In addition, one or more factors interact in the system data processing. The value of one or more factors influences the values of other factors, the system's outputs, or the processing performed. For example, on typical multiscreen forms or business logic, you have the different fields and operations, you can fill the fields in various orders, and so forth. The value of one field can determine the way subsequent fields are handled.

- The factors should not interact. The system should process data in substantially the same way no matter what value the factors take on. For example, to test application compatibility, you have to consider platforms, operating systems, printers, cohabitating applications, networks, and modems. The application should work the same in all supported configurations.

In Chapter 16, I discussed a technique that works when the factors should interact. In this chapter on orthogonal arrays and all-pairs testing, I'll examine two test techniques that work when the factors should not interact but might do so incorrectly. And, after all, if parts of the system never interacted incorrectly, we would only have to run unit tests!

Both techniques rely on a simple assumption about bugs: that most bugs will arise from single options for any given factor or from pairs of options across pairs of factors. You make the simplifying — and, in many cases, essential — assumption that bugs will not arise from triples of options, quadruples of options, or other high-order combinations of options.

In my years of experience with compatibility testing of systems and applications with interoperating and cohabiting systems or applications, I've found this assumption to be reasonable. I can recall only one case where a bug relied on the specific options chosen for three factors. The case involved a laptop computer that my associates and I tested for compatibility with about 100 applications, add-on hardware items, networks, and servers. The laptop passed most of these tests. For the tests that failed, we reported back to the client that they should not support the applications, hardware, or networks involved.

After the laptop was released, one salesperson had an embarrassing sales call. While he was demonstrating the laptop for a potential client, the system repeatedly rebooted. Later analysis showed that the following was required to see the failure:

- A specific network card
- A specific network card speed setting
- A specific server

We had tested this specific network card with each possible network connection speed. However, we had not tested each type of card with each possible connection speed attached to each possible type of server.

The number of such tests would have been very large. At the time, I estimated we would have needed thousands if not tens of thousands of test combinations — at a very high price — to find such bugs reliably. The lost sale was regrettable, but it was a risk that my client was well advised to take. My client could have spent more money testing that laptop than they stood to make in profits. The testing of common and affordable options across all factors, along with an attempt wherever possible to test all pairs of options across all pairs of factors, is a reasonable way to address the compatibility risks while intelligently reducing the number of potential test cases.

Orthogonal Arrays and All-Pairs Tables

There are two general techniques for ensuring that we test all options for each factor and all pairs of options across all pairs of factors. One technique is called orthogonal arrays. The other is called all-pairs tables.

I'm not going to explain how to construct orthogonal arrays or all-pairs tables. Like a mechanic, who doesn't need to know how to make high-carbon steel to use a wrench, you don't need to know how to construct these tools to use them. You can find arrays and tools on the Internet by entering "orthogonal arrays" or "all-pairs tables" into a search engine. Instead, I'm going to focus on how to apply these tools to your projects.[1]

NOTE Orthogonal arrays and all-pairs tables differ in the number of times each pair of options is represented, which is usually not important for compatibility testing. Orthogonal arrays figure prominently in some quality management disciplines, like Six Sigma, as Design of Experiments. In these disciplines, the number of times each pair of options occurs is important.

Two Orthogonal Arrays

Table 18-1 shows a simple orthogonal array. There are two factors. There are two options per factor. Each option is represented at least once for each factor. Each pair of options across the two factors is represented in one (and only one) row. It's obvious, if you think about it, why there must be four rows.

---

[1] You can find one library of orthogonal arrays at www.research.att.com/~njas/oadir. You can find a freeware all-pairs tool at www.satisfice.com.

Table 18-1 Simple Orthogonal Array

	Factor	
Test	1	2
1	0	0
2	0	1
3	1	0
4	1	1

Table 18-2 shows a larger orthogonal array. There are three factors. There are two options per factor. Each option is represented at least once for each factor. Each pair of options across the three pairs of factors is represented in one (and only one) row. Notice that I added a factor without increasing the tests. The reason is that I'm not going to try to cover all the triples, just all the pairs.

Table 18-2 A Slightly Larger Orthogonal Array

	Factor		
Test	1	2	3
1	0	0	0
2	0	1	1
3	1	0	1
4	1	1	0

You might think that as the number of factors increases, the number of rows would have to increase too. However, in a moment, you'll see a striking example of how often you can get away with adding more factors without increasing the number of rows. This is important because each row represents an additional test case or test configuration. Restraining any increase in the number of rows, then, represents a significant time and cost savings to the project.

If you're having trouble imagining how to use an orthogonal array, suppose you're planning on testing the compatibility of various web clients with an e-commerce system. The factors of interest might be the operating system, the browser, and the connection speed. Suppose that you only care about Windows and Linux, Internet Explorer and Netscape, and dial-up and DSL for each of these three factors.

Take a look at Table 18-3. By doing a quick search-and-replace on the factor headings and the options in each column, I've created an orthogonal array that you can use to cover all pairs of options across these three factors. It took me less than 60 seconds.

Table 18-3   A Simple Application of Orthogonal Arrays

	Factor		
Test	OS	Browser	Speed
1	Windows	Internet Explorer	Dial-up
2	Windows	Netscape	DSL
3	Linux	Internet Explorer	DSL
4	Linux	Netscape	Dial-up

Selecting an Orthogonal Array

You must start by selecting a suitable orthogonal array in which to fit your factors and options. Here are three simple rules for selecting an orthogonal array.

1. The chosen array must have at least as many columns as the factors you are testing. If there are too many columns, you can drop the extra column because it maps to a factor that doesn't exist.

2. The chosen array must have at least enough unique numbers in the columns to hold all of the options for each factor. You can replace any "spare" numbers that don't map to any option with any valid option for that factor. However, you may not omit the option because each factor must take on some value, in most cases. You certainly must not delete the row with the spare option unless that row contains only "spare" numbers and other pairs of options that are represented somewhere else in the table.

3. The chosen array must have at least as many rows as the multiplicative product of the number of options for the two factors with the most options. In some cases, you'll find that you have too many rows. Again, you must not delete any extra rows, except rows that contain only "spare" numbers and other pairs of options that are represented somewhere else in the table.

Pay close attention to these rules and all will go well. The search-and-replace operations are trivial given the right array. If you select the wrong array, the search-and-replace operation will probably fail and you'll have to start over at step 1.

Applying Orthogonal Arrays to a Complicated Real-World Example

Consider a system for constructing e-commerce sites that must support various client and server configurations. Suppose you have the following seven factors with the options shown:

- Browser (A, B, C)
- Host OS (A, B, C)
- Speed (A, B, C)
- Web server (A, B, C)
- Application server (A, B, C, D, E)
- Database server (A, B, C, D, E)
- Server OS (A, B, C, D)

Note that I have labeled the options A, B, C, and so on to avoid putting specific names on each option. In the real world, you'd use the actual names.

While there are only a few options per factor, there are many combinations.

$$3x3x3x3x5x5x4=8,100$$

From a test point of view, that's an entirely unreasonable number of configurations to test.

Applying the rules given earlier to select an orthogonal array, Table 18-4 shows the orthogonal array I found at the website referenced earlier. It has 8 columns, though I only needed 7. It has 7 options per column, though I only needed 5. It has 49 rows, though I only need 25. It is a simple block of text, quick and easy to download.

Table 18-4   The Library Version of an Orthogonal Array

00000000
01123456
02234561
03345612
04456123
05561234
06612345
10111111
11352064
12520643

13206435

14064352

15643520

16435206

20222222

21546301

22463015

23630154

24301546

25015463

26154630

30333333

31265140

32651402

33514026

34140265

35402651

36026514

40444444

41031625

42316250

43162503

44625031

45250316

46503162

50555555

51604213

52042136

53421360

54213604

Continued

Table 18-4 (continued)

55136042
56360421
60666666
61410532
62105324
63053241
64532410
65324105
66241053

I started by importing this chunk of text into Excel, which makes working with it easy. I added labels for the factor columns and the test rows, shown in Table 18-5.

Table 18-5 Using an Orthogonal Array, First Step

				Factor				
Test	**1**	**2**	**3**	**4**	**5**	**6**	**7**	**8**
1	0	0	0	0	0	0	0	0
2	0	1	1	2	3	4	5	6
3	0	2	2	3	4	5	6	1
4	0	3	3	4	5	6	1	2
5	0	4	4	5	6	1	2	3
6	0	5	5	6	1	2	3	4
7	0	6	6	1	2	3	4	5
8	1	0	1	1	1	1	1	1
9	1	1	3	5	2	0	6	4
10	1	2	5	2	0	6	4	3
11	1	3	2	0	6	4	3	5
12	1	4	0	6	4	3	5	2
13	1	5	6	4	3	5	2	0
14	1	6	4	3	5	2	0	6
15	2	0	2	2	2	2	2	2

				Factor				
Test	1	2	3	4	5	6	7	8
16	2	1	5	4	6	3	0	1
17	2	2	4	6	3	0	1	5
18	2	3	6	3	0	1	5	4
19	2	4	3	0	1	5	4	6
20	2	5	0	1	5	4	6	3
21	2	6	1	5	4	6	3	0
22	3	0	3	3	3	3	3	3
23	3	1	2	6	5	1	4	0
24	3	2	6	5	1	4	0	2
25	3	3	5	1	4	0	2	6
26	3	4	1	4	0	2	6	5
27	3	5	4	0	2	6	5	1
28	3	6	0	2	6	5	1	4
29	4	0	4	4	4	4	4	4
30	4	1	0	3	1	6	2	5
31	4	2	3	1	6	2	5	0
32	4	3	1	6	2	5	0	3
33	4	4	6	2	5	0	3	1
34	4	5	2	5	0	3	1	6
35	4	6	5	0	3	1	6	2
36	5	0	5	5	5	5	5	5
37	5	1	6	0	4	2	1	3
38	5	2	0	4	2	1	3	6
39	5	3	4	2	1	3	6	0
40	5	4	2	1	3	6	0	4
41	5	5	1	3	6	0	4	2
42	5	6	3	6	0	4	2	1
43	6	0	6	6	6	6	6	6

Continued

Table 18-5 *(continued)*

Test	Factor							
	1	**2**	**3**	**4**	**5**	**6**	**7**	**8**
44	6	1	4	1	0	5	3	2
45	6	2	1	0	5	3	2	4
46	6	3	0	5	3	2	4	1
47	6	4	5	3	2	4	1	0
48	6	5	3	2	4	1	0	5
49	6	6	2	4	1	0	5	3

I dropped the extra column, column eight, since I only have seven factors, to obtain Table 18-6.

Table 18-6 Using an Orthogonal Array, Second Step

Test	Factor						
	1	**2**	**3**	**4**	**5**	**6**	**7**
1	0	0	0	0	0	0	0
2	0	1	1	2	3	4	5
3	0	2	2	3	4	5	6
4	0	3	3	4	5	6	1
5	0	4	4	5	6	1	2
6	0	5	5	6	1	2	3
7	0	6	6	1	2	3	4
8	1	0	1	1	1	1	1
9	1	1	3	5	2	0	6
10	1	2	5	2	0	6	4
11	1	3	2	0	6	4	3
12	1	4	0	6	4	3	5
13	1	5	6	4	3	5	2
14	1	6	4	3	5	2	0
15	2	0	2	2	2	2	2
16	2	1	5	4	6	3	0
17	2	2	4	6	3	0	1

			Factor				
Test	1	2	3	4	5	6	7
18	2	3	6	3	0	1	5
19	2	4	3	0	1	5	4
20	2	5	0	1	5	4	6
21	2	6	1	5	4	6	3
22	3	0	3	3	3	3	3
23	3	1	2	6	5	1	4
24	3	2	6	5	1	4	0
25	3	3	5	1	4	0	2
26	3	4	1	4	0	2	6
27	3	5	4	0	2	6	5
28	3	6	0	2	6	5	1
29	4	0	4	4	4	4	4
30	4	1	0	3	1	6	2
31	4	2	3	1	6	2	5
32	4	3	1	6	2	5	0
33	4	4	6	2	5	0	3
34	4	5	2	5	0	3	1
35	4	6	5	0	3	1	6
36	5	0	5	5	5	5	5
37	5	1	6	0	4	2	1
38	5	2	0	4	2	1	3
39	5	3	4	2	1	3	6
40	5	4	2	1	3	6	0
41	5	5	1	3	6	0	4
42	5	6	3	6	0	4	2
43	6	0	6	6	6	6	6
44	6	1	4	1	0	5	3
45	6	2	1	0	5	3	2

Continued

Table 18-6 *(continued)*

46	6	3	0	5	3	2	4
47	6	4	5	3	2	4	1
48	6	5	3	2	4	1	0
49	6	6	2	4	1	0	5

I mapped the factors to columns to create Table 18-7.

Table 18-7 Using an Orthogonal Array, Third Step

				Factor			
Test	**Browser**	**Host**	**Speed**	**Web**	**App**	**DBMS**	**Server**
1	0	0	0	0	0	0	0
2	0	1	1	2	3	4	5
3	0	2	2	3	4	5	6
4	0	3	3	4	5	6	1
5	0	4	4	5	6	1	2
6	0	5	5	6	1	2	3
7	0	6	6	1	2	3	4
8	1	0	1	1	1	1	1
9	1	1	3	5	2	0	6
10	1	2	5	2	0	6	4
11	1	3	2	0	6	4	3
12	1	4	0	6	4	3	5
13	1	5	6	4	3	5	2
14	1	6	4	3	5	2	0
15	2	0	2	2	2	2	2
16	2	1	5	4	6	3	0
17	2	2	4	6	3	0	1
18	2	3	6	3	0	1	5
19	2	4	3	0	1	5	4
20	2	5	0	1	5	4	6
21	2	6	1	5	4	6	3

				Factor			
Test	Browser	Host	Speed	Web	App	DBMS	Server
22	3	0	3	3	3	3	3
23	3	1	2	6	5	1	4
24	3	2	6	5	1	4	0
25	3	3	5	1	4	0	2
26	3	4	1	4	0	2	6
27	3	5	4	0	2	6	5
28	3	6	0	2	6	5	1
29	4	0	4	4	4	4	4
30	4	1	0	3	1	6	2
31	4	2	3	1	6	2	5
32	4	3	1	6	2	5	0
33	4	4	6	2	5	0	3
34	4	5	2	5	0	3	1
35	4	6	5	0	3	1	6
36	5	0	5	5	5	5	5
37	5	1	6	0	4	2	1
38	5	2	0	4	2	1	3
39	5	3	4	2	1	3	6
40	5	4	2	1	3	6	0
41	5	5	1	3	6	0	4
42	5	6	3	6	0	4	2
43	6	0	6	6	6	6	6
44	6	1	4	1	0	5	3
45	6	2	1	0	5	3	2
46	6	3	0	5	3	2	4
47	6	4	5	3	2	4	1
48	6	5	3	2	4	1	0
49	6	6	2	4	1	0	5

To build Table 18-8, I mapped the options in each column using search-and-replace. For those numbers in the columns that do not correspond to any option, I used the tilde ~ to represent "tester's choice" in terms of which option to select.

Table 18-8 Using an Orthogonal Array, Fourth Step

				Factor			
Test	**Browser**	**Host**	**Speed**	**Web**	**App**	**DBMS**	**Server**
1	A	A	A	A	A	A	A
2	A	B	B	C	D	E	~
3	A	C	C	~	E	~	~
4	A	~	~	~	~	~	B
5	A	~	~	~	~	B	C
6	A	~	~	~	B	C	D
7	A	~	~	B	C	D	~
8	B	A	B	B	B	B	B
9	B	B	~	~	C	A	~
10	B	C	~	C	A	~	~
11	B	~	C	A	~	E	D
12	B	~	A	~	E	D	~
13	B	~	~	~	D	~	C
14	B	~	~	~	~	C	A
15	C	A	C	C	C	C	C
16	C	B	~	~	~	D	A
17	C	C	~	~	D	A	B
18	C	~	~	~	A	B	~
19	C	~	~	A	B	~	~
20	C	~	A	B	~	E	~
21	C	~	B	~	E	~	D
22	~	A	~	~	D	D	D
23	~	B	C	~	~	B	~
24	~	C	~	~	B	E	A
25	~	~	~	B	E	A	C
26	~	~	B	~	A	C	~

			Factor				
Test	Browser	Host	Speed	Web	App	DBMS	Server
27	~	~	~	A	C	~	~
28	~	~	A	C	~	~	B
29	~	A	~	~	E	E	~
30	~	B	A	~	B	~	C
31	~	C	~	B	~	C	~
32	~	~	B	~	C	~	A
33	~	~	~	C	~	A	D
34	~	~	C	~	A	D	B
35	~	~	~	A	D	B	~
36	~	A	~	~	~	~	~
37	~	B	~	A	E	C	B
38	~	C	A	~	C	B	D
39	~	~	~	C	B	D	~
40	~	~	C	B	D	~	A
41	~	~	B	~	~	A	~
42	~	~	~	~	A	E	C
43	~	A	~	~	~	~	~
44	~	B	~	B	A	~	D
45	~	C	B	A	~	D	C
46	~	~	A	~	D	C	~
47	~	~	~	~	C	E	B
48	~	~	~	C	E	B	A
49	~	~	C	~	B	A	~

Now comes the hard part. Since this orthogonal array was "too big" in terms of options and rows, I have lots of extra test rows. I'd like to drop extra rows with no interesting singletons or pairs. This can often be done by combining rows where "tester's choice" values allow us to merge the rows. Notice that the test cases get new numbers as shown in the second column of Table 18-9.

Table 18-9 Using an Orthogonal Array, Fifth Step

Old Test	Test	Factor Browser	Host	Speed	Web	App	DBMS	Server	Comments
1	1	A	A	A	A	A	A	A	
2	2	A	B	B	C	D	E	**B**	
3	3	**A**	C	C	~	E	**B**	**C**	
4		A	~	~	~	~	~	B	*Move (A,B) up to test 2.*
5		A	~	~	~	~	B	C	*Move (A,B,C) up to test 3.*
6	4	A	~	~	~	B	C	D	
7	5	A	~	~	B	C	D	~	
8	6	B	A	B	B	B	B	B	
9	7	B	B	~	~	C	A	~	
10	8	B	C	~	C	A	**C**	**A**	
11	9	B	~	C	A	~	E	D	
12	10	B	~	A	~	E	D	~	
13	11	B	~	**A**	~	D	**C**	C	
14		B	~	~	~	~	C	A	*Move (B, C, A) up to test 8.*
15	12	C	A	C	C	C	C	C	
16	13	C	B	~	**A**	**C**	D	A	
17	14	C	C	**A**	**C**	D	A	B	
18	15	C	~	~	~	A	B	~	
19	16	C	~	**C**	A	B	**A**	~	
20	17	C	~	A	B	~	E	~	
21	18	C	~	B	~	E	~	D	
22	19	~	A	~	~	D	D	D	
23	20	~	B	C	~	~	B	~	
24	21	~	C	~	~	B	E	A	
25	22	~	~	**B**	B	E	A	C	

		Factor							
Old Test	**Test**	**Browser**	**Host**	**Speed**	**Web**	**App**	**DBMS**	**Server**	**Comments**
26	23	~	~	B	~	A	C	~	
27		~	~	~	A	C	~	~	*Move (A,C) up to test 13.*
28		~	~	A	C	~	~	B	*(Move A,C) up to test 14 (match B).*
29	24	~	A	~	~	E	E	~	
30	25	~	B	A	~	B	~	C	
31	26	~	C	~	B	~	C	~	
32	27	~	~	B	~	C	~	A	
33	28	~	~	~	C	~	A	D	
34	29	~	~	C	~	A	D	B	
35	30	~	~	~	A	D	B	~	
36		~	A	~	~	~	~	~	*Delete — no pairs here.*
37	31	~	B	~	A	E	C	B	
38	32	~	C	A	~	C	B	D	
39	33	~	~	~	C	B	D	~	
40	34	~	~	C	B	D	~	A	
41		~	~	B	~	~	A	~	*Move (B) up to test 22 (match A).*
42	35	~	~	~	~	A	E	C	
43		~	A	~	~	~	~	~	*Delete — no pairs here.*
44	36	~	B	~	B	A	~	D	
45	37	~	C	B	A	~	D	C	

Continued

Table 18-9 *(continued)*

		Factor							
Old Test	**Test**	**Browser**	**Host**	**Speed**	**Web**	**App**	**DBMS**	**Server**	**Comments**
46		~	~	A	~	D	C	~	*Move (A,C), up to test 11 (match D).*
47	**38**	~	~	~	~	C	E	B	
48	**39**	~	~	~	C	E	B	A	
49		~	~	C	~	B	A	~	*Move (C,A) up to test 16 (match B).*

And here's the final orthogonal array, in Table 18-10. Notice that I managed to shrink the array to 39 rows, which is a 20 percent reduction. Might there be more shrinking you could do? Sure, it's possible. The question is how much work you want to put into trying to squeeze it. The longer each test takes to set up and run, the more sense it makes to invest more time up front trying to shrink the array.

Table 18-10 Final Orthogonal Array

	Factor						
Test	**Browser**	**Host**	**Speed**	**Web**	**App**	**DBMS**	**Server**
1	A	A	A	A	A	A	A
2	A	B	B	C	D	E	**B**
3	A	C	C	~	E	**B**	**C**
4	A	~	~	~	B	C	D
5	A	~	~	B	C	D	~
6	B	A	B	B	B	B	B
7	B	B	~	~	C	A	~
8	B	C	~	C	A	**C**	**A**
9	B	~	C	A	~	E	D
10	B	~	A	~	E	D	~
11	B	~	**A**	~	D	**C**	C

	Factor						
Test	Browser	Host	Speed	Web	App	DBMS	Server
12	C	A	C	C	C	C	C
13	C	B	~	**A**	**C**	D	A
14	C	C	**A**	**C**	D	A	B
15	C	~	~	~	A	B	~
16	C	~	**C**	A	B	**A**	~
17	C	~	A	B	~	E	~
18	C	~	B	~	E	~	D
19	~	A	~	~	D	D	D
20	~	B	C	~	~	B	~
21	~	C	~	~	B	E	A
22	~	~	**B**	B	E	A	C
23	~	~	B	~	A	C	~
24	~	A	~	~	E	E	~
25	~	B	A	~	B	~	C
26	~	C	~	B	~	C	~
27	~	~	B	~	C	~	A
28	~	~	~	C	~	A	D
29	~	~	C	~	A	D	B
30	~	~	~	A	D	B	~
31	~	B	~	A	E	C	B
32	~	C	A	~	C	B	D
33	~	~	~	C	B	D	~
34	~	~	C	B	D	~	A
35	~	~	~	~	A	E	C
36	~	B	~	B	A	~	D
37	~	C	B	A	~	D	C
38	~	~	~	~	C	E	B
39	~	~	~	C	E	B	A

At runtime, you can fill in any remaining spare cells (those with tildes ~) with easy tests, popular configurations, or options that are likely to reveal bugs. In fact, whatever criteria you want to use to pick these is fine.

All-Pairs Tables

The orthogonal arrays technique is simple, but finding the right orthogonal array can be a challenge. Further, there is the issue that you tend to end up with a larger set of tests than you really wanted, as in the preceding example. All-pairs tables are a simpler and often more compact alternative and can be prepared by downloading a freeware tool such as the one referenced earlier. I used that tool to create the all-pairs table in Table 18-11 to solve the same problem I solved earlier with the orthogonal array. Notice that this table has only 30 rows, a savings of an additional 20 percent or so over the improved 39-row orthogonal array compared to the original 49-row array.

Table 18-11   An All-Pairs Solution

Test	Browser	Host	Speed	Web	App	DBMS	Server	Pairings
1	A	A	A	A	A	A	A	21
2	B	B	B	B	A	B	B	21
3	C	C	C	C	A	C	C	21
4	B	C	A	C	B	A	B	18
5	C	B	C	A	B	B	A	18
6	A	A	A	B	B	C	D	17
7	C	A	B	B	C	A	C	17
8	A	B	A	C	C	B	D	16
9	B	C	B	A	C	C	A	16
10	A	C	C	B	D	D	B	17
11	B	A	B	C	D	E	C	15
12	C	B	B	A	D	D	D	12
13	B	B	A	A	E	D	C	12
14	C	A	C	A	E	E	B	13
15	B	C	C	B	E	E	D	10
16	A	B	B	C	E	A	A	8

Test	Browser	Host	Speed	Web	App	DBMS	Server	Pairings
17	C	B	A	B	B	E	A	6
18	A	A	B	C	B	D	C	6
19	~A	~B	C	~A	C	A	B	3
20	~C	C	A	~C	D	B	A	4
21	~A	A	~C	~A	A	B	C	2
22	~C	B	~B	~C	A	C	B	2
23	~B	~A	~C	~B	A	D	A	2
24	A	~C	~B	~A	A	E	D	3
25	~C	~A	~C	~C	C	D	~D	1
26	~A	~C	~A	~B	C	E	~C	1
27	~B	~B	~C	~B	D	A	D	2
28	~A	~A	~A	~A	D	C	~B	1
29	~C	~C	~B	~B	E	B	~C	1
30	~B	~A	~C	~C	E	C	~A	1

Other Thoughts on Configuration Testing

Obviously, orthogonal arrays and all-pairs tests are very useful for configuration and compatibility testing. In addition, here are some other ideas.

Pick the key configuration options for each factor. Identify the options that you really care about. Consider customer usage, the likelihood and impact of failures of those options, each option's test availability and costs, and the long-term usefulness of each option in the test lab. Balance the total number of options you intend to cover against the risks posed by other test areas. If you try to cover too many configurations, you'll end up without enough time, money, or people to test other important quality risks.

Use "tester's choice" options — the tildes ~ in the orthogonal array or all-pairs tables — to try to increase the number of interesting triples, quadruples, and other higher-order combinations that you cover. Change the lab configuration in terms of the "tester's choices" selected frequently to increase your chances of happening upon a bug that somehow is related to triples, quadruples, and so on.

If you're still concerned about triples, quadruples, and so forth, plan your beta or field test to cover as wide a sample of configurations as possible, especially those that you can't cover in the test lab. Of course, the added complexity of outsourcing test work to nonprofessional testers will make isolating bugs challenging. However, you'll get a chance to obtain some coverage that is otherwise impossible in the test lab.

CHAPTER 19

Orthogonal Arrays Exercise

Let's apply the orthogonal array test technique to the Omninet project. Suppose you need to test compatibility of various kiosk configurations. According to the Omninet System Requirements Document, we intend to support kiosks running configurations based on three major factors, each set to one of the options shown:

- Operating System: Windows XP or Linux
- Browser: Internet Explorer (Windows only), Netscape, or Opera
- Connection: DSL, dial-up, or cable

The next few pages show orthogonal arrays you might use to test this. The exercise consists of four steps.

1. Select the appropriate array from Table 19-1, Table 19-2, and Table 19-3.
2. Map the factors (OS, browser, and connection) on to the column headings.
3. Map the options within each factor into the array cells.
4. Handle rows with spare cells and pairs that represent impossible configuration combinations.

Of these, you've seen how to handle steps 1 through 3. Step 4 will be clear if you keep in mind the rules about handling rows and tester's choice (tilde ~) cells. I suggest 30 minutes as a time limit. When you're done, keep reading to see my solution.

Table 19-1 Orthogonal Array 1

	Factors		
Test	1	2	3
1	0	0	0
2	0	1	1
3	1	0	1
4	1	1	0

Table 19-2 Orthogonal Array 2

	Factors			
Test	1	2	3	4
1	0	0	0	0
2	0	1	1	2
3	0	2	2	1
4	1	0	1	1
5	1	1	2	0
6	1	2	0	2
7	2	0	2	2
8	2	1	0	1
9	2	2	1	0

Table 19-3 Orthogonal Array 3

	Factors				
Test	1	2	3	4	5
1	0	0	0	0	0
2	0	1	1	1	1
3	0	2	2	2	2
4	0	3	3	3	3
5	1	0	1	2	3
6	1	1	0	3	2

Test	Factors 1	2	3	4	5
7	1	2	3	0	1
8	1	3	2	1	0
9	2	0	2	3	1
10	2	1	3	2	0
11	2	2	0	1	3
12	2	3	1	0	2
13	3	0	3	1	2
14	3	1	2	0	3
15	3	2	1	3	0
16	3	3	0	2	1

My Solution and Comments

I selected the second array, shown in Table 19-4. It has one extra column, which I deleted from the table. It has exactly the right number of options in two of the three columns, with an extra option in one of the columns. It has exactly the right number of rows. I could use the third array, too, but it would be too big and would result in a lot of painful shrinking work at the last step. Since this has the exact number of rows I need, no shrinking is possible or required.

Table 19-4   Selected Orthogonal Array

Test	Factors 1	2	3
1	0	0	0
2	0	1	1
3	0	2	2
4	1	0	1
5	1	1	2
6	1	2	0

Continued

Table 19-4 *(continued)*

	Factors		
Test	*1*	*2*	*3*
7	2	0	2
8	2	1	0
9	2	2	1

Now I mapped the factors on to the column headings, as shown in Table 19-5.

Table 19-5 Orthogonal Array with Factors Mapped

	Factors		
Test	*Operating System*	*Connection Speed*	*Browser*
1	0	0	0
2	0	1	1
3	0	2	2
4	1	0	1
5	1	1	2
6	1	2	0
7	2	0	2
8	2	1	0
9	2	2	1

Since the left-side column of an orthogonal array tends to change the most slowly, put the factor that is hardest to change there. The operating system is the hardest to change because it requires a reinstall if I want to change it on a lab system. I'll probably configure a system with either Linux or Windows XP and leave it that way unless severe hardware shortages require me to swap configurations.

Next, I mapped the options within each factor into the array cells, as seen in Table 19-6. For ease of reference, I left the old numbers there, crossed out. I replace unused numbers with tilde ~ to represent tester's choice.

Table 19-6   Orthogonal Array with Options Mapped

	Factors		
Test	Operating System	Connection Speed	Browser
1	0 Windows XP	0 Dial-up	0 Internet Explorer
2	0 Windows XP	+ DSL	+ Netscape
3	0 Windows XP	2 Cable	2 Opera
4	+ Linux	0 Dial-up	+ Netscape
5	+ Linux	+ DSL	2 Opera
6	+ Linux	2 Cable	0 Internet Explorer
7	2 ~	0 Dial-up	2 Opera
8	2 ~	+ DSL	0 Internet Explorer
9	2 ~	2 Cable	+ Netscape

Finally, I have to do something we haven't discussed before. Notice that row six contains an impossible pairing of Linux with Internet Explorer. That pairing is inevitable in at least one row, regardless of which order you map the columns, since you're guaranteed to get all possible pairs of options across all possible pairs of factors. How do we deal with this?

Remember, you can't simply delete a row. In this case, row six contains two important pairs. One is Linux with cable. The other is cable with Internet Explorer.

The general solution is to add one or more rows where those pairings you want to preserve are kept and those pairings that are disallowed are not represented. After doing so, you fix the original row to eliminate the disallowed pairings.

However, in this case, the tester's choice option in row nine makes it possible to handle the problem without adding any rows, as shown in Table 19-7. Notice that row eight does not actually have a tester's choice option since the browser constrains the operating system.

Table 19-7 Orthogonal array with Impossible Configurations Resolved

	Factors		
Test	*Operating System*	*Connection Speed*	*Browser*
1	0 Windows XP	0 Dial-up	0 Internet Explorer
2	0 Windows XP	+ DSL	+ Netscape
3	0 Windows XP	2 Cable	2 Opera
4	+ Linux	0 Dial-up	+ Netscape
5	+ Linux	+ DSL	2 Opera
6	+ ~~Linux~~ Windows XP	2 Cable	0 Internet Explorer
7	2 ~	0 Dial-up	2 Opera
8	2 ~ Windows XP	+ DSL	0 Internet Explorer
9	2 ~ Linux	2 Cable	+ Netscape

If you prefer to use an all-pairs tool, you will have the same challenge. However, the only step you'll have to do manually will be the last one, resolving the "impossible configurations" rows. A similar approach will work for an all-pairs table generated with an all-pairs tool.

Reactive Testing

In this last chapter on behavioral or black-box test design, I'll cover an approach to test design that focuses on reacting to what happens during test execution. These techniques are typically employed as part of what I described in an earlier chapter as a dynamic test strategy.

To me, reactive tests are particularly interesting to address the inevitable gaps in my carefully designed, prewritten tests. Any one approach to testing won't reveal all bugs. It's important to have a blended approach to testing to ensure adequate risk mitigation. To fill the gaps in your predesigned tests during the test execution period, a combination of inspiration, experience (yours or others), and cunning are required.

General Facts about Reactive Tests

Reactive tests of the kind I discuss in this chapter often rely heavily on the tester's skill and intuition, experience with similar applications, and experience with similar technologies. Since you are trying to fill gaps that appear (or at least can be found) during the test execution, the tests I describe are not pre-designed to a great level of detail. Instead, the specifics of these tests are created during test execution. As I wrote in an earlier chapter, the test strategy for such tests is dynamic. The test cases themselves can be described as reactive, since to a great extent testers create the test details on-the-fly in reaction to the reality presented by the system under test.

Now, while the testers create the specifics during test execution, most professional approaches to running reactive test cases do not entirely forego any structure or advanced preparation. Often, the test manager and test engineers put a framework in place for the tests, giving a general idea of the areas they will test and the conditions they will cover. In creating this framework, they may be guided by bug taxonomies, by a list of common system weaknesses or past successful attacks, by a bug hunting method, by a set of test charters, by checklists, and by other sources of inspiration. The test manager and the test engineers typically prepare this framework in advance to some level of detail.[1]

When such open-ended and imprecisely described tests are run, two key challenges relate to managing the effort and time required and keeping track of coverage. To handle the first challenge, many practitioners run these reactive tests in a "time-boxed" fashion. The size of the time box depends on factors like the risks associated with the test conditions to be covered, the complexity of the area tested, the time required to carry out a typical use case, and so on. To handle the second challenge, high-level descriptions of the test cases, sometimes called test charters, are used to track what was covered. For example, the test manager might allocate 90 minutes to test the check printing function of a personal finance application. In this case, "test check printing" is the charter and the time box is 90 minutes. The tester will spend 90 minutes testing the check printing function and will exceed that time box only if her testing reveals an unexpected number of bugs.

In the next few sections, let's examine some specific approaches to reactive testing. After that, I'll make some observations on the general advantages and disadvantages of reactive tests. I'll close this chapter with a case study of reactive testing in action.

Error Guessing, Attacks, and Bug Taxonomies

Error guessing is the name that Glenford Myers gave, years ago, to inspirational testing.[2] You have a list — written or unwritten — of errors you expect or suspect. You look for errors in the system based on this list. The approach you use may be standardized if the list remains relatively constant from one system to another. However, error guessing can also take a more dynamic form. For example, experienced users may sit down in front of a system and, knowing what aspects of the business problem are complex, attack those areas first.

---

[1] That said, purely on-the-fly testing by unqualified individuals with no clear strategy or framework is quite common. You will hear some test professionals, myself included, refer to this as ad hoc testing, typically in a derisive way. That derision is well deserved, because an unqualified person banging away at a keyboard with no framework before, no insight or oracle during, and no documented results after their testing is doing simply manual random testing of the most ineffective form.

[2] See Myers's *The Art of Software Testing*, Chapter 4.

James Whittaker's concept of attacks exemplifies an attempt to systematize the error-guessing approach.[3] The central idea is that you identify ways in which software typically fails and then generalize the failures (the bugs) into high-level procedures (i.e., rules of thumb for designing and running tests) that will often locate these failures. For example, one attack is to overflow input buffers. This often results in a failure because not all programmers are meticulous about checking the size of inputs.

You might notice something interesting about this example: You could design a buffer overflow test from knowledge that programs often fail when confronted by excessively large input. However, you could also design such a test based on equivalence partitioning and boundary value analysis (as I mentioned in an earlier chapter). In fact, you'll see in a later chapter that you could also design a buffer overflow test based on branch and condition coverage, a structural or white-box technique (at least if the code cooperates). It is a general rule that many test techniques lead to similar tests.

A standard list of attacks is helpful, but you might want to develop your own list of attacks to augment such a standard list. To do so, you can start with a bug taxonomy. This is a classification of bugs from which your system tends to suffer. You would then figure out a general, high-level procedure for locating each type of bug in the list. If you create your bug taxonomy from a database (or databases) of bugs reported during testing and after release, the steps to reproduce the bug from the bug report are the starting point of developing this procedure.[4]

Bug Hunting

I mentioned in an earlier chapter on test strategies that one key to hunting and fishing is to hunt where the birds are and fish where the fish are. The fanciest shotgun in the wrong meadow does you no good, while even a primitive-style muzzle-loading shotgun in a field teaming with quail can lead to an exciting and successful outing.

---

[3] See Whittaker's book *How to Break Software* for his complete list of functional testing attacks and his book, with Herbert Thompson, *How to Break Software Security* for a variation of these attacks focused on finding security bugs.

[4] To see an example of a bug taxonomy, check out Boris Beizer's *Software Testing Techniques*. For a case study on applying the taxonomy technique to creating specific tests or attacks for e-commerce software, see Giri Vijayaraghavan and Cem Kaner's presentation, "Bugs in Your Shopping Cart," www.kaner.com/pdfs/giri2002qw.pdf.

A bug hunt, like a bird hunt, involves a cunning search for bugs. Like a hunter or a fisherman, you examine clues and follow them to the bugs. If you're good, you often find bugs while searching for other bugs, leading to more and new searches. This dynamic approach is evolving all the time, reacting to the behavior of the system under test as you observe it.[5]

Okay, so where do you find the clues and how do you follow them? The way I and others often do this is by combining classical test design techniques like equivalence partitioning; other reactive techniques like attacks and bug taxonomies; knowledge or educated guesses of the internal structure of the system under test; knowledge or educated guesses of the users, operators, and other people who will interact with the system under test; and knowledge of the developers. As with hunting, it doesn't matter so much which end of the field you start in, usually, provided that you visit all the right places as your hunt progresses.

Exploratory Tests

Its most vocal advocate, James Bach, has defined exploratory testing as "an interactive process of simultaneous learning, test design, and test execution."[6] The exploratory testing process is simple to describe but challenging to perform.

1. Learn a bit about the system by using it, reading source documents like requirements specifications, asking people how the system works, looking at past and current test results, and exploiting any other source of information you have.

2. Make an educated guess about where you might find some bugs or observe some other interesting behavior. This guess (some might call it a heuristic or bug hypothesis or theory of error) would be influenced by your own past experiences as a tester and the field performance of previous, similar products.

3. Design a test to check for the presence or absence of those bugs or to observe those behaviors.

4. Run the test, observing carefully for the bugs you guessed were there, other bugs that might also be there, and the various behaviors the system exhibits.

---

[5] Examples of this technique can be found in Elisabeth Hendrickson's courses "Bug Hunting" and "Creative Software Testing."

[6] See James Bach's website, www.satisfice.com, for this definition and more on exploratory testing.

5. Reflect on the meaning of your observations, then return to step 1 to revise your learning about the system, your guess about where other bugs might be, and your concept of what interesting behaviors might be worth seeing.

In some forms of exploratory testing, step 2 is restricted to a predetermined area of the system. This is based on what is called the test charter. Skilled testers perform these steps mostly in parallel and, sometimes, almost unconsciously.

Exploratory testing often proceeds in a sequence of testing sessions. Each session ranges in duration from an hour to two or three hours. The session must last long enough to iterate this process a few times, otherwise you'll never get fully immersed in the testing and the results and you won't make the same kind of sharp, intelligent guesses about where the bugs are as you would during a longer session.[7]

Checklists

Up to this point, all the reactive test types I've described suffer from one major flaw: They are almost entirely focused on finding bugs. While in some cases the test team's mission is to find as many bugs as possible, nothing more, the more general test team mission is to help the project team manage risk. In Chapter 6 , I mentioned that a common mistake that people make with risk-based testing is to focus exclusively on technical risk; that is, where bugs are most likely. People fall into that trap often by complete reliance on the reactive test approaches described so far in this chapter.

There are a couple ways to guard against that mistake. One way is to use reactive tests only in combination with written, predesigned tests based on a quality risk analysis that address both business and technical risk. This is the approach that I typically use, and I'll elaborate on why shortly.

Suppose, though, for whatever reason, you have chosen to use a purely reactive test set. Perhaps you have no time or budget for advance test planning and preparation. Perhaps you are simply checking another test group's work and you want to gain some confidence in what they have done. Perhaps what you planned to test was quickly proven to be inadequate when you started test execution.

In such a case, you could base your reactive tests not only on finding lots of bugs, but also on what the system needs to do or what it would mean for the

---

[7] See also Cem Kaner, James Bach, and Bret Pettichord's book *Lessons Learned in Software Testing*.

system to have quality. For example, consider the ISO 9126 standard of quality characteristics and subcharacteristics (mentioned in an earlier chapter):

- Functionality
  - Suitability
  - Accuracy
  - Interoperability
  - Compliance
  - Security
- Reliability
  - Maturity
  - Recoverability
  - Fault Tolerance
- Usability
  - Learnability
  - Understandability
  - Operability
- Efficiency
  - Time Behavior
  - Resource Behavior
- Maintainability
  - Stability
  - Analyzability
  - Changeability
  - Testability
- Portability
  - Installability
  - Conformance
  - Replaceability
  - Adaptability

To use this as a testing checklist, you could go through this hierarchy and identify those subcharacteristics that apply to your system. You could then identify one or more test charters (to borrow the exploratory testing term) associated with each subcharacteristic. The number of test charters and thus the amount of effort for each subcharacteristic could be driven by a formal or informal risk analysis or simply by your sense of what was most important to stakeholders or most likely to contain bugs.[8]

Other Sources of Inspiration for Reactive Testing

I implied earlier that some people consider exploratory testing a form of risk-driven or risk-based testing. What they usually mean by this is that exploratory testing is based on tester experience and opinions about technical risk. Technical risk varies, as I mentioned in Chapter 6, based on the likelihood of a bug.

At the start of a reactive testing session, a tester might think, "The last time I tested a personal finance package, I found lots of bugs in checkbook-reconcile function, so I'll start testing there." Or, a tester might read the design specification or even run a McCabe complexity tool on the source code (see Chapter 21), then decide, "The database access subsystem is complex, so I'll start testing there."

There's no reason you can't use a quality risk analysis document as a roadmap for exploratory testing. A tester working with a formal risk analysis might have a prioritized list of possible failure modes or quality risk items. A less formal analysis, such as notes from conversations with stakeholders about what they're worried about, could work, too.

Of course, if one of the things you're trying to accomplish with reactive testing is filling the gaps in your predesigned tests, you might use the quality risk analysis in a complementary way, more like a photographic negative. What I mean is that you could say, "Okay, these are the areas we thought were *low risk* in our quality risk analysis. Therefore, we have little if any coverage in those areas. To check out the validity of our quality risk analysis, let's do some reactive testing in those areas to make sure there are not a large number of bugs or any major, important bugs hiding there." This is often an approach I use for exploratory testing.

Some testers like to use worst-case scenarios as the start of their exploratory testing sessions. A tester might try to log in all the valid accounts at once.[9] However, that's something you might wait to do until you have some number of more basic testing sessions completed. If you start with complex tests against an unstable product, it can be difficult to isolate bugs or even to complete a test session.

---

[8] James Bach and Michael Bolton's course "Rapid Software Testing" teaches a variation of this technique where a checklist that involves quality characteristics and more is used as the framework for exploratory testing.

[9] Made more complex and elaborate, such a test becomes what Hans Buwalda referred to as "soap opera testing," the construction of scenarios that force all sorts of bad things to happen to the system under test at once or in a sequence.

Advantages and Disadvantages

Ractive testing has its supporters and detractors. I consider myself a supporter of reactive testing, but with caveats.

Here are the advantages of reactive testing done properly:

Effectiveness. I have some anecdotal evidence that reactive testing performed by skilled, experienced testers is significantly more effective at finding bugs than scripted tests run by less-experienced testers is (see the case study at the end of this chapter).

Robustness. The pesticide paradox of testing is that tests tend to lose their effectiveness over time. Tests that once found bugs stop finding bugs after a while. Something interesting about tests that are more dynamic and reactive is that, because of their natural variance over time, they tend to resist the pesticide paradox.[10] In addition, since the tests grow from observations of actual system behavior, reactive testing is effective even under conditions of poor system documentation and severe time pressure.

Efficiency. Due to the limited paperwork, reactive testing is cheaper when measured in terms of cost per bug found as well as being easier to maintain.

Safety. Reactive testing is a useful way to find and fill gaps in your written tests. Any process has holes, including even the best processes for creating written tests; so reactive testing gives you a chance to find those gaps before release.

Creativity. Reactive testing is a fun and innovative experience and can provide a productive break from running scripted manual tests, which can be drudgery when those scripts are not finding bugs.

Here are some disadvantages of reactive testing:

Coverage gaps. Most people miss major areas of testing if they follow a purely reactive testing approach. People can easily become stuck in a rut, testing similar areas or in similar ways.

Missing oracle. With predesigned tests, there is typically a defined expected result or some other way of determining whether the test passed. In some cases with reactive testing, the only test oracle is the judgment of the tester during test execution. The possibility of mistaken interpretation of results is high, and these mistakes lead to false positives (bad bug reports) and false negatives (test escapes to the field).

---

[10] For more on the pesticide paradox, see Boris Beizer's *Software Testing Techniques* or my own forthcoming book, coauthored with Isabel Evans, Dorothy Graham, and Erik van Veenendaal, titled *Foundations of Software Testing*.

Estimation problems. It's difficult to estimate the amount of testing needed without up-front analysis. Test estimation is hard enough without the added complication of not being able to guess during the project-planning period how many test cases you'll need.[11]

No prevention. Reactive testing is a good, cheap way to find bugs, but it's better and cheaper to prevent bugs. Reactive testing involves simultaneous test planning, design, and execution and so does not create opportunities to find bugs prior to code being written.

Nonscalable, nondistributable. Many test management approaches for reactive testing involve debriefing each tester at the end of each testing session. That approach doesn't scale up to larger teams and is challenging if not impossible when some or all of the test team is strewn across the globe, as happens so often with offshore outsourcing.

Limited expertise. Perhaps most importantly, a good reactive tester must have significant ability to analyze the system and design tests on-the-fly. This means significant testing, technical, and application domain skills. Not all testers have the necessary level of skill and experience, and when these testers become involved in reactive testing, the result is a toxic mishmash of bad bug reports, false confidence, and frustration.

Limited repeatability. Unless the detail notes are taken during testing — which can reduce the efficiency allure of reactive techniques — it is often difficult to repeat a test precisely after it is run.

Limited visibility and manageability. When using reactive techniques heavily, most managers and project teams find it difficult to track the testing done so far, manage the remaining testing work to be done, and measure progress toward precisely defined test exit criteria. Some techniques, like session-based exploratory testing, exist to address these problems, but they are not widely practiced.

Now, some of these disadvantages are manageable or preventable. For example, given a sufficiently skilled test team, there are no disadvantages associated with limited expertise. However, the difficulties of estimation remain, and lacking a time machine, there is simply no way for reactive tests to prevent bugs.

To obtain the advantages while minimizing the disadvantages, I typically allocate between 10 and 20 percent of the test execution effort to reactive forms of testing. The bulk of the test execution effort is reserved for testing that follows written test cases.

---

[11] Test management issues are, for the most part, outside the scope of this book, but I cover the topic of test estimation in depth in *Critical Testing Processes*.

As I have mentioned before, these written tests often leave a fair amount to the discretion of the tester. My directive to a tester is typically, "A written test case is a road map to interesting places, and when you get someplace interesting, stop and look around." This embeds a significant amount of reactive testing into the written test cases themselves. Therefore, I consider my approach to testing one that blends the advantages of proactive and reactive testing without suffering from the disadvantages of either.

A Case Study of Exploratory Testing

In an Internet appliance project that I managed, our team consisted of a mixture of test technicians and test engineers. The technicians had less experience with testing than the engineers, though we hired people we thought had a natural bent for the testing task. The test engineers were true professional testers.

During the test execution period, the technicians followed precise test cases, albeit with the directive to vary their testing within the script and to explore interesting behaviors they came across. The technicians showed varying levels of ability and inclination to react intelligently while running written test cases. The test engineers, having written the test cases during the test preparation period (based on an informal risk analysis), supported the technicians while running the tests, answering questions, debriefing them on test results, updating tests where the cases were wrong or the behavior of the system had changed, and so forth.

I was concerned, though, because the most-skilled and most-experienced testers on the team would not do any test execution. To counter that, I instructed the test engineers (and myself) to spend one or two hours per day doing exploratory testing. The framework of the exploratory testing was simple: Complement the scripted testing being done; focus on finding bugs we might otherwise miss. Table 20-1 shows a comparison of the reactive testing against the predesigned testing. The effectiveness metric is computed by dividing the number of bugs found by the test hours per day.

Table 20-1 Analysis of the Bug-Finding Effectiveness of Reactive Testing

Staff	7 Technicians	3 Engineers + 1 Manager
Experience	<10 years total	> 20 years total
Test Type	Precise scripts	Complimentary exploratory
Test Hours per Day	42	6
Bugs Found (% of Total)	928 (78%)	261 (22%)
Effectiveness	22	44

This case study showed that, on this project, the exploratory testing was about twice as effective at finding bugs on an hour-per-hour basis. It was also significantly more efficient, because the scripted tests required extensive effort to create and maintain while the exploratory tests had no such overhead.

Given that, you might say that my overall approach of blending scripted and exploratory testing was a mistake — and some probably would say that. You might say, "You should have simply foregone the test scripts and had the test technicians and the test engineers spend all their time doing exploratory testing." That's a fair criticism, but one that misses important points that I raised in the previous section and would like to reinforce here.

First, a high level of skill, discipline, and experience is critical to do any form of reactive testing effectively. I have seen people who were not skilled testers waste phenomenal amounts of time on exploratory testing, yielding few if any real bugs and establishing no confidence in the system by their testing.[12] I have every reason to believe, based on the limited ability of some of the technicians to exercise effectively the exploratory discretion they already had in the test scripts, that collectively the technicians would almost certainly have done more harm than good without the scripts.

"But the technicians *did* do more harm than good," you might say at this juncture, "because they clearly distracted the test engineers who otherwise would have been finding more bugs." That brings up the second point, though, which is that the value of testing goes beyond finding bugs. The scripted tests covered a large number of risk areas. Simply because those areas turned out to be sparser in terms of bugs doesn't mean they weren't worth testing. A test case that passes is still a valuable test case because you know something you didn't know before and, if the test case is connected to an important quality risk, the overall level of risk is reduced.

This is connected to the third point. Through traceability, we knew what our scripted tests covered. We could inspect them, down to the test condition level. In fact, the test engineers frequently debriefed the test technicians to make sure they had properly tested the test conditions in each test case they ran. (And, in fact, those test technicians gradually became skilled testers through the guidance of the well-defined processes and test cases along with the coaching of their more-skilled colleagues.) But what did the exploratory tests cover? Well, where the exploratory tests revealed important bugs, we often added written test cases to our test set. These test cases not only covered the bugs found, they were based on a general analysis of what we had missed that we should have covered to begin with. However, those exploratory tests that did not reveal bugs had no documented coverage. As I mentioned earlier, it is possible

---

[12] In fact, my negative comments about exploratory testing in the first edition of *Managing the Testing Process* grew out of my reaction to most of the exploratory testing I had seen up to that point, which was of this unproductive variety.

through test charters to address this issue somewhat, but the fact remains that there's not much of a detailed coverage record associated with a test charter.[13]

As a final point, note that there is some value to the test scripts themselves. During the period immediately before release, my two most senior test technicians — who were more like test engineers after their experience on this project — guided the technical support staff through all of our test cases and all of the known bugs. The test cases helped the technical support team know what had been tested so they could recognize user error when someone called with a problem in a known-good feature. Furthermore, after the release, some of the test team, myself and most of the test engineers included, went off to do other things. The test cases became a useful tool to ramp up the new test technicians and engineers who came on board. These test cases were also useful to the test automation effort that was launched during the maintenance period.

Reflecting back on this project and other projects where I have — and have not — used forms of reactive testing wisely, I am now aware of its strengths and its weaknesses. As a test manager or test engineer, I would encourage you to use reactive testing as part of your test approach. In some cases, you may find that it makes sense as a primary or even a sole technique. However, the more general case is that some blend of reactive and proactive, predesigned tests will work best and that the degree to which the predesigned tests contain reactive elements (i.e., the "test case as a road map to interesting places to explore" directive) will vary depending on the test team.

---

[13] Of course, the details of a test charter can vary. I've used test charters as short as two or three words. Michael Bolton, when reviewing this chapter, mentioned that his test charters are more like two or three sentences. The extent of documentation you gather on test coverage and traceability will give you and others insight into what has been covered. How much documentation you need depends on the project. Some exploratory testers, like Bolton, Jon Bach, and others, use a technique called session-based test management to capture detailed coverage information for exploratory tests. Again, more information on session-based test management can be found at www.satisfice.com.

PART

V

Structural Testing

In this Part

Control-Flow Testing

In this chapter, I cover some basics related to white-box testing of the control-flows in units. By control flows in units, I mean the sequence of execution of statements. In many cases, one statement follows the previous statement. However, in some cases the sequencing of statements is determined by decisions. Some of these decisions are made in branches like *if* statements and *switch* statements. Some of these decisions are made in loops like *for* statements and *while* statements and function calls.

Control-flow-based white-box testing is the cheapest way to find many types of coding bugs because many bugs are errors in control flows that exist entirely within a line or a few lines of a unit. Why wait until you have a "needle in a haystack" situation, where bugs lurk among millions of lines of code during system test? Early white-box unit testing by programmers can greatly increase the quality of the system and reduce the costs of poor quality later in the project.

If you are a tester, you might not find this section applicable to your daily work. However, I encourage you to skim this chapter and Chapter 23, on data-flow-based white-box testing. A basic familiarity with good unit testing practices can help you have an intelligent conversation with your programmer colleagues and assess the unit test coverage.

If you are a programmer, you'll find this chapter and the next two chapters helpful. The example programs run on either Windows or Linux systems or both, so you can get some hands-on, computer-based experience.

White-box tests are based on how the system works internally. To build them, you can examine the code to find the control flows through each unit.

You can also examine the code and data structures to find the data flows through each unit or between units. You can also look at application program interfaces, class member functions, or class methods to find how a component, library, or object interfaces with the rest of the system. This and the next couple of chapters look at these topics in more detail.

Code Coverage

Code-based or control-flow-based tests are often designed to achieve a particular level of code coverage. There are seven major ways to measure code coverage:

Statement coverage. You have achieved 100 percent statement coverage when you have executed every statement.

Branch (or decision) coverage. You have achieved 100 percent branch coverage when you have taken every branch (or decision) each way. For *if* statements, you'll need to make sure the expression that controls the branching evaluates both true and false. For *switch/case* statements, you'll need to cover each specified case as well as at least one unspecified case or the default case.

Condition coverage. Some branching decisions in programs are made not based on a single condition but on multiple conditions. You have achieved 100 percent condition coverage when you have evaluated behavior with each of these conditions both true and false. For example, if the conditional expression controlling an *if* statement is (A>0) && (B<0), then you need test both (A>0) true and false and (B<0) true and false. This can be done in two tests: true && true and false && false.

Multicondition coverage. When compound conditions apply to branching, you can move beyond condition coverage to multicondition coverage by requiring testing all possible combination of conditions. To continue our example in which the conditional expression controlling an *if* statement is (A>0) && (B<0), then you need to test all four possible combinations: true && true, true && false, false && true, and false && false.

Multicondition decision coverage. For languages like C++ where the subsequent conditions might not be evaluated depending on the preceding conditions, 100% condition coverage doesn't always make sense. In this case, you cover the conditions that can affect the decision made in terms of control flow. To finish our example in which the conditional expression controlling an *if* statement is (A>0) && (B<0), then you can test three combinations: true && true, true && false, and false && true. The extra combination, false && false, is now unneeded because the second condition cannot influence the decision.

Loop coverage. For loop paths, you must also iterate each loop zero, once, and multiple times. Ideally, you'll iterate the loop the maximum possible number of times. Sometimes it's possible to predict the maximum number of times a loop will iterate; sometimes it is not possible.

Path coverage. You have achieved 100 percent path coverage when you have taken all possible control paths. For functions with loops, path coverage is very difficult.

To some extent, you can rank these in order of increasing levels of coverage. If you achieved path coverage, you are guaranteed to have achieved loop, branch, and statement coverage (but not vice versa). If you achieved branch coverage, you are guaranteed to have achieved statement coverage (but not vice versa). If you achieved multicondition coverage, you are guaranteed to have achieved multicondition decision and condition coverage (but not vice versa). Notice that path coverage does not guarantee multicondition coverage, nor does multicondition coverage guarantee path coverage.

Let's look at an example. In Listing 21-1, you see a simple C program that runs on a Windows or Linux system. This program accepts an integer input and prints the factorial of that integer.

```
1.   main()
2.   {
3.       int i, n, f;
4.       printf("n = ");
5.       scanf("%d", &n);
6.       if (n < 0) {
7           printf("Invalid: %d\n", n);
8.           n = -1;
9.       } else {
10.          f = 1;
11.          for (i = 1; i <= n; i++) {
12.            f *= i;
13.          }
14.          printf("%d! = %d.\n", n, f);
15.      }
16.      return n;
17. }
```

Listing 21-1 A program calculating factorials

What test values for *n* do you need to cover all the statements? Two values for *n* will work: *n* less than 0 and *n* greater than 0. Do those two values get you branch coverage? No, you also need to test *n* equal to zero to cover the "never iterate the loop" branch. Do those three values get you condition coverage? Yes, in this case, as there are no compound conditions in the program. How about loop coverage? Well, not quite. You need to cover *n* equal 1 and *n* equal to whatever the maximum number of iterations would be.

If you have access to a Windows or Linux system, give it a try.

What value for *n* did you use to achieve loop coverage? What happened to the factorial at the maximum value?

Here's what happened on my Windows 2000 system:

```
n = 12
12! = 479001600.
n = 13
13! = 1932053504.
```

However, the real answer for 13! is 6,227,020,800.

Is that a bug? If you understand how computers store integers, you can certainly see how the integer value of *f* would overflow eventually. However, there are other Windows applications, including the bundled calculator that comes with Windows, that can handle larger integers. And a routine for calculating factorials that only calculates the first 12 factorials isn't good for much.

This example illustrates one danger of white-box testing. I did not specify the expected results in advance. The output might appear reasonable, but is it correct? Beware of white-box unit testing without some reliable oracle that can help you determine test pass/fail status.

McCabe Cyclomatic Complexity

Another common kind of control-flow testing derives from work done by Thomas McCabe in the 1970s. McCabe created a metric called Cyclomatic Complexity, which measures program unit complexity in terms of control flows, specifically branching. You can measure Cyclomatic Complexity by drawing a directed graph to represent the unit under test. Nodes or bubbles represent entries, exits, and branching decision points. Edges or arrows represent nonbranching statements.

McCabe was trying to understand why programs are so hard to write and maintain. However, Cyclomatic Complexity has some useful testing implications. First, high-complexity modules are inherently buggy and regression prone. Second, the Cyclomatic Complexity number also tells you the number of basis paths through the graph, which is equal to the number of basis tests needed to cover the graph. McCabe basis test coverage is used as a testing-completeness standard for unit testing in some situations, including avionics software regulated by the Federal Aviation Administration.

Let's take a look at an example, using the factorial program again. In Figure 21-1, you can see how I turned the factorial program into a McCabe-style directed graph. I've used arrows to connect chunks of code with the nodes and edges that represent them.

Program   Flow Diagram   Cyclomatic Complexity

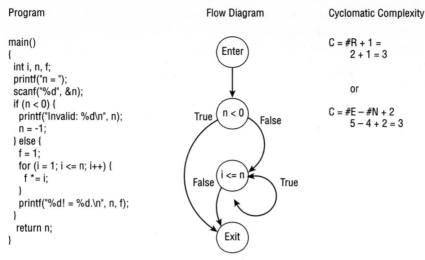

```
main()
{
  int i, n, f;
  printf("n = ");
  scanf("%d", &n);
  if (n < 0) {
    printf("Invalid: %d\n", n);
    n = -1;
  } else {
    f = 1;
    for (i = 1; i <= n; i++) {
      f *= i;
    }
    printf("%d! = %d.\n", n, f);
  }
  return n;
}
```

$C = \#R + 1 =$
$\quad 2 + 1 = 3$

or

$C = \#E - \#N + 2$
$\quad 5 - 4 + 2 = 3$

Figure 21-1: Control flow graph for factorial program

Given such a McCabe-style directed graph, you can calculate the McCabe Cyclomatic Complexity. It's the number of enclosed regions (R) in the graph plus one, or the number of edges (E) minus the number of nodes (N) plus two. For the factorial program, the Cyclomatic Complexity is 3. Since the Cyclomatic Complexity is 3, that means three basis paths, and thus three basis tests.

Figure 21-2 shows the basis paths and tests. I've lettered the nodes in the bubbles and described the basis paths in terms of the sequence of nodes traversed. You can arbitrarily pick values for n to cover the basis paths, though I used boundary value analysis.

Program   Flow Diagram   Basis Paths

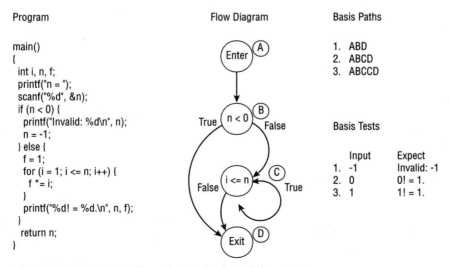

```
main()
{
  int i, n, f;
  printf("n = ");
  scanf("%d", &n);
  if (n < 0) {
    printf("Invalid: %d\n", n);
    n = -1;
  } else {
    f = 1;
    for (i = 1; i <= n; i++) {
      f *= i;
    }
    printf("%d! = %d.\n", n, f);
  }
  return n;
}
```

1. ABD
2. ABCD
3. ABCCD

Basis Tests

	Input	Expect
1.	-1	Invalid: -1
2.	0	0! = 1.
3.	1	1! = 1.

Figure 21-2: Basis paths and tests for factorial program

If you compare the basis tests against the tests I needed to achieve branch coverage earlier in this chapter, you can see that McCabe basis tests satisfy branch coverage. This makes the McCabe technique a useful one when branch coverage is a requirement. It's also a quick way to ensure that you've covered the major control flows.[1]

---

[1] For more on the McCabe technique, see the report written by Thomas McCabe and Arthur Watson, "Structured Testing: A Testing Methodology Using the Cyclomatic Complexity Metric," available at www.nist.gov.

## CHAPTER 22

Control-Flow Testing Exercise

It's time to apply the white-box control-flow testing concepts you've learned to a simple program. In Listing 22-1, you'll find a simple C program that converts hexadecimal character input into an integer. It displays the number of hexadecimal characters converted and their value (in hexadecimal). It ignores nonhexadecimal characters. This program will run on a Windows or Linux system if you have a compiler available to you.

The exercise is in three parts:

1. Understand the number of potential test cases.

2. Create a set of test cases for full statement, branch, condition, and loop coverage.

3. Calculate the McCabe complexity, write the basis paths, and create the basis tests.

I suggest 30 minutes as a time limit. When you're done, keep reading to see my solution.

```
1. main()
2. /* Convert hex digits to a number */
3. {
4.     int c;
5.     unsigned long int hexnum, nhex;
6.
7.     hexnum = nhex = 0;
8.
9.     while ((c = getchar()) != EOF) {
10.      switch (c) {
11.         case '0': case '1': case '2': case '3': case '4':
12.         case '5': case '6': case '7': case '8': case '9':
13.           /* Convert a decimal digit */
14.           nhex++;
15.           hexnum *= 0x10;
16.           hexnum += (c - '0');
17.           break;
18.         case 'a': case 'b': case 'c':
19.         case 'd': case 'e': case 'f':
20.           /* Convert a lower case hex digit */
21.           nhex++;
22.           hexnum *= 0x10;
23.           hexnum += (c - 'a' + 0xa);
24.           break;
25.         case 'A': case 'B': case 'C':
26.         case 'D': case 'E': case 'F':
27.           /* Convert an upper case hex digit */
28.           nhex++;
29.           hexnum *= 0x10;
30.           hexnum += (c - 'A' + 0xA);
31.           break;
32.        default:
33.         /* Skip any non-hex characters */
34.          break;
35.      }
36.    }
37.    printf("Got %d hex digits: %x\n", nhex, hexnum);
38.    return 0;
39. }
```

Listing 22-1   Hex converter program

My Solution and Comments

1. Understand the number of potential test cases.

The set of potential tests is infinite. To be mathematically precise, the set of potential tests is countably infinite. To see how, attempt to construct a set of tests that you say is complete and exhaustive for this program.

I can find a test in your test set that has the most input characters, hexadecimal and nonhexadecimal. I can then add one more character to this test. I have thus created a new test. This test is different from all other tests in your test set.

I can repeat this process for any given set of tests. That includes the set I just constructed from your test set plus my one additional test. So, we have an infinite loop that will never run out of new tests to create. Since I create the new tests one at a time, I could keep track of the number of tests and count them, all the way up to infinity.

Clearly, it's not efficient to try to run an infinite number of tests for such a small program. It's not very effective, either, as many tests are redundant in terms of the bugs they can reveal.

2. Create a set of test cases for full statement, branch, condition, and loop coverage.

The set of tests I created is shown in Table 22-1.

Table 22-1   Statement, Branch, Condition, and Loop Coverage

TEST #	TESTER ACTION AND DATA	EXPECTED RESULT
Statement Coverage		
1	Input "0"	Output "Got 1 hex digits: 0" Returns 0.
2	Input "a"	Output "Got 1 hex digits: a" Returns 0.
3	Input "F"	Output "Got 1 hex digits: f" Returns 0.
4	Input "g"	Output "Got 0 hex digits: 0" Returns 0.
Branch Coverage		
5	Input "" (empty input)	Output "Got 0 hex digits: 0" Returns 0.
Condition Coverage		
6	Input "0123456789"	Output "Got 10 hex digits: 123456789" Returns 0.

Continued

Table 22-1 *(continued)*

TEST #	TESTER ACTION AND DATA	EXPECTED RESULT
Condition Coverage		
7	Input " abcdef"	Output "Got 6 hex digits: abcdef" Returns 0.
8	Input " ABCDEF"	Output "Got 6 hex digits: abcdef" Returns 0.
Loop Coverage		
9	Very large input with a known number (n) of hexadecimal digits with a known hexadecimal value (x).	Output "Got n hex digits: x" Returns 0.

3. Calculate the McCabe complexity, write the basis paths, and create the basis tests. These are shown in Figure 22-1.

My expected results for the coverage and the basis test solutions come from the (briefly stated) requirements given for the program:

▪ Converts hexadecimal character input into an integer.

▪ Displays the number of hexadecimal characters and their value (in hexadecimal).

▪ Ignores nonhexadecimal characters.

Some automated white-box tools and some people doing white-box testing derive the expect results from the code itself. Maybe you did too?

That would be okay for an exercise like this. The idea is to apply specific techniques. As a general rule, though, the system under test is not the right oracle to use. If I use the system under test as the test oracle, all I'm really testing is whether the compiler and the hardware work!

For this program, there are a couple bugs. Most importantly, any time you input more than eight hexadecimal digits, the most significant digits begin to "fall off the left end" of the *hexnum* variable. This happens with one of the condition tests, the loop test, and one of the basis tests. In addition, if you input enough hexadecimal digits, you will overflow the hexadecimal digit counter. Making sure that you test such limits on variables is a data test, not a control test. We'll get to that in a subsequent chapter.

Program

```
main()
/* Convert hex digits to a number */
{
    int c;
    unsigned long int hexnum, nhex;
    hexnum = nhex = 0;

    while ((c = getchar()) != EOF) {
        switch (c) {
            case '0': case '1': case '2': case '3': case '4':
            case '5': case '6': case '7': case '8': case '9':
                /* Convert a decimal digit */
                nhex++;
                hexnum *= 0x10;
                hexnum += (c - '0');
                break;

            case 'a': case 'b': case 'c':
            case 'd': case 'e': case 'f':
                /* Convert a lower case hex digit */
                nhex++;
                hexnum *= 0x10;
                hexnum += (c - 'a' + 0xa);
                break;

            case 'A': case 'B': case 'C':
            case 'D': case 'E': case 'F':
                /* Convert an upper case hex digit */
                nhex++;
                hexnum *= 0x10;
                hexnum += (c - 'A' + 0xA);
                break;

            default:
                /* Skip any non-hex characters */
                break;
        }
    }

    printf("Got %d hex digits: %x\n", nhex, hexnum);
    return 0;
}
```

Flow Diagram

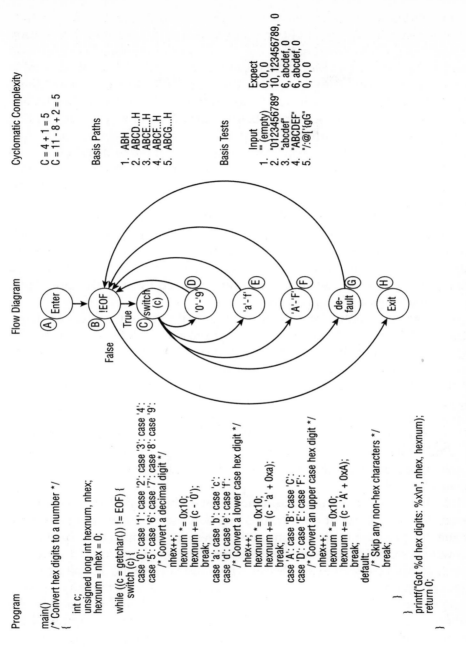

Cyclomatic Complexity

$C = 4 + 1 = 5$
$C = 11 - 8 + 2 = 5$

Basis Paths

1. ABH
2. ABCD...H
3. ABCE...H
4. ABCF...H
5. ABCG...H

Basis Tests

	Input	Expect
1.	"" (empty)	0, 0, 0
2.	"0123456789"	10, 123456789, 0
3.	"abcdef"	6, abcdef, 0
4.	"ABCDEF"	6, abcdef, 0
5.	"/:@['lgG"	0, 0, 0

Figure 22-1: McCabe Cyclomatic Complexity, basis paths, and basis tests

In the condition coverage section, notice that tests 6, 7, and 8 supercede tests 1, 2 and 3, respectively. You could drop any two of tests 1, 2, and 3. If you drop all three, though, you won't satisfy the "once around the loop" rule for loop coverage. You can see that McCabe basis tests, since they model loops as simple branches, do not require anything other than "not doing the loop" and "doing the loop at least once." I don't have a "once around the loop" test in the McCabe basis tests, which you can see by the basis paths that contain ellipses (…) that omit (or elide) repeated portions of the path.

For condition coverage, I've interpreted each case of the switch statement as a separate condition. To see why, rewrite the program using a ladder-*if-else-if* type of structure. Use only equality comparisons in your conditions, not ranges, and do not use macros like *isdigit*(). Since you can model the default case as the final *else* in the ladder, you do not need more than one test for the default.

In the McCabe flow diagram, to show the switch block, I've included a separate edge leading into a node for the switch. The switching among various input characters that leads to different processing is then shown with an extra node representing each *case* statement itself followed by an extra edge representing the various actions performed.

I could have drawn this same diagram without the separate edges and nodes for the *switch* and *case* statements. I've used those extra edges and nodes for drawing clarity. If it makes it clearer to include nonbranching statements as one or more edge-and-node pair, you can always do so because adding a single edge balanced by a single node does not affect the cyclomatic complexity or the basis paths.

As with the condition coverage tests, I included each case value in the McCabe basis tests. However, I could have covered the basis paths with only one value for each test. In other words, an empty input, a single decimal digit, a single lowercase hexadecimal digit, and a single uppercase hexadecimal digit would suffice.

While this might satisfy the requirement that each basis path be covered, it is not sufficient. Think about one obvious bug that such a test would miss. Suppose that the program neglected one of the cases. For example, the 2 digit could be missing as a case in the decimal digit section. The program would discard any 2 from any input containing a '2' because it would fall into the default case.

For a program with a *switch* statement, you could assume that any test that got you into each case body would find bugs in the case body. Such bugs in the case body would include a missing break statement, which is a common bug. However, it is better to include the additional bug assumption that bugs are also likely to involve not getting to the proper case body in every possible case.

This is a key point for any test design technique. These techniques can and should help you develop your tests, but your most powerful test design tool is a curious and skeptical mind. Think about the assumptions you're making about where bugs are — and are not — as you design your tests. Ask yourself if those assumptions are valid.

## CHAPTER 23

Data-Flow Testing

In this chapter, we move on to white-box testing based on the data flows. Data-flow-based white-box testing is a good complement to control-flow-based white-box testing because there are certain types of bugs related to data handling that control-flow-based tests will not reveal.

In chapters 21 and 22, we looked at how to build white-box tests based on how the control flows through the code. However, there is more than just control flowing through programs. Most programs exist to deal with data. Programs accept data as input, process data, store data, retrieve data, and output data. In the course of this data being handled, it flows through the system. Perhaps we should figure out how to test these data flows?

You can analyze data flows using a technique called set-use pairs. To do this, you first identify each data item in the unit to be tested; that is, local variables, class members, and so on. For each data item, you identify pairs of lines in the unit where the item is first assigned a value, and then the item's value is used. These are set-use pairs. Two lines are not a set-use pair if the data item will be set in some other line after being set in the first line and before being used in the second line. To test data flows, you need to cover all the set-use pairs.

Let's look at an example. In Listing 23-1, you see our simple C program that accepts an integer input and prints the factorial of that input. The program uses three integer variables, which are the only data items for this program. I'll identify the set-use pairs for each of these variables, and then identify the test inputs that will cover these set-use pairs.

```
1. main()
2. {
3.     int i, n, f;
4.     printf("n = ");
5.     scanf("%d", &n);
6.
7.     if (n < 0) {
8.             printf("Invalid: %d\n", n);
9.             n = -1;
10.    } else {
11.            f = 1;
12.            for (i = 1; i <= n; i++) {
13.            f *= i;
14.            }
15.            printf("%d! = %d.\n", n, f);
16.    }
17.      return n;
18. }
```

Listing 23-1   Factorial program

The first variable is i, the loop counter. It is set and used in line 12, the *for* loop. There are two different sets that can happen. One is the initial assignment. The other is the increment. In each case, the subsequent use is the comparison. n equals 0 covers the assign-compare set-use pair. n equals 1 covers the increment-compare set-use pair. (It also covers the assign-compare set-use pair, but for conciseness, I'll only mention previously uncovered set-use pairs that are covered by additional test inputs.)

i also has a set use pair at (12,13). You can cover this set-use pair with n equals 1, but not in an interesting way. Multiplying a number by 1 doesn't do anything to it. You can have lots of coincidental correctness problems with your test results if you test at values where the result does not bear the obvious hallmarks of the operation you are testing. For multiplication, classic coincidental correctness problems exist when one term is 1 and when the two terms multiplied have the same sum. For example, 2+2 is the same as 2*2. n equals *max* gives you a more interesting test, provided you resolve the overflow bug identified previously.

The second variable is n, the input number for which to calculate a factorial. It has six set-use pairs, at (6,7), (6,8) (6,12), (6,15), (6,17), and (9,17). n equals -1 covers (6,7), (6,8), and (9,17). n equals 0 adds (6,12), (6,15), and (6,17). Notice that (9,15) is not a set-use pair since it's unreachable.

The third variable is f, the factorial. It has four set-use pairs, at (11,13), (13,13), (11,15), and (13,15). n equals 0 covers (11,15). n equals 1 covers (11,13) and (13,15). To cover (13,13), you need to iterate the loop at least twice. Again, n equal to the maximum loop iteration value covers this.

You may have noticed that McCabe basis test coverage does not guarantee set-use pair data-flow coverage. McCabe basis tests coverage would require you to iterate the loop only once. In fact, it isn't until the third time around the loop that both f and i have values greater than 1, resulting in two terms greater than 1 being multiplied together.[1]

This point brings us to PIE — not the food, the test-related acronym. PIE stands for propagation, infection, execution. PIE is key to finding bugs. To find a bug, you must execute the line, lines, or unit that contains the bug. That bug must infect the rest of the system. That infection must propagate to some point at which it's observable by the tester.

For the factorial program, the bug is the overflow of f. It is a data flow bug. It lives at line 13. You certainly must execute line 13 to see the bug. However, infection is also required. The necessary condition for infection is such that f multiplied by i exceeds the maximum value storable in f, so line 12 is also implicated. Propagation occurs when the value of f, which has overflowed, is printed in line 15.

To satisfy the PIE condition, you need to have n equal to at least 13, given a 32-bit signed integer. So, again you see that simply satisfying a test criterion will not necessarily reveal a bug. You could cover the set-use pairs with n equals –1, 0, 1, and 2, but that won't reveal this bug. However, by using the set-use analysis, you can set how data flows. This can lead you to formulate a bug assumption that you can then test. In this case, the bug assumption is that integer overflow might happen in this program. You must then design a specific set of tests that will reveal the bug.

---

[1] A good resource for additional reading on set-use pairs, as well as other interesting test coverage ideas, is Richard Bender's article "How Do You Know When You Are Done Testing?" available at www.benderrbt.com.

## CHAPTER 24

Data-Flow Testing Exercise

It's time to apply the white-box data-flow testing concepts you've learned to a simple program. Again, we'll use our simple C program that converts hexadecimal input, shown in Listing 24-1. To refresh your memory, this program converts hexadecimal character input into an integer. It displays the number of hexadecimal characters it received and their value (in hexadecimal). It ignores nonhexadecimal characters. It accepts as many characters as you want to give it. This program will run on a Windows or Linux system if you have a compiler available to you.

The exercise consists of five major activities:

1. Identify the data items.

2. For each data item, identify the set-use pairs.

3. For each data item and set-use pair, identify test inputs to cover those set-use pairs.

4. Compare those test inputs to the test inputs you created for control-flow testing, for both statement, branch, condition, and loop (SBCL) coverage and basis test coverage.

5. Identify any additional data-flow-related tests you'd like to run to investigate other bug assumptions.

I suggest 60 minutes as a time limit. When you're done, keep reading to see my solution.

```
1. main()
2. /* Convert hex digits to a number */
3. {
4.    int c;
5.    unsigned long int hexnum, nhex;
6.
7.    hexnum = nhex = 0;
8.
9.    while ((c = getchar()) != EOF) {
10.       switch (c) {
11.          case '0': case '1': case '2': case '3': case '4':
12.          case '5': case '6': case '7': case '8': case '9':
13.             /* Convert a decimal digit */
14.             nhex++;
15.             hexnum *= 0x10;
16.             hexnum += (c - '0');
17.             break;
18.          case 'a': case 'b': case 'c':
19.          case 'd': case 'e': case 'f':
20.             /* Convert a lower case hex digit */
21.             nhex++;
22.             hexnum *= 0x10;
23.             hexnum += (c - 'a' + 0xa);
24.             break;
25.          case 'A': case 'B': case 'C':
26.          case 'D': case 'E': case 'F':
27.             /* Convert an upper case hex digit */
28.             nhex++;
29.             hexnum *= 0x10;
30.             hexnum += (c - 'A' + 0xA);
31.             break;
32.          default:
33             /* Skip any non-hex characters */
34.            break;
35.       }
36.    }
37.    printf("Got %d hex digits: %x\n", nhex, hexnum);
38.    return 0;
39. }
```

Listing 24-1: Hexadecimal converter program

My Solutions and Comments

Identify the data items. Identify the set-use pairs. Identify test inputs to cover those set-use pairs. Compare those test inputs to the test inputs for statement, branch, condition, and loop (SBCL) coverage and basis test coverage.

My solution is shown in Table 24-1.

Table 24-1 Set-Use Pair Coverage for Hexadecimal Converter

DATA ITEM	SET-USE PAIR(S)	COVERING INPUT	SBCL TEST ID	BASIS TEST ID
c	(9,9)	Any, including the empty input.	1-9	1-5
	(9,11 ['0']), (9,11 ['1']), (9,11 ['2']), (9,11 ['3']), (9,11['4']), (9,12 ['5']), (9,12 ['6']), (9,12 ['7']), (9,12 ['8']), (9,12 ['9'])	Any with at least one decimal digit will cover at least one of these pairs.	1 (9, 11 ['0'] only), 6 (all), 9 (ideally all)	2 (all)
	(9,18 ['a']), (9,18 ['b']), (9,18 ['c']), (9,19 ['d']), (9,19 ['e']), (9,19 ['f'])	Any with at least one lowercase hexadecimal digit from 'a' through 'f' will cover at least one of these pairs.	2 (9,18 ['a'] only), 7 (all), 9 (ideally all)	3 (all)
	(9,25 ['A']), (9,25 ['B']), (9,25 ['C']), (9,26 ['D']), (9,26 ['E']), (9,26 ['F'])	Any with at least one upper-case hexadecimal digit from 'A' through 'F' will cover at least one of these pairs.	3 (9,26 ['F'] only), 8 (all), 9 (ideally all)	4 (all)
	(9,32)	Any with at least one nonhexadecimal digit character.	4, 9	5
nhex	(7,7)	Any, including the empty input.	1-9	1-5
hexnum	(7,15)	At least one digit, the first of which is decimal.	1, 6	2
nhex	(7,14)			
hexnum	(7,22)	At least one digit, the first of which is lower-case hexadecimal 'a'-'f' digit.	2, 7	3
nhex	(7,21)			

Continued

Table 24-1 (continued)

DATA ITEM	SET-USE PAIR(S)	COVERING INPUT	SBCL TEST ID	BASIS TEST ID
hexnum	(7,29)	At least one digit, the first of which is an uppercase hexadecimal 'A'-'F' digit.	3, 8	4
nhex	(7,28)			
hexnum	(15,16)	At least one decimal digit.	1, 6, 9	2
hexnum	(22,23)	At least one lowercase hexadecimal 'a'-'f' digit.	2, 7, 9	3
hexnum	(29,30)	At least one uppercase hexadecimal 'A'-'F' digit.	3, 8, 9	4
hexnum	(16,15)	At least two decimal digits with no hexadecimal digits between them.	6	2
nhex	(14,14)			
hexnum	(23,22)	At least two lowercase hexadecimal 'a'-'f' digit with no decimal digits or uppercase hexadecimal 'A'-'F' digits between them.	7	3
nhex	(21,21)			
hexnum	(30,29)	At least two uppercase hexadecimal 'A'-'F' digit with no decimal digits or lowercase hexadecimal 'a'-'f' digits between them.	8	4
nhex	(28,28)			

DATA ITEM	SET-USE PAIR(S)	COVERING INPUT	SBCL TEST ID	BASIS TEST ID
hexnum	(16,22)	At least two digits, one decimal digit followed by one or more lowercase hexadecimal 'a'-'f' digit(s), with no uppercase hexadecimal digit between them.	9 (if so designed)	No cover
nhex	(14,21)			
hexnum	(16,29)	At least two digits, one decimal digit followed by one or more uppercase hexadecimal 'A'-'F' digit(s), with no lowercase hexadecimal digit between them.	9 (if so designed)	No cover
nhex	(14,28)			
hexnum	(23,15)	At least two digits, one lowercase hexadecimal 'a'-'f' digit followed by one or more decimal digit(s), with no uppercase hexadecimal digit between them.	9 (if so designed)	No cover
nhex	(21,14)			
hexnum	(23,29)	At least two digits, one lowercase hexadecimal 'a'-'f' digit followed by one or more uppercase hexadecimal 'A'-'F' digit(s), with no lowercase hexadecimal digit between them.	9 (if so designed)	No cover
nhex	(21,28)			

Continued

Table 24-1 *(continued)*

DATA ITEM	SET-USE PAIR(S)	COVERING INPUT	SBCL TEST ID	BASIS TEST ID
hexnum	(30,15)	At least two digits, one uppercase hexadecimal 'A'–'F' digit followed by one or more decimal digit(s), with no lowercase hexadecimal digit between them.	9 (if so designed)	No cover
nhex	(28,14)			
hexnum	(30,22)	At least two digits, one uppercase hexadecimal 'A'–'F' digit followed by one or more lowercase hexadecimal 'a'–'f' digit(s), with no decimal digit between them.	9 (if so designed)	No cover
nhex	(28,21)			
hexnum	(16,37)	At least one digit, the last of which is decimal.	1, 6	2
nhex	(14,37)			
hexnum	(23,37)	At least one digit, the last of which is a lowercase hexadecimal 'a'–'f' digit.	2, 7	3
nhex	(22,37)			
hexnum	(30,37)	At least one digit, the last of which is an uppercase hexadecimal 'A'–'F' digit.	3, 8	4
nhex	(28,37)			

For ease of reference, my statement, branch, condition, and loop coverage tests are in Table 24-2.

Table 24-2   Set-Use Pair Tests for Hexadecimal Converter

TEST #	TESTER ACTION AND DATA	EXPECTED RESULT
Statement Coverage		
1	Input "0"	Output "Got 1 hex digits: 0" Returns 0.
2	Input "a"	Output "Got 1 hex digits: a" Returns 0.
3	Input "F"	Output "Got 1 hex digits: f" Returns 0.
4	Input "g"	Output "Got 0 hex digits: 0" Returns 0.
Branch Coverage		
5	Input "" (empty input)	Output "Got 0 hex digits: 0" Returns 0.
Condition Coverage		
6	Input "0123456789"	Output "Got 10 hex digits: 123456789" Returns 0.
7	Input " abcdef"	Output "Got 6 hex digits: abcdef" Returns 0.
8	Input " ABCDEF"	Output "Got 6 hex digits: abcdef" Returns 0.
Loop Coverage		
9	Very large input with a known number (n) of hexadecimal digits with a known hexadecimal value (x).	Output "Got n hex digits: x" Returns 0.

For ease of reference, my McCabe basis tests are shown in Table 24-3.

Table 24-3   McCabe Basis Tests for Hexadecimal Converter

TEST #	TESTER ACTION AND DATA	EXPECTED RESULT
1	Input "" (empty input)	Output "Got 0 hex digits: 0" Returns 0.
2	Input "0123456789"	Output "Got 10 hex digits: 123456789" Returns 0.
3	Input " abcdef"	Output "Got 6 hex digits: abcdef" Returns 0.
4	Input " ABCDEF"	Output "Got 6 hex digits: abcdef" Returns 0.
5	Input "/:@['{gG"	Output "Got 0 hex digits: 0" Returns 0.

Identify any additional data-flow-related tests you'd like to run to investigate other bug assumptions.

This is a unit test for the input classifier, not *getchar()*. I'm not testing the integration of *getchar()* with the input classifier, either. (I'll get to integration testing in Chapter 25.) So I can probably safely ignore the possibility of weird data flows from *getchar()* into *c*.

In addition to overflowing *hexnum*, I might want to overflow *nhex*. This is an integer variable, like *f* in the factorial example. An extremely large file (on the order of a gigabyte) will overflow this variable. However, this scenario, unlike the overflow of *hexnum*, probably falls into the "no real user will ever do that" category. I generally encourage my testers to spend little if any time testing highly unlikely scenarios, especially when the impact of the failure is likely to be low. Clearly, overflowing *nhex* is a low-likelihood, low-impact and thus low-risk bug.

For the switch variable *c*, I'm counting each possible case as a separate use. This is consistent with what I did in the control-flow exercise, where I said you could model the switch statement as a ladder-*if-else-if* with each comparison as a single condition. Those conditions would look like

```
(c == ' ')
```

so each condition *is* a separate use. Ultimately, in the CPU, this is how the switch is evaluated.

On line 7, *nhex* is both set and used, in the sense that I use the value of the assignment expression to set the variable to the left of "nhex=0" (which is *hexnum*). In this case, you can't help but evaluate line 7 in exactly one way. However, conditional expressions and other trickery could make this complex.

In my solution, I've shown all the tests that cover each set-use pair. For example, all tests cover the (9,9) set-use pair for *c*. You don't need to do this to satisfy the set-use pair technique. What's necessary to satisfy set-use pair coverage is that you have at least one test case that covers each interesting variation of any set-use pair.

In general, you can view each set-use pair as creating a data-flow coverage test requirement. As Brian Marick points out in his book *The Craft of Software Testing*, under many circumstances, you can cover multiple test requirements with a single test. In his book, he illustrates a technique for devising test requirements. Many of his rules for generating test requirements are based on data and data flows. He then shows ways to cover each requirement with at least one test.

Another thing Marick mentions in his book is the benefit of test variety. Test variety means that not only will you find bugs you're looking for, but you're also more likely to stumble across bugs for which you didn't deliberately design tests. In this example, you can see that the tests created to achieve statement, branch, condition, and loop coverage show more variety in terms of data flow coverage than do the McCabe basis tests.

However, they will contain enough variety only if I'm careful to include that variety. Through the set-use pair analysis, I know that I need to have various mixed-and-matched sequences of decimal, uppercase hexadecimal, and lowercase hexadecimal inputs in test 9 to ensure that all the set-use pairs for *hexnum* and *nhex* are uncovered.

The situation with the McCabe basis tests is actually worse than it looks in this exercise. In my solution in the control-flow exercise, I included each case value in the McCabe basis tests. However, I could have covered the basis paths with only one value for each test. An empty input, a single decimal digit, a single uppercase hexadecimal digit, a single lowercase hexadecimal digit, and a single non-digit character would satisfy the McCabe basis tests requirements. This would result in even more set-use pairs for *hexnum* and *nhex* not being covered. As a general rule, achieving 100 percent statement, branch, condition, and even loop coverage does not guarantee 100 percent set-use pair coverage.

All of this analysis and careful test design to cover set-use pairs might seem like a lot of work for very little payoff. However, in an earlier chapter I mentioned a pernicious type of regression risk. Regression can occur when a change to one module affects another module through a shared data record or even only a shared data field or subfield in a record. Designing tests to target this kind of regression requires set-use pair analysis. Without such analysis, you will not be able to effectively and efficiently select a subset of tests for repetition during regression testing.

## CHAPTER 25

Integration Testing

In this chapter, I cover some techniques for white-box integration testing of builds. By builds, I mean the sequence of integrated sets of communicating, interoperating, or interdependent units that make up part or all of the system under test. The sequence of these builds is usually driven by the architecture and also, ideally, by the risks posed to the system itself by failures that may occur in interactions between some set of units. I also discuss factors that influence the number of units you add in each build on your way toward integrating the entire system under test.

As with unit testing, integration testing is about saving money and controlling risk. Many bugs are errors in interactions between units. These interactions may occur through data, control flows, or communications between units. Two or more units that pass their unit tests may nevertheless exhibit bugs when they must work together.

A classic example of this occurred with one of the United States Mars missions in the late 1990s, which I mentioned in the earlier chapter on reviews. In that mission, the craft survived its entire trip to Mars only to crash into the surface. It turned out that one subsystem involved in the process of decelerating on landing performed its calculations in metric units. Another subsystem used English units. The result, understandably, was catastrophic. While the NASA team could have detected this bug through design, or code reviews, the earliest opportunity to detect the bug during dynamic testing was in integration test.

The bug could also have been detected during system test, but typically isolating a problem between two or three units is much harder when dozens, hundreds, or even thousands of units are involved. Again, why wait until the bugs can hide in the interfaces and interactions between many units? White-box integration testing, whether by programmers or skilled testers, can greatly increase the quality of the system and reduce the costs of poor quality later in the project or after release.

If you are a tester, you might not find this chapter applicable to your daily work. However, I encourage you to skim this chapter at least. A basic familiarity with good integration testing practices can help you have an intelligent conversation about such tests with your programmer colleagues, and as a tester, you have a vested interest in the order of integration.

If you are a programmer, you'll find this chapter very helpful. The example programs run on Linux systems, so you can get some hands-on, computer-based experience. I've included an exercise to reinforce your knowledge.

Drivers and Stubs

When testing, if the parts of the system that would ultimately send or receive control or data to the unit under test are not ready, you need to simulate them. This is a general problem. During unit, component, and integration testing — and anytime you want to test through an API — you'll often find it necessary to simulate parts of the call or data flow involved with the units or builds under test. In addition, you might need to set up or clean up data for such a test. So, you can use drivers and stubs to fill in for the missing parts of the system.

A driver is a function or sequence of functions that call or send data to the units or builds under test. A stub is a function or sequence of functions that are called or receive data from the units or builds under test. Figure 25-1 shows the relationships between the drivers, stubs, and units under test.

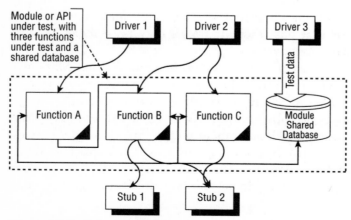

Figure 25-1: Drivers and stubs

Collections of drivers and stubs along with other software that supports unit or build testing are sometimes called test harnesses. In addition, such collections are sometimes referred to as mock objects in object oriented programming, because they provide a mock-up or simulation of those parts of the whole system with which the object under test will interact.

Integration Techniques

Drivers, stubs, harnesses, and mock objects all serve to allow you to isolate a single unit or a collection of units from other parts of the system. This improves isolation of bugs. Except for those software and hardware components in the test environment, only the unit or units included in the build under test can contain any bugs that you see. Therefore, you know where to look.

However, the approach of using drivers, stubs, harnesses, and mock objects has its costs. The creation of these software items — which are not part of the delivered system — takes time and attention. Though drivers, stubs, harnesses, and mock objects needn't work perfectly, they must work well enough to support the testing you intend to use them for. So they must be tested, albeit minimally. You can reuse these items later, but they deliver only information, not a valuable portion of the system.

In addition, each cycle of producing a build with the drivers, stubs, harnesses, or mock objects; installing that build in a test environment; running the tests; and fixing any bugs you find takes time and ties up human and system resources. Now, I would argue that the time spent fixing bugs found in unit or integration test is typically well spent because it saves a larger amount of time that the organization might spend later, in system test or after release. Nevertheless, the time and resources are committed and spent before this payback is in evidence.

So you need an integration strategy that balances these considerations. There are four major integration strategies, each of which has its strengths and weaknesses.

The first strategy is called big bang integration (often with a sneer). In such an approach, you assemble all the units that make up the system at once. Hopefully, they've been individually unit-tested. After working through the obvious integration problems that the compiler and linker will not let you ignore, you have a running system. You then test that system.

This has the obvious advantage of being cheap and apparently quick. No drivers, stubs, harness, or mock objects are needed. No special effort building and deploying intermediate builds of parts of the system are needed. These advantages are often outweighed by the disadvantages for large systems.

First, should you see a problem, where is the bug? In which module does it live? Extensive debugging might be required to find it. Second, the appearance of quickness might be illusory. With large systems, I've seen it take longer to get an installable, runnable, testable build of all the units together and deployed in the test environment than it would have taken to test pieces of the overall system over time. This is something that the agile methodologies practitioners have recognized for some time in approaches like test-driven development and the use of reusable test harnesses.

Third, since you must wait until all the units are ready for integration to start integration testing, you have delayed the discovery of any integration bugs until that time. Why wait until all code is written to start integration? After all, the later you find the bug, the longer it will take to fix and the more it will cost. Why introduce such delays and cost into the system test phase, when the daily project cost is often at its highest, delays are often felt most acutely in the project team and the organization, and costs of fixing are the highest that they will be prior to release?

Except for small systems or minor modifications during maintenance releases, big bang integration is usually a false economy of time and money. However, for small systems and minor modifications, the savings can outweigh the increased risks to the schedule, cost, and quality of the system.

As an alternative to big bang integration, you can integrate from the bottom up. The bottom is established by the architecture of the system under test. Often it is the database or hardware access layer of the system.

In bottom-up integration, you start with bottom-layer units and produce an installable, runnable, testable build consisting of some or all of the units at that layer. Around the same time, you construct appropriate drivers. However, since you are at the bottom layer of the system, interacting with database or hardware elements that already exist, the need for stubs should be minimal if any. You then test that build.

The process is then repeated. You can proceed layer by layer if you are bold. Alternatively, you can build portions of a layer at a time. The choice of how many units you add in each build should be driven by considerations like the risk of integration bugs between the current and the added units of the build, the need for easy isolation of bugs within current and added units, and the cost and time associated with testing each build. The required set of drivers will change with each build. Each build tends to replace existing drivers with new integration units. Above those units may sit new drivers. The process continues until you perform the final cycle of integration testing against the fully integrated system.

This approach offers the advantage of good bug isolation. However, it has a potential disadvantage. If the nasty bugs exist at the top levels of the system, you will not see them until the last cycle. For example, if the graphical user interface is clumsy and hard for users to understand, then you might have to make changes that have architectural implications. Those changes could invalidate some of your integration testing in lower layers.

Similarly, you could integrate from the top down. The top is often the user interface, but it can be whatever the top layer of the architecture is. Rather than using drivers, top down integration uses stubs. You again have good bug isolation, if you proceed slowly and deliberately, but if the nasty bugs are at the bottom levels, you will not see them until the last cycle. For example, if the database schema is such that the system is very slow when realistically sized data sets are loaded, you might have to make changes that limit functionality that was presented to users in the graphical user interface. Perhaps the usability testing you did with the first build is now invalid?[1]

Backbone Integration

An alternative to integration strategies that use the system architecture as the sole driver, backbone integration uses business and technical risk as the prime driver. You select the most critical units in the first build, which is called the first backbone. By most critical, I mean those units that, should they fail, would most likely call into question the feasibility or business value of the system. You might then need to create both drivers and stubs to test the first backbone.

From that point, you add units to each subsequent backbone. Of course, it only makes sense to add units that communicate with each other and with any other units already in the build. However, within those constraints, you try always to select additional units based on risk considerations. If your risk analysis is accurate, you should find the bugs in risk priority order as well as having the bug isolation advantages inherent in top-down and bottom-up integration.

Let me walk you through an example from a real project. In this project, we tested a network of interactive voice response servers. These interactive voice response servers provided interactive voice messaging and real-time connectivity to groups of users. The production systems were to be spread across North America and connected by a wide area network. The wide area network would also tie in a call center, which would allow users to obtain customer services through the interactive voice response servers or by calling a toll-free number.

So, in the first integration backbone, we tested the communication APIs and the basic networking architecture. After all, if the interactive voice response servers couldn't communicate, the design of the system was untenable. Not only did the wide area network have to provide all the necessary communication functions, it had to provide those functions reliably, to handle and recover from error conditions, and to provide sufficient throughput for voice communications across the wide area network.

The design of backbone zero is shown in Figure 25-2.

---

[1] A good discussion of top-down and bottom-up integration techniques is found in Rick Craig's book *Systematic Software Testing*.

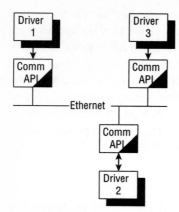

Figure 25-2: Backbone 0

For the next backbone, backbone 1, shown in Figure 25-3, we added the modules that implemented the most critical core operations and services on top of the communication infrastructure. Once again, we tested the basic functionality of those operations and services and also error handling and recovery, reliability, and performance. The key risk to the quality of the system at this stage was whether the core operations and functions integrated properly with the communication layer.

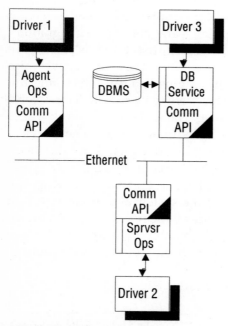

Figure 25-3: Backbone 1

This process of building and testing backbones includes eight builds, each with its key risks. At each backbone level, the overall risk to the quality of the system due to integration problems was reduced.

The final backbone was the fully integrated system, shown in Figure 25-4. Through careful design of our test harnesses, we were able to reuse them, along with other commercial and home-built test tools, to perform end-to-end testing through the graphical user interface at the call center to the telephone user interface at the interactive voice response servers.

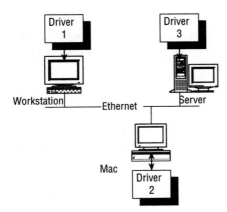

Figure 25-4: Backbone *N*

This final backbone looked for integration bugs related to the entire system. It also provided the first fully integrated build for system test.[2]

McCabe Basis Paths for Integration

Just as there are McCabe basis paths for unit testing, there is also a form of McCabe basis paths for integration testing. Where unit test basis paths recognize entry, exit, sequences of statements, and branching, integration basis paths are based on four types of design predicates. Each design predicate represents a kind of caller/callee relationship that can exist between units. You can represent any real-world caller/callee relationships using a design predicate or some combination of design predicates.[3]

Each design predicate has an associated integration complexity. Together, the integration complexities for all the design predicates represent the integration complexity for the integrated build. As Cyclomatic Complexity predicts

---

[2] The first and I believe best discussion of integration testing, including the backbone integration approach, is found in Boris Beizer's *Software System Testing and Quality Assurance*.

[3] This technique is also covered in McCabe and Watson's "Structured Testing: A Testing Methodology Using the Cyclomatic Complexity Metric," available at www.nist.gov.

the number of basis tests needed to cover the statements and branches of a unit, the integration complexity predicts the number of integration basis tests needed to test the caller/callee relationships in the build.

Let's look at the four design predicates and how they can combine, then work through an example.

The simplest design predicate is an unconditional call. A call is unconditional when one unit will always call another unit. There is no integration complexity increase associated with an unconditional call since you don't have to keep in mind whether the call will occur or not.

The unconditional call is represented as shown in Figure 25-5. Notice the arrow representing the caller/callee relationship, unit 0 calls unit 1, and the number representing the integration complexity of the design predicate.

Figure 25-5: Unconditional call

The next design predicate is the conditional call. A conditional call exists when a unit might call another unit, depending on some condition. There is an integration complexity increase of 1 associated with a conditional call since you do have to keep in mind whether the call occurs.

The conditional call is represented as shown in Figure 25-6. Notice the arrow representing the caller/callee relationship, unit 0 might call unit 1, with the dot on the tail of the arrow representing the possibility that the call might not occur. Again, the number representing the integration complexity of the design predicate appears next to it.

Figure 25-6: Conditional call

A similar but more complex design predicate is the mutually exclusive conditional call. A mutually exclusive conditional call exists when a unit will call one and only one of some number of units. Which exact unit is called depends on some condition. Assuming there are n units in the mutually exclusive conditional callee relationship with the caller, then there is an integration complexity increase of $n-1$ associated with a mutually exclusive conditional call because have to remember which of the n units is called.

The mutually exclusive conditional call is represented as shown in Figure 25-7. The arrows represent the caller/callee relationship, unit 0 will call either unit 1 or unit 2 or...unit n, with the dot on the tail of the arrows representing the possibility that the call might not occur. Again, the number representing the integration complexity of the design predicate appears next to it.

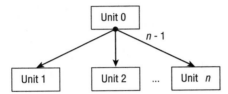

Figure 25-7: Mutually exclusive conditional call

A different type of design predicate is the iterative call. An iterative call exists when a unit will call one unit at least once and perhaps more than once. There is an integration complexity increase of 1 associated with an iterative call because you have to remember how many times the unit is called.

The iterative call is represented as shown in Figure 25-8. The downward arrow represents the caller/callee relationship, unit 0 will call unit 1 at least once. The arrow looping around the downward arrow represents the possibility of multiple calls to unit 1. The number representing the integration complexity of the design predicate appears next to it.

Figure 25-8: Iterative call

This last design predicate probably had you thinking, "Hey, sometimes one unit calls another unit zero, one, or more times, since that's the nature of most loop iteration. How do you handle that?" The way you handle that is by combining basic design predicates.

For example, to handle the situation of calling a unit zero, one, or more times, you can combine the conditional call and the iterative call. This combined design predicate shows the situation when a unit may call another unit zero, one, or more than one times. For the integration complexity increase, you add the combined design predicates.

The combined iterative-condition call design predicate is represented as shown in Figure 25-9. The downward arrow represents the caller/callee relationship, unit 0 might call unit 1. The dot on the downward arrow represents the fact that unit 0 might not call unit 1. The arrow looping around the downward arrow represents the possibility of multiple calls to unit 1. The number representing the integration complexity of the design predicate appears next to it, being the sum of the conditional call complexity, 1, and the iterative call complexity, also 1.

Figure 25-9: Iterative conditional call

Enhanced Hex Converter Program

In Listing 25-1, you see an enhanced version of the hexadecimal converter program that you used in the white-box unit test control flow exercise. This version allows the user, when running the program in the foreground, to send an interrupt in order to undo the last hexadecimal character input. It also complains with an error message if it doesn't receive any hexadecimal character.[4]

```
1. #include <stdio.h>
2. #include <signal.h>
3. #include <setjmp.h>
4.
5. jmp_buf sjbuf;
6. unsigned long int hexnum;
7. unsigned long int nhex;
8.
9. main()
10.   /* Classify and count input chars */
11.   {
12.     int c, gotnum;
13.     void pophdigit();
14.
15.     hexnum = nhex = 0;
```

Listing 25-1 Interruptible hexadecimal converter program

---

[4] Sorry, Windows users, but this version only runs on Linux or Unix systems. You'd have to change the interrupt-handling code to make it portable to Windows.

```
16.
17.    if (signal(SIGINT, SIG_IGN) != SIG_IGN) {
18.        signal(SIGINT, pophdigit);
19.        setjmp(sjbuf);
20.    }
21.
22.    while ((c = getchar()) != EOF) {
23.        switch (c) {
24.            case '0': case '1': case '2': case '3': case '4':
25.            case '5': case '6': case '7': case '8': case '9':
26.                /* Convert a decimal digit */
27.                nhex++;
28.                hexnum *= 0x10;
29.                hexnum += (c - '0');
30.                break;
31.            case 'a': case 'b': case 'c':
32.            case 'd': case 'e': case 'f':
33.                /* Convert a lower case hex digit */
34.                nhex++;
35.                hexnum *= 0x10;
36.                hexnum += (c - 'a' + 0xa);
37.                break;
38.            case 'A': case 'B': case 'C':
39.            case 'D': case 'E': case 'F':
40.                /* Convert an upper case hex digit */
41.                nhex++;
42.                hexnum *= 0x10;
43.                hexnum += (c - 'A' + 0xA);
44.                break;
45.            default:
46.                /* Skip any non-hex characters */
47.                break;
48.        }
49.    }
50.
51.    if (nhex == 0) {
52.        fprintf(stderr, "hexcvt: no hex digits to convert!\n");
53.    } else {
54.        printf("Got %d hex digits: %x\n", nhex, hexnum);
55.    }
56.
57.    return 0;
58. }
59.
60. void pophdigit()
61.0/* Pop the last hex input out of hexnum if interrupted */
62. {
63.    signal(SIGINT, pophdigit);
64.    hexnum /= 0x10;
65.    nhex—;
66.    longjmp(sjbuf, 0);
67. }
```

Listing 25-1 (continued)

Call Flow

Figure 25-10 shows the call flow diagram drawn with the McCabe design predicates. *main* first calls *signal*, and *main* calls *signal* at least once. If *signal* tells *main* that SIGINT is not currently ignored, then *main* will call *signal* again to set *pophdigit* as the signal handler for SIGINT. *main* will then call *setjmp* to save the program condition in anticipation for a *longjmp* back to this spot.

main then calls *getchar* at least once. If *getchar* returns EOF, then *main* bypasses the loop and, having received no input, calls *fprintf* to report an error.

If *getchar* instead returns a character, *main* will convert (or trash) that character to hexadecimal and call *getchar* again. *main* repeats that action until *getchar* finally returns EOF, at which time *main* calls *printf* to report the number of hexadecimal characters received and their value.

If at any time after calling *setjmp* the user sends *main* an interrupt, *main* will call *pophdigit*. *pophdigit* then calls *signal* to reset the signal handle, then *longjmp* to return to the *setjmp* point. As a practical matter, the user is unlikely to send an interrupt except during a call to *getchar*, while the program is waiting for input.

I've also labeled the design predicates with letters in ovals. I'll use the labels later to document the basis tests.

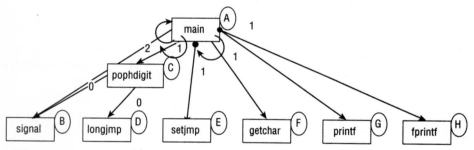

Figure 25-10: Integration call flow for hexadecimal converter

Integration complexity is computed as shown in Figure 25-11. This is the maximum number of basis tests needed to cover all the possible types of caller/callee relationships in the build or backbone. The +1 means there's always at least one integration test required, even for the simplest of programs, the single unconditional call to *printf* in the "hello world" program.

An integration basis path can be said to cover a design predicate when it shows a control flow through the units that covers some element of that design predicate. For example, it takes two basis paths to fully cover a conditional call design predicate. One basis path covers the "do call" caller/callee relationship possibility. Another basis path must cover the "don't call" caller/callee relationship possibility.

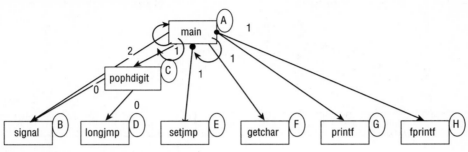

Integration Complexity
IC = Sum(Design Predicates) + 1 =
       2 + 1 + 1 + 1 + 1 + 0 + 0 + 1 = 7

Figure 25-11: Integration complexity

So, a single basis path can only fully cover an unconditional call design predicate. However, a single basis path can — and often must — cover more than one design predicate partially. For example, the same basis path that represents main calling *getchar* only once must also include the call to *fprintf*. If *getchar* is called only once, then no input was received and *getchar* returned EOF immediately. That's an error, according to *main*, and *main* will use *fprintf* to send the user an error message.

It is often possible to construct hypothetical basis paths that have no corresponding reality. For example, I could construct a basis path where *main* called *pophdigit* before calling *getchar*. However, the likelihood of *main* receiving an interrupt in the time after calling *setjmp* but before calling *getchar* is infinitesimally small. Be careful to subject your basis paths to a reality check before trying to test them.

A basis test is a set of inputs and other conditions that force control to flow along a certain basis path. I tend to be a bit sloppy and use the terms *basis path* and *basis test* interchangeably, but the test also includes the input, other conditions, and expected results.

One possible set of McCabe integration basis paths and tests is shown in Figure 25-12. Notice that I managed to cover the design predicates with three basis tests.

I mentioned that some basis tests can't help but cover multiple design predicates. However, in some cases, it is up to the tester how many previously uncovered design predicate elements are covered in each basis test. If I maximize the number of previously uncovered design predicate elements covered in each basis tests, that will minimize the number of basis tests. If I try to cover as few as possible previously uncovered design predicate elements in each basis test, I will get the largest possible number of basis tests, usually equal to the integration complexity.

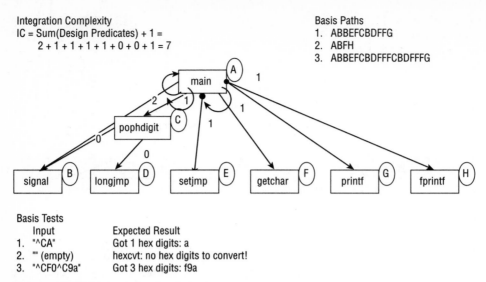

Integration Complexity
IC = Sum(Design Predicates) + 1 =
     2 + 1 + 1 + 1 + 1 + 0 + 0 + 1 = 7

Basis Paths
1.   ABBEFCBDFFG
2.   ABFH
3.   ABBEFCBDFFFCBDFFFG

Basis Tests

	Input	Expected Result
1.	"^CA"	Got 1 hex digits: a
2.	"" (empty)	hexcvt: no hex digits to convert!
3.	"^CF0^C9a"	Got 3 hex digits: f9a

Figure 25-12: Integration basis tests

Why wouldn't I want to minimize the number of basis tests? Well, the risk of running few tests is that you won't be able to isolate bugs if you see them. This is back to the classic rule of integration testing, which I hinted at in the early material on integration strategies. The fewer integration builds there are, the fewer integration stubs and drivers we use, and the fewer integration tests we run, the more difficult it is to isolate whatever bugs you find. This means that, the more complex the system or the more difficult the system is to debug, the more slowly you should proceed.

As a bonus exercise, compile and test the input classifier on a Linux system. You will notice at least one bug. You might notice two. The second bug has to do with interrupt handling and is subtle. It's easy to miss if you use a minimal set of test conditions. If you use a more complex sequence of inputs and interrupts, it'll jump right out at you. This carries an important lesson: Like McCabe Cyclomatic Complexity and unit basis tests, integration basis tests can miss important bugs. Integration basis tests cover only the caller/callee relationships. They might not fully reveal problems like the ones hiding in this program.

## CHAPTER 26

Integration Basis Test Exercise

It's time to apply the McCabe integration basis path testing concepts you've learned to the Omninet example. Integration basis paths and tests aren't just for code. In this exercise, you'll use the technique for the Omninet kiosk module flow described in the Omninet System Requirements Document (Appendix B) and shown in Figure 26-1.

The exercise consists of three steps:

1. Rework the module flow into standard and combined design predicates by referring to the Omninet Marketing Requirements Document and Omninet System Requirements Document.

2. Calculate the integration complexity for the call flow you've drawn.

3. Design basis tests to cover the design predicates.

You can minimize or maximize tests as you see fit. I suggest 30 minutes as a time limit. When you're done, keep reading to see my solution.

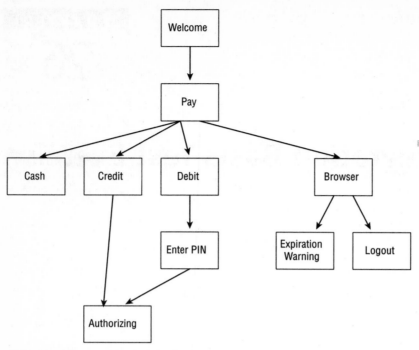

Figure 26-1: Omninet screen flow

Integration Complexity
IC   = sum(Design Predicates) + 1
     = 1 + 2 + 1 + 1 + 1 + 1 + 2 + 1 + 1
     = 11

Basis Tests
1.   A
2.   ABC
3.   ABD
4.   ABDG
5.   ABE
6.   ABEF
7.   ABEFG
8.   ABCHI
9.   ABDGHJ
10. ABEFGHIIJ

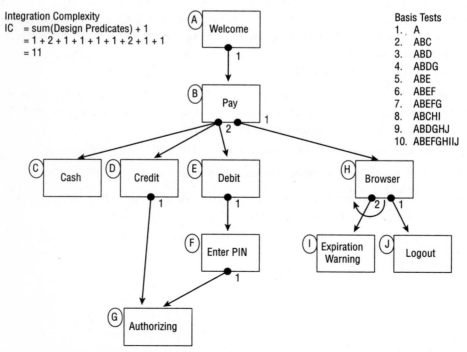

Figure 26-2: Omninet screen flow solution

My Solution and Comments

Figure 26-2 shows my version of the module flow with standard and combined design predicates, the integration complexity calculation, and the basis paths.

I've shown the calls to the Authorizing and Enter PIN modules as conditional. Even though the requirements aren't clear on this point, I think it's reasonable to expect that the user be allowed to cancel or abandon a purchase of time at any point. The conditional nature of the calls to those modules reflects that.

You might have noticed that it's possible to construct basis paths that have no relationship to reality. For example, ABCH appears to be possible based on the flow graph. However, the user must exit the browser one way or another. Either the user logs out or her time expires.

That being so, why isn't the relationship between Browser, Expiration Warning, and Logout a mutually exclusive one? It's not mutually exclusive because it's possible for Browser to call Expiration Warning, for the user to purchase more time, and for the user ultimately to use the Logout screen to exit. In addition, how could you construct a combined design predicate that expressed the iterative nature of the call to Expiration Warning when Logout can only be called once? This is also why the McCabe integration complexity number exceeds the number of basis paths and tests.

Here are my basis tests covering each path:

1. Boot the kiosk. Check that the Welcome screen displays properly. Let the kiosk run untouched overnight. Verify that neither the Pay screen nor the Browser screen are started.

2. Boot the kiosk. From the Welcome screen, go to the Pay screen. Check the Pay screen. Select Cash. Check the Cash screen. Cancel the transaction. Verify that the kiosk returns to the Welcome screen.

3. Repeat step 2, but go the Credit screen. Check the Credit screen. Cancel the transaction. Do not proceed to the Authorizing screen. Verify that the kiosk returns to the Welcome screen.

4. Repeat step 3, but do proceed to the Authorizing screen. Check the Authorizing screen as accessed from the Credit module. Cancel the transaction at the Authorizing screen. Verify that the kiosk returns to the Welcome screen.

5. Repeat step 3, but go the Debit screen. Check the Debit screen. Cancel the transaction. Do not proceed to the Enter PIN screen. Verify that the kiosk returns to the Welcome screen.

6. Repeat step 5, but do proceed to the Enter PIN screen. Check the Enter PIN screen. Cancel the transaction at the Enter PIN screen. Do not proceed to the Authorizing screen. Verify that the kiosk returns to the Welcome screen.

7. Repeat step 6, but do proceed to the Authorizing screen. Check the Authorizing screen as accessed from the Debit module. Cancel the transaction at the Authorizing screen. Verify that the kiosk returns to the Welcome screen.

8. Repeat step 2, but do not cancel the transaction. Proceed to the Browser screen. Check the Browser screen. Browse the Web until the Expiration Warning screen appears. Check the Expiration Warning screen. Allow time to expire without purchasing more time. Verify that the kiosk returns to the Welcome screen.

9. Repeat step 4, but do not cancel the transaction. Proceed to the Browser screen. Check the Browser screen. Browse the Web for some time, but before the Expiration Warning screen appears, select Logout. Check the Logout screen. Verify that the kiosk returns to the Welcome screen.

10. Repeat step 8, but do purchase more time after the Expiration Warning is given. Allow time to almost expire again, triggering the Expiration Warning, but again purchase more time before the time completely expires. Browse the Web for some time, but before the Expiration Warning screen appears, select Logout. Verify that the kiosk returns to the Welcome screen.

A final note: McCabe's integration test technique does not guarantee that all interesting possible sequences of flows are covered. For example, what happens if, while purchasing additional time, the user changes his mind and cancels? Should the system return to the browser and allow the user to use the rest of his time, or should it go to the Welcome screen? That might be an interesting test.

So, when using the McCabe integration test technique, it often makes sense to add more tests. Using basis paths as a foundation for your integration tests will guarantee that you test all caller/callee relationships. From there, you can add more tests.

PART

VI

Appendixes

NOTE Both the Omninet Marketing Requirements Document and the Omninet System Requirements Document contain some defects. I introduced most of these accidentally when writing them, but I deliberately left them in. That may seem strange, but remember that one of the main themes of this book is testing as a *preventive* activity. During some of the static and black-box exercises, you will find these mistakes. I have been told by course attendees around the world that the quality of these two requirements documents is about the same as the quality of requirements documents they typically receive — when they are lucky enough to receive requirements documents!

Omninet:
The Internet Everywhere
Marketing Requirements
Document

VER.	DATE	AUTHOR	DESCRIPTION	APPROVED BY	APPROVAL DATE
0.1	June 6, 2003	Rex Black	First Draft		
0.2	June 6, 2003	Rex Black	Second Draft		
0.3	July 1, 2003	Rex Black	Third Draft		

Table of Contents

1 Scope

This document specifies the requirements for a family of Internet kiosks called Omninet. These kiosks shall provide cash, credit card, and debit card customers with simple, fast, reliable Internet access in public places for reasonable prices per minute of usage.

1.1 Terms, Acronyms, and Abbreviations

For the purposes of this project, the following abbreviations apply:

AS	Application Server
Cable	Cable high-speed Internet connection at least 128Kbps
CC	Credit card (for payment): American Express, Visa, or MasterCard
CS	Communication Server
DBMS	Database Management System (server)
DC	Debit card (for payment): PLUS or Cirrus networks.
DSL	Digital Subscriber Line high-speed Internet connection (either asymmetric or symmetric) at least 128Kbps
IE	The Internet Explorer Internet browser
Kbps	Kilobits per second
Kiosk	The free-standing Omninet Internet access point
Linux	Red Hat Linux Release 8.0 operating system
Opera	The Opera freeware Internet browser
PIN	Personal Identification Number (for debit card)
PSTN	Public Switched Telephone Network Internet connection (ordinary dial-up connectivity) at least 50 KBPS
URL	Universal resource locator
WS	Web Server
WXP	Windows XP Professional operating system

1.2 Applicable Documents

[1] See the Omninet System Requirements Document for system design requirements.

[2] See the Omninet Screen Prototype Document for the kiosk and call center screens (currently unavailable).

2 Required release date

The first set of 1,000 Omninet kiosks shall be live, accepting payment and accessing the Internet, as of the financial third quarter.

3 Description of requirements

3.1 General technical requirements

Omninet shall give customers in airports, malls, theaters, and other public places access to the Internet.

Omninet shall provide call center agents with access to information about current and past kiosk sessions as well as the ability to control current sessions.

3.1.1 Welcome

Between sessions, each Omninet kiosk shall display an inviting welcome message (see screen prototype K.1).

3.1.2 Payment

Once a user navigates past the Welcome screen, the kiosk shall give the user the option to purchase a block of browser time in the Payment screen (see screen prototype K.2). The kiosk shall sell blocks of time in five (5) minute increments, up to one (1) hour.

The system accepts the following forms of payment:

- Cash (bills only) (see screen prototype K.3)

- Credit card (American Express, Visa, or MasterCard only) (see screen prototype K.4 and K.7)

- Debit card (PLUS or Cirrus networks only) (see screen prototype K.5 and K.7)

Once the current block of time is within sixty (60) seconds of expiration, the kiosk shall pop up a message asking if the user wants to purchase more time (see screen prototype K.9).

3.1.3 Internet Browser

At the Welcome screen, each Omninet kiosk shall provide the user with a choice of the latest version of Netscape, Opera, or Internet Explorer (available on Windows kiosks only).

3.1.4 Performance

On kiosks operating with a PSTN connection, users shall have greater than 50Kbps connection speed.

On kiosks operating with DSL or cable connections, users shall have greater than 128Kbps connection speed.

3.1.5 Localization

Each Omninet kiosk shall be configured to operate in the primary local language for its installed locale.

In locales where multiple languages are commonly used, the Welcome screen shall present the user with the option to select the language for the session.

Each Omninet kiosk browser shall be configured to support all languages supported by the operating system and browser.

3.1.6 Content Control

Because Omninet users will access the Internet in public places, Omninet shall implement site blocking that prevents the display of pornographic, objectionable, lewd, obscene, or violent material.

Omninet shall protect each kiosk against sending or receiving a virus, worm, or other malicious code.

3.1.7 Session Termination

Users may terminate sessions in one of two ways:
   Logging out (no refund is given for unused time)
   Allowing time to expire.

3.1.8 Confidentiality

To protect user confidentiality — e.g., URLs visited — once a session terminates, each kiosk shall clear all cookies and other downloaded files, clear the URL history, exit the browser, and restart the browser at the Welcome screen.

3.2 Administration

3.2.1 Software Updates

Under ordinary circumstances, software updates will take place automatically. At 2:00 A.M. local time, each kiosk shall connect to the server farm and ask for updates. Those updates include:

- Operating system or browser patches
- New network, modem, or graphics drivers
- New logos
- Updated per-minute payment rate tables
- Virus, worm, malicious code, or other firewall definitions
- Blocked websites.
- If there are no updates available, the kiosk shall disconnect.

If the update application on the application server tells the kiosk that it is overloaded, the kiosk shall disconnect, then retry at a later time. The delay for retry is a random period between ten (10) and sixty (60) minutes.

Call center agents may also push software updates to kiosks.

3.2.2 View Kiosks

Call center agents shall be able to browse a list of kiosks. For each kiosk, call center agents shall be able to see:

- Current operating system version
- Current browser version
- Total uptime since installation
- Total uptime since last software update
- Number of crashes, reboots, or other hard failures since last software update.

Kiosks shall connect to the server farm once per hour to report status.

If a kiosk is not connected to the server farm, the call center agent may force a connection to check status.

If a kiosk is down, that kiosk shall show up at the top of the list of kiosks, highlighted in red.

3.2.3 View Users

For those kiosks that have active users, call center agents shall have access to the following information:

- Current and past URLs.
- Credit or debit card number (if applicable)
- Name (if available from credit card validation)
- Amount paid for this session
- Blocks of time purchased
- Previous session (if available from credit card number and name)
- Paid time remaining

3.2.4 Modify User

Call center agents shall be able to modify a user's session by adding blocks of time.

Supervisory override is required for an agent to add more than sixty (60) minutes of time per day.

3.2.5 Terminate User

If a call center agent believes that a user is engaged in illegal, inappropriate, or fraudulent use of a session, the agent may terminate that session.

The user shall receive a refund for any unused time at the point of termination.

The user shall receive a message that the session was terminated for inappropriate activity. The message shall specify the amount of the refund.

Omninet:
The Internet Everywhere
System Requirements Document

VER.	DATE	AUTHOR	DESCRIPTION	APPROVED BY	DATE
0.1	June 14, 2003	Rex Black	First Draft		
0.2	July 1, 2003	Rex Black	Second Draft		

Functionality System Requirements

The capability of the system to provide functions that meet stated and implied needs when the software is used under specified conditions.

ID.	VER	MRD	DESCRIPTION	PRIORITY*
010-010			*Suitability*	
010-010-010	1.0	3.1	Kiosk design shall be suitable for installation in public places.	1
010-010-020	1.0	3.1	Kiosks shall allow access to Internet sites through all supported URLs.	1
010-010-030	1.0	3.1	Kiosks shall provide a standard keyboard-video-mouse graphical user interface.	1
010-010-040	1.0	3.1	Call center desktops shall provide agents with a standard keyboard-video-mouse graphical user interface.	2
010-010-110	1.0	3.1.6	Kiosks shall accept payment in local currencies.	2
010-010-210	1.0	3.1.5	Kiosks shall be configured to interact with customers entirely in the primary local language from the Welcome screen until session termination.	1
010-010-220	1.0	3.15	At the Welcome screen, kiosks shall allow users to select a secondary local language where appropriate. Once this language is selected, the kiosk shall interact with customers entirely in this language until session termination.	2
010-010-230	1.0	3.15	All kiosk web browsers shall be able to display web pages in (US) English, (Mexican) Spanish, and (Canadian) French in addition to all primary and secondary local languages for which the kiosk is configured.	2

*Priorities are: 1 Very high   2 High   3 Medium   4 Low   5 Very low

ID.	VER	MRD	DESCRIPTION	PRIORITY*
010-010-240	1.0	3.15	All kiosk web browsers shall be able to display web pages in Hebrew, Arabic, German, (Mandarin) Chinese, (Hong Kong) Chinese, Japanese, and Russian.	3
010-010-250	1.0	3.15	All kiosk Web browsers shall be able to display Web pages in languages other than those specified in 010-010-230 and 010-010-240.	4
010-010-910	1.0	3.1.7	Kiosks shall allow users to terminate sessions at any time by clicking the "Log Out" icon on the taskbar.	1
010-010-920	1.0	3.1.2	At any time while the user is browsing the Web, kiosks shall allow users to purchase more time by clicking on the "Buy Time" icon on the taskbar.	3
010-010-930	1.0	3.1.2	Exactly 60 seconds before a session expires, kiosks shall present users with a message that gives them the option to return to the payment screen and purchase additional time. The user may accept the option or decline.	1
010-010-940	1.0	3.1.7	Kiosks shall automatically terminate a user's sessions within 1 second of the expiration of the user's currently purchased blow of time.	1
			[More TBD]	
010-020			*Accuracy*	
010-020-010		3.1.3	All supported email attachments and web pages (see section 010-030) shall be visible on kiosks without any noticeable distortion from their sources on their originating systems. Scrolling shall not be considered distortion.	2
			[More TBD]	
010-030			*Interoperability*	

*Priorities are: 1 Very high   2 High   3 Medium   4 Low   5 Very low

Continued

(continued)

ID.	VER	MRD	DESCRIPTION	PRIORITY*
010-030-010		3.1.3	The kiosks shall allow users to send and receive email to and from other Omninet kiosks.	1
010-030-020		3.1.3	The kiosks shall allow users to send and receive email to and from other Windows and Linux PCs running email and operating system software not more than two years old.	2
010-030-030		3.1.3	The kiosks shall allow users to send and receive e-mail to and from Macintosh PCs.	3
010-030-040		3.1.3	The kiosks shall allow users to send and receive email to and from other systems such as mainframes, Unix servers, VMS servers, PCs (those running email or operating system software more than two years old or those not running Windows, Linux, or Mac) and other systems.	5
			[More TBD]	
010-040			*Security*	
010-040-010	1.0	3.16	A firewall running on the kiosk shall protect each kiosk against inbound or outbound virii, worms, other malicious code, and hacking via a firewall. Upon detection of any such item, the firewall shall report such security events to the application server.	1
010-040-020	1.0	3.16	Filtering software running at the server farm shall protect each kiosk against inbound or outbound pornographic, objectionable, lewd, obscene, violent, or other inappropriate material. Upon detection of any such item, the filtering software shall report such security events to the application server.	1
010-040-030	1.0	3.16	Upon report of a security event, the application server shall send a log entry to the database server to place the event in a database table.	1

*Priorities are: 1 Very high   2 High   3 Medium   4 Low   5 Very low

ID.	VER	MRD	DESCRIPTION	PRIORITY*
010-040-040	1.0	3.16	Logged security events in the database table shall be maintained for at least one year.	3
010-040-040	1.0	3.16	Upon report of a security event, the application server shall escalate the event to an active call center agent desktop. (*Active* is defined as currently logged in and not locked.) The agent so alerted shall take action in accordance with the current security policies for handling security events.	1
010-040-050	1.0	3.16, 3.2.5	Subject to the current security policies for handling security events, a call center agent shall be able to terminate the session for a user who sends malicious code or inappropriate material or who uses the kiosk to hack other systems. The user whose session is so terminated shall receive a message that includes a toll-free number to call to appeal the decision.	2
010-040-060	1.0	N/A	Subject to the current security policies for handling security events, a call center agent shall be able to log in to their desktop system at the beginning of each shift and log out at the end of each shift.	1
010-040-070	1.0	N/A	Subject to the current security policies for handling security events, a call center agent shall be able to lock her current login session on her desktop system prior to leaving her desk.	2
			[More TBD]	
010-050			*Compliance (functionality standards/laws/regs)*	
			[TBD]	

*Priorities are: 1 Very high   2 High   3 Medium   4 Low   5 Very low

Reliability System Requirements

The capability of the system to maintain a specified level of performance when used under specified conditions.

ID.	VER	MRD	DESCRIPTION	PRIORITY
020-010			*Maturity*	
020-010-010	1.0	3.1.3	Except as noted in 020-010-030, the server farm shall make available to the kiosks the latest drivers, patches, and other updates for Linux or Windows (as appropriate) only after each update has been available for at least 30 days, Technical Support has documented all known issues, and the Change Control Board has approved the update.	3
020-010-020	1.0	3.1.3	Except as noted in 020-010-030, the server farm shall make available to the kiosks the latest drivers, patches, and other updates for Internet Explorer, Netscape, or Opera (as appropriate) only after each update has been available for at least 30 days, Technical Support has documented all known issues, and the Change Control Board has approved the update.	3
020-010-030	1.0	3.1.6	The server farm shall make available to the kiosks the latest virus, worm, malicious code, and blocked website definitions.	1
			[More TBD]	
020-020			*Fault-tolerance*	
020-020-010	1.0	3.1.2	Should the network connection fail during payment approval, the kiosk shall complete the transaction if the customer has been charged. The kiosk shall not complete the transaction if the customer has not been charged.	1

ID.	VER	MRD	DESCRIPTION	PRIORITY
020-020-020	1.0	3.1.2	Should the network connection fail during payment approval, the kiosk shall not complete the transaction if the customer has not been charged.	2
			[More TBD]	
020-030			*Recoverability*	
			[TBD]	
020-040			*Compliance (reliability standards/laws/regs)*	
			[TBD]	

Usability System Requirements

The capability of the system to be understood, learned, used, and attractive to the user and the call center agents when used under specified conditions.

ID.	VER	MRD	DESCRIPTION	PRIORITY
030-010			*Understandability*	
030-010-010	1.0	3.1	The kiosk user interface shall preserve the commonly understood Microsoft Windows look and feel.	2
030-010-010	1.0	3.1	Call center agent desktop user interface shall preserve the commonly understood Microsoft Windows look and feel.	2
			[More TBD]	
030-020			*Learnability*	
			[TBD]	
030-030			*Operability*	
030-030-010	1.0	3.1	The kiosk user interface shall not require the user to navigate through more than five unique pages before accessing the web browser.	2

Continued

(continued)

ID.	VER	MRD	DESCRIPTION	PRIORITY
030-030-020	1.0	3.1	The call center desktop agent user interface shall not require the user to navigate through more than five unique pages before accessing any of the major call-center functions.	2
			[More TBD]	
030-040			*Attractiveness*	
			[TBD]	
030-050			*Compliance (usability standards)*	
	1.1		System shall comply with local handicap-access laws.	5

Efficiency System Requirements

The capability of the system to provide appropriate performance relative to the amount of resources used under stated conditions.

ID.	VER	MRD	DESCRIPTION	PRIORITY
040-010			*Time behavior*	
040-010-010	1.0	3.1.1	The kiosk shall present the Welcome screen within 120 seconds of initial kiosk power-up 95% of the time. In no case shall the time exceed 240 seconds.	1
040-010-020	1.0	3.1.1	The kiosk shall present the Welcome screen within 15 seconds of completion of the previous session 95% of the time. In no case shall the time exceed 30 seconds.	1
040-010-030	1.0	3.1.2	The kiosk shall present the first payment screen within 0.5 seconds of a potential customer touching the screen, mouse, or keyboard 95% of the time. In no case shall the time exceed 1.5 seconds.	2

ID.	VER	MRD	DESCRIPTION	PRIORITY
040-010-040	1.0	3.1.2	Excluding any user and credit/debit card approval delays, the kiosk shall complete payment processing no more than 15 after presenting the first payment screen 95% of the time. In no case shall the time exceed 30 seconds. Should any credit/debit card approval delay exceed 30 seconds, the kiosk shall present the user with the option of canceling the transaction.	2
040-010-050	1.0	3.1.2	In the case that any user or credit/debit card approval delay reaches 60 seconds, the kiosk shall cancel (timeout) the transaction. The user may reattempt the transaction.	2
			[More TBD]	
040-020			*Resource utilization*	
040-020-010	1.0	2	The server farm shall support 1,000 kiosks, all of which may be simultaneously active.	2
040-020-020	1.0		The server farm shall support 25 call center agent desktops, all of which may be simultaneously active.	2
			[More TBD]	
040-030			*Compliance (performance standards)*	
			[TBD]	

Maintainability System Requirements

The capability of the system to be modified. Modifications may include corrections, improvement, or adaptations of the software changes in environments and in requirements and functional specifications.

ID.	VER	MRD	DESCRIPTION	PRIORITY
050-010			*Analyzability*	
	1.0		The development and maintenance organizations shall maintain traceability between marketing requirements, system requirements, quality risks, test suites, and test cases.	1
			[More TBD]	
050-020			*Changeability*	
050-020-010	1.1		The server farm shall support up to 100 call center agents.	2
050-020-020	1.1		The server farm shall support up to 5,000 kiosks.	2
			[TBD]	
040-030			*Compliance (performance standards)*	
			[TBD]	

Portability System Requirements

The capability of the system to be transferred from one environment to another.

ID.	VER	MRD	DESCRIPTION	PRIORITY
060-010			*Adaptability*	
060-010-010	1.0		The kiosk hardware shall support Linux.	1
060-010-010	1.1		The kiosk hardware shall support Windows XP.	2
			[More TBD]	
060-020			*Installability*	

ID.	VER	MRD	DESCRIPTION	PRIORITY
060-020-010	1.0		The server farm shall push appropriate updates (for OS, browser, and kiosk software) to the kiosks upon identifying a back-level version of software in a kiosk.	1
			[More TBD]	
060-030			*Coexistence*	
060-030-010	1.0		The kiosks shall support viewing Adobe Acrobat documents on web pages.	3
			[More TBD]	
060-040			*Replaceability*	
060-040-010	1.0		The server software shall be written to be portable across web server, application server, and database server vendors.	2
			[More TBD]	
060-050			*Compliance*	
060-050-010	1.0		The kiosk software shall be implemented to work on any standards-compliant browser.	3
060-050-020	1.0		The server software shall be written using industry-standard database and programming languages.	1
			[More TBD]	

Design Models

Omninet System Architecture

Figure B-1: shows the Omninet system architecture.

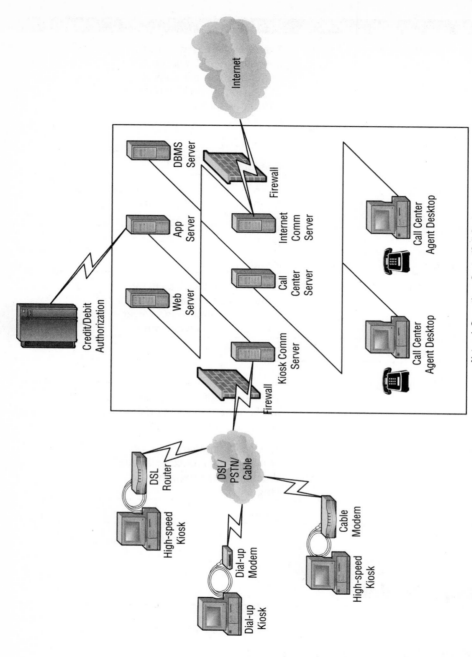

Figure B-1: Omninet system architecture

Payment Processing Decision Table

Table B-1 shows the business rules that govern processing of payments. The processing of payments logic that authorizes credit and/or debit cards runs on the application server. The processing of payments logic that verifies legitimate currency or correct card runs on the kiosk.

Table B-1: Payment Processing Decision Table

| | Business Rule | | | | | |
Condition	1	2	3	4	5	6
Valid money	No	Yes	-	-	-	-
Valid card	-	-	No	Yes	Yes	Yes
Valid PIN (for debit) or no PIN required (for credit)	-	-	-	No	Yes	Yes
Amount approved	-	-	-	-	No	Yes
Action						
Reject cash	Yes	No	No	No	No	No
Reject card	No	No	Yes	Yes	No	No
Prompt for lower amount	No	No	No	No	Yes	No
Sell time block	No	Yes	No	No	No	Yes

Kiosk Module Flow

Figure B-2: shows the kiosk module flow.

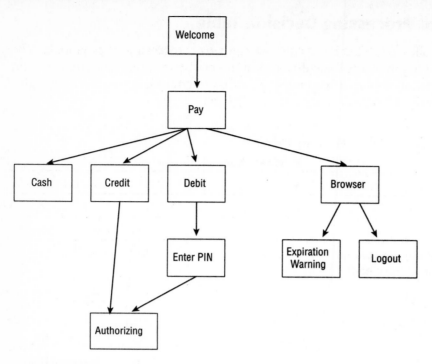

Figure B-2: Kiosk module flow

Kiosk State-Transition Diagram

The following diagram shows the states that the kiosk can be in, the transitions that can occur between states, and the events, conditions, and actions associated with those transitions.

TBD

Kiosk State-Transition Table

The following table shows the state transitions that can occur based on the events and conditions that can influence the kiosks' behavior.

NB: The following events can occur:

Logout	The user terminates the active kiosk session.
Terminate	A call center agent terminates the active kiosk session.
URL	The user enters a URL (which may be browseable or blocked)
Pay	The user submits some form of payment (currency, credit card, or debit card, any of which may be valid or invalid) to the kiosk to begin or continue a kiosk session
TBD	
Starting State	Event [Condition] Action New State

Kiosk OS/Browser/Connection Speed Configuration Orthogonal Array

The following orthogonal array shows the configuration options (singletons and pairs) that will need to be tested.

TBD: One of these arrays will work.

	Factors		
Config	1	2	3
1	0	0	0
2	0	1	1
3	1	0	1
4	1	1	0

	Factors			
Config	1	2	3	4
1	0	0	0	0
2	0	1	1	2
3	0	2	2	1
4	1	0	1	1
5	1	1	2	0
6	1	2	0	2
7	2	0	2	2
8	2	1	0	1
9	2	2	1	0

	Factors				
Config	1	2	3	4	5
1	0	0	0	0	0
2	0	1	1	1	1
3	0	2	2	2	2
4	0	3	3	3	3
5	1	0	1	2	3
6	1	1	0	3	2
7	1	2	3	0	1
8	1	3	2	1	0
9	2	0	2	3	1
10	2	1	3	2	0
11	2	2	0	1	3
12	2	3	1	0	2
13	3	0	3	1	2
14	3	1	2	0	3
15	3	2	1	3	0
16	3	3	0	2	1

Bibliography and Other Recommended Readings

The following are books and articles I referenced in this book. I have selected 10 books as essential reading for pragmatic software testers, especially hands-on test engineers. I have marked the titles of these books with asterisks (*). For people with test management responsibilities, I consider 4 additional books as essential and have marked the titles of these books with daggers (†).

Beizer, Boris. *Software System Testing and Quality Assurance.** New York: Van Nostrand Reinhold, 1984.

Beizer, Boris. *Software Testing Techniques, 2e.** New York: Van Nostrand Reinhold, 1990.

Binder, Robert. *Testing Object-Oriented Systems.* Reading, Mass.: Addison-Wesley, 1999.

Black, Rex. *Managing the Testing Process, 2e.** New York: John Wiley & Sons, 2001.

Black, Rex. *Critical Testing Processes.†* Reading, Mass.: Addison Wesley 2003.

Black, Rex et al. *Foundations of Software Testing.** London: Thomson, 2006.

Brooks, Frederick P., Jr. (1975). *The Mythical Man-Month*,* Addison-Wesley: Reading, MA.

Copeland, Lee. *A Practitioner's Guide to Software Test Design.** Norwood, Mass.: Artech House, 2003.

Craig, Rick et al. *Systematic Software Testing.*† Norwood, Mass.: Artech House, 2002.

Crispin, Lisa et al. *Testing Extreme Programming*. Reading, Mass.: Addison-Wesley, 2002.

Crosby, Phillip. *Quality Is Free*. New York: McGraw-Hill, 1979.

Drabick, Rodger. *Best Practices for the Formal Software Testing Process*. New York: Dorset House, 2003.

English, Larry. *Improving Data Warehouse and Business Information Quality*. New York: John Wiley & Sons, 1999.

Fewster, Mark, and Dorothy Graham. *Software Test Automation.** Harlow: Addison-Wesley, 1999.

Holmes, Jeff. "Identifying Code-Inspection Improvements Using Statistical Black Belt Techniques." *Software Quality Professional*, Volume 6, Issue 1 (December 2003).

Hetzel, Bill. *The Complete Guide to Software Testing*. New York: John Wiley & Sons-QED, 1998.

Jones, T. Capers. *Estimating Software Costs.*† New York: McGraw-Hill, 1995.

Juran, J. M. *Juran on Planning for Quality*. New York: Free Press, 1988.

Kan, Stephen. *Metrics and Models in Software Quality Engineering.*† Reading, Mass.: Addison-Wesley 1995.

Kaner, Cem et al. *Lessons Learned in Software Testing.** New York: John Wiley & Sons, 2001.

Marick, Brian. *The Craft of Software Testing*. New York: Prentice Hall PTR, 1994.

McCabe, Thomas et al. *Structured Testing: A Testing Methodology Using the Cyclomatic Complexity Metric*. Gaithersburg, Md.: National Institutes of Standards and Technology, 1996.

McLean, Harry. *HALT, HASS & HASA Explained*. Milwaukee: ASQ Press, 2000.

Myers, Glenford. *The Art of Software Testing*. New York: John Wiley & Sons, 1979.

Neumann, Peter. *Computer-Related Risks.** New York: Addison-Wesley, 1995.

Nielsen, Jakob. *Usability Engineering*. San Francisco: Academic Press, 1993.

Norman, Donald. *The Invisible Computer*. Cambridge, Mass.: The MIT Press, 1999.

Petzold, Charles. *Code*. Seattle: Microsoft Press, 2000.

Pol, Martin et al. *Software Testing.*† New York: Addison-Wesley, 2001.

Pressman, Roger. *Software Engineering, 4e.* New York: McGraw-Hill, 1997.

Rubin, Jeffrey. *Handbook of Usability Testing.* New York: John Wiley & Sons, 1994.

Splaine, Steve. *Testing Web Security.* New York: John Wiley & Sons, 2001.

Stamatis, D. H. *Failure Mode and Effect Analysis.* Milwaukee, Wis.: ASQC Quality Press, 1995.

Weigers, Karl. *Software Requirements, 2e.* Seattle: Microsoft Press, 2003.

Whittaker, James. *How to Break Software.** Reading, Mass.: Addison-Wesley, 2001.

Whittaker, James et al. *How to Break Software Security.* Reading, Mass.: Addison-Wesley, 2003.

Zuckerman, Amy. *International Standards Desk Reference.* New York: Amacom, 1996.

RBCS Company Profile

This book draws upon experiences and materials that my associates and I developed while performing consulting, training, and project work for various RBCS clients. To help you understand a bit more about RBCS, I've included this brief company profile.

After a diverse career as a programmer, system administrator, test engineer, and test manager in organizations spanning academia, small businesses, large businesses, and third-party test labs, I founded Rex Black Consulting Services, Inc., in 1994. In the years since then, RBCS has offered world-class consulting services worldwide, focusing exclusively on software, hardware, and systems testing and quality assurance. RBCS provides services in the areas of quality assurance and testing, including consulting, outsourcing assessment, and training.

RBCS prides itself in taking a flexible approach that allows my associates and I to apply best practices to leading companies in a wide range of industries. RBCS consultants and associates have successfully applied these best practices in small, medium, and large organizations across a wide range industries, including banks and insurance; retail and entertainment; defense; servers and data center equipment; PCs and PC components; consumer-electronics, embedded, and telephony systems; large and specialty-market software; web technologies; software development, consulting, and testing services; and education.

Our principals and associates include world-recognized leaders in the field of testing and quality assurance. In addition to its extensive library of resources, proven best practices and methodologies, and global presence, the level of expertise of its principals and associates is a key reason why clients choose RBCS. This level of expertise can be measured in terms of projects completed and customers satisfied as well publications released, courses taught, and speeches made.

Rex Black Consulting Services, Inc.
31520 Beck Road
Bulverde, TX 78163
USA
Web: www.rexblackconsulting.com
E-mail: sales@rexblackconsulting.com

Index